NO ERRORS IN MY BIBLE,

SORRY ABOUT YOURS

NO ERRORS IN MY BIBLE,

SORRY ABOUT YOURS

MARK JOHANSEN

Electric Tactics

Monroe, Michigan

No Errors in My Bible, Sorry About Yours

ISBN: 978-0-9830859-0-4
Library of Congress Control Number: 2010940681

Questions or comments about this book may be sent to:
mark@electrictactics.com

CONTENTS

These are the days when the Christian is expected to praise every creed except his own.

G. K. Chesterton, *Illustrated London News*, 1928

DETAILED CONTENTS

I would like to thank my daughter Arianna for her many suggestions during the writing of this book. Her comments were often cruel but always helpful.

1. Introduction

1.1. What's Here

Critics of the Bible routinely claim that it is filled with errors and contradictions. In this book, I list over ninety such criticisms and give a Christian response to each.

Some of these criticisms are easy to rebut. Some are so easy to rebut that I find them rather silly. Others are tough. In a few cases I don't know any truly satisfying reply. I've only included a few of those that are trivially easy, partly because they are generally boring, and partly because I don't want to look like I'm fighting a straw man. It's far more interesting and satisfying to tackle the serious questions. (I considered labeling criticisms as easy or hard. But then I decided that it was better to let the reader judge that for himself.)

There have been many attacks on the Bible over the centuries. Trying to discuss them all in a book of readable length is not practical. So I've had to select which ones to include.

I've concentrated on criticisms that I've heard many times. I've included a few just because I think they're interesting.

Many criticisms are very similar to each other. For example, the Old Testament books of Samuel, Kings, and Chronicles cover the same time period, and so they often have overlapping stories. Some numbers given – like the number of chariots in an army or the number of years in a king's reign – appear to be inconsistent. Going through every one of these sorts of numerical discrepancies can get pretty tedious, so I just picked a few representative examples. (See issues 7.5, 7.6, and 7.7.)

There is one big challenge to the Bible that I do not cover in this book: Evolution and Creation. This is a very big and complex subject. Many books have been written on this subject alone. Trying to cover it here would leave no room for anything else. (I do nibble around the edges of it a little, discussing the age of the Earth, First Cause, etc.)

1.2.   Who Cares?

I have often heard religious people dismiss claims of errors in the Bible with statements like, "Well, the Bible wasn't intended to be a science textbook" or "a history textbook" or whatever. "We shouldn't get wrapped up in these trivial details. Rather, we should look for the deeper meaning, the spiritual lesson that God is trying to teach us."

With all due respect: No.

The position of these folks seems to be that when the Bible talks about pragmatic things, like history and science, it cannot be expected to be reliable, and it is not important whether it is true or not. But when it talks about spiritual things, like morality and angels and eternity, then it is authoritative.

This can sound very profound and spiritual. But I can't help but wonder if some people who take this position don't adopt it out of fear. They want to believe the Bible, but they are afraid that if it is put to the test, it may fail. So they say that the Bible is not necessarily accurate when it talks about things where we might really be able to test it, like history and science, where we might be able to find evidence to prove it true or false. But when it talks about things that we cannot possibly test, like the supernatural, or that are not subject to objective evaluation, like moral precepts, *then* it is infallible divine revelation. The spiritual message is carefully protected from challenge. They declare in advance that any error that anyone could possibly find doesn't count. Thus, they don't need to worry about defending the accuracy of the Bible. They can safely believe the spiritual parts without having to defend the mundane parts.

One catch to this is that it is unlikely to be convincing to anyone who doubts the Bible. As Jesus said, "If I have told you earthly things and you do not believe, how will you believe if I tell you heavenly things?" [John 3:12]

Atheists recognize this quite well. As one atheist put it (in an imagined conversation with conservative Christians):

> I would like to acknowledge that there are many points on which you and I agree. We agree, for instance, that if one of us is right, the other is wrong. The Bible is either the word of God, or it isn't. ...
>
> Of course, there are Christians who do not agree with either of us. ... According to liberals and moderates, faith is about mystery and meaning, and community, and love. People make religion out of the full fabric of their lives, not out of mere beliefs.
>
> I have written elsewhere about the problems I see with religious liberalism and religious moderation. ... Either the Bible is just an ordinary book, written by mortals, or it isn't.
>
> Harris, Sam. *Letter to a Christian Nation.* New
> York: 2006. pp. 3-5.

As this atheist points out, on this question we find ourselves in the interesting position that conservative Christians and atheists are on one side and liberal Christians are on the other. To the conservative Christian and the atheist, the Bible can be objectively tested and evaluated. To the liberal Christian, this is not a question of fact, but of feeling. What is true for me may not be true for you.

I believe in facts. In the history of mankind there have been only two institutions that have consistently stood for objective truth: science and Christianity. Neither has been without flaw, of course. Sometimes they have made mistakes. Sometimes they have even lied. But as a whole these two have recognized the existence of objective truth and tried to find it. Compare them to advertising, politics, or Hollywood.

I think that Christians should boldly state that we will take on all comers. The Bible is either true or false. No weaseling, no equivocating. If it is not accurate when it talks about history and science, then we can't trust it when it talks about the supernatural and the moral. But if it is accurate when it talks about history and science, then we should seriously consider what it has to say about the supernatural and the moral.

1.3.   What about Faith?

Some Christians say that we don't need to defend the Bible, but should simply accept it on faith. If we could prove that the Bible is true, we wouldn't need faith. They say that the Bible repeatedly criticizes people for seeking proof rather than relying on faith. For example, Jesus criticized Thomas for wanting proof: "Thomas, because you have seen Me, you have believed. Blessed are those who have not seen and yet have believed." [John 20:29]

Again I politely reply: No.

Why should we accept the Bible on blind faith? If we are going to believe the Bible without evidence, why not believe the Koran, or the Bhagavad Gita, or the Humanist Manifesto, or the Seldon Plan? How do you decide who or what to believe, without looking at the evidence? You can't tell me that you will believe the Bible because it is the word of God. Without looking at the evidence, how do you know that it is the word of God, and that the sacred book of some other religion is not?

The Bible never tells us that we should accept it on blind faith. Quite the contrary. Peter says, "[A]lways be ready to give a defense to everyone who asks you a reason for the hope that is in you." [1 Peter 3:15] The word translated "defense" is the Greek word "apologia", meaning a reasoned argument. It was a legal term: In a trial, the prosecution lawyer first gave the "kategoria", the case against the accused person. Then the defendant's lawyer replied with the "apologia", his defense against these charges. Peter is telling us that Christians should be prepared to reply to criticisms of Christianity with an argument like a defense lawyer would use in court: a point-by-point reply to the charges.

Jesus never asked people to accept him on blind faith. "Believe me when I say that I am in the Father and the Father is in me; or at least believe on the evidence of the miracles themselves." [John 14:11]

Luke tells us that when Jesus came back from the dead, he didn't demand that the disciples accept this without evidence: "After his suffering, he showed himself to these men and gave many convincing proofs that he was alive." [Acts 1:3]

So what about the condemnations of lack of faith? Look at the specific examples. Nowhere does the Bible condemn anyone for failing to believe in the complete absence of evidence.

Rather, when we read, for example, that Jesus said to Peter, "O you of little faith, why did you doubt?" [Matthew 14:31], consider the context. Peter had just seen Jesus walking on water. He asked Jesus to enable him to walk on water also. Jesus did, Peter walked on water for a few steps ... and then his faith failed. He had just seen the evidence: He saw Jesus do it. Jesus enabled him to do it. But despite the evidence of his own eyes – of his own feet! – he didn't believe.

For a harsher example, Jesus said, "And you, Capernaum, who are exalted to heaven, will be brought down to Hades; for if the mighty works which were done in you had been done in Sodom, it would have remained until this day." [Matthew 11:23] Capernaum was condemned, not because they failed to believe without evidence, but because they refused to believe despite being shown all sorts of evidence.

This is what God means by "faith". Not that you should believe without evidence, but just the opposite: That you should believe what the evidence shows. What your intuition says or what is popular to believe or what you want to believe or what you find consistent with your "world view" doesn't matter. What matters is the evidence.

1.4.   Who's the Boss?

Some Christians object to using history and science to confirm the Bible. They say that the Bible is the ultimate authority, and if we use history or science to prove the Bible, then we are saying this other source is more authoritative than the Bible. We are judging the accuracy of the Bible by this other source. We are putting a human scientist or historian above God.

I disagree. When I use a history book or a scientific experiment to confirm the Bible, I am not saying that I believe that this other source is more authoritative than the Bible. Rather, I am seeking common ground with the person I am speaking to.

In any attempt to persuade, we have to start with something we both agree on. Suppose you were trying to convince a friend that *Bob's Car Repair Guide* is the best car repair book available. (I just made up that title – the Bible is controversial enough without getting into debates about car repair books here.) If your friend questions the value of *Bob's Car Repair Guide*, for you to point out that the introduction says, "This book is based on the latest and most accurate information" would not convince him of anything. He is not going to be convinced because the book claims to be accurate. What would you expect it to say about itself? You would have to find some other source that he trusts. You might get an endorsement from a mechanic he trusts. You might take him through a repair to an actual damaged vehicle, showing that following the instructions in *Bob's* actually works. One way or another, in order to convince him that this book is accurate, you have to appeal to some standard that your friend already agrees is a valid standard. By doing this, you are not saying that you think the standard you are using is better than *Bob's*, just that your friend is already convinced that this other standard is reliable, while he is not yet convinced that *Bob's* is reliable.

When I am discussing theology with Christian friends, I start with the Bible because we both agree that that is the authority. Debates among Christians tend to center on, "What Bible verses can I find that support my position?"

But when I am talking to an atheist, obviously he does not already believe the Bible. Quoting Bible verses that say "All scripture is given by inspiration of God" is a pointless waste of time. If he doesn't believe the Bible, why would be believe the Bible when it says that you should believe the Bible? I'm sure there are plenty of books written by charlatans and con artists that claim that they are true. This proves nothing.

When I talk to people who don't believe the Bible, to convince them that the Bible is true I have to start with something that they do believe. If they respect science, we can use scientific evidence to back up the Bible. If they are knowledgeable about history, we can discuss how well events in the Bible match up with historical records and archaeology. Whatever the other person already believes and accepts we can use as the starting point and build from there.

Once someone is convinced that the Bible is reliable, *then* we can use it as an authority.

1.5.   Defensiveness

The point of this book is to offer replies to criticisms of Christianity. By its nature, this book might sound rather "defensive". I present no affirmative reasons to believe the Bible or to become a Christian, I just reply to criticisms.

Of course there are many positive arguments one can make for Christianity. Others have written such books. Perhaps at some other time I'll write one, too. But you can't do everything all at once. This is a book about defense.

1.6. Disclaimer

Need I point out the obvious? I claim that the Bible is without error. I don't claim that I am without error. If you find errors here, that proves that the author of this book made a mistake, not that the Author of the Bible made a mistake.

1.7. Style Notes

I include this little section in case you're wondering why I used certain style conventions in this book. If you don't care, my feelings won't be hurt if you skip it.

Terminology

For convenience, in this book I refer to people who believe the Bible to be literally true and correct as "Christians", and to people who challenge the accuracy of the Bible as "critics".

Of course there are people who call themselves "Christians" who do not believe the Bible to be literally true and completely correct. As is obvious from the fact that I have written this book, I disagree with such people. While I do not believe that everyone who calls himself a "Christian" really is one, I'm sure there are many people who are legitimate and sincere Christians who disagree with me on any number of points. I don't question someone's salvation just because we disagree. But if every time I wanted to express the idea, I wrote "people who believe the Bible to be literally true and correct", there would be a lot of extra words and it would get very tedious. I considered using an alternative word, like "literalists" or "inerrantists", but these seemed too awkward and unfamiliar. Many of my defenses relate to the Old Testament, so many Orthodox and Conservative Jews would agree with what I say in those sections. So please understand that my use of the word "Christian" here to refer to those who hold to a literal interpretation of the Bible – Old or New Testament – is not meant to imply that anyone who does not agree with such a position is not a Christian. It is just a convenient terminology. (With all due apologies to like-minded Jews.)

Likewise I kicked around exactly what to call people taking the opposite position. I don't like the term "skeptic". I consider myself a "skeptic" in the sense that I practice healthy skepticism: I want to see evidence for something before I will believe it. "Atheist" is inappropriate because there are many people who do not believe the Bible to be literally true who are not atheists, such as Moslems and liberal Christians. "Errantists" is a good word, but too strange to most readers, and when you use a strange word over and over it tends to be distracting. (Like when one uses the word "one" in a sentence once, one finds oneself forced to use it over and over so one is not inconsistent with what one said previously.) "Critic" seemed appropriate. Of course there are many sorts of critic in the world – I am certainly not referring to movie critics in this book – so the word could be too vague. But again, to avoid having to write a paragraph describing someone's position every time I need to refer to one group or the other, I simply picked this word and used it consistently.

Translation

Most of the Bible quotes in this book are from the New King James Version -- the "Jimmy 2".

This translation is good for this sort of discussion because it strives to be as close to a word-for-word translation as is possible while giving readable and comprehensible English. (The New American Standard Bible is also rated as very literal.)

The original King James is widely recognized as the "standard" English translation. Both critics and Christians often use the King James because everyone agrees that this is the "real" Bible, that it is the real source of Christian beliefs. If someone in this sort of debate used a less popular or widely-acknowledged translation or paraphrase, the other side might dismiss their arguments on the grounds that they are not quoting from the "real" Bible. But the King James has the obvious problem that the language is seriously out of date and is often difficult for modern Americans to read. Anyone who tries to read the King James finds himself stumbling over the "thou"s and the "hast"s, and words that most modern Americans don't even know the meaning of, like "ambassage" or "froward". The New King James replaces these with modern words. Thus, it combines the "traditional authority" of the King James with the readability of a modern translation.

I am not saying that the New King James is the only valid translation or even that it is the "best" translation. I think it is the best translation that I know of for the present purpose.

In a few cases I use the New International Version where I thought it was more clear. The New International strives more for clarity of the English translation. Bible translators routinely struggle with the balance between word-for-word accuracy and capturing the sense of a sentence or paragraph as a whole. The NKJV leans more toward word for word, and the NIV toward the sense of the whole.

Statements of Criticism

My original intention was to state each criticism of the Bible with a published quote from a critic. I was thinking that this would protect me from any accusation that I was misstating a criticism to make it weaker, or inventing lame criticisms just so I could shoot them down.

But this quickly proved impractical and unproductive.

First, I found it surprisingly difficult to get clear, concise statements of the criticisms. Critics often take a lot of words to explain their argument, and I found that to get it down to a quote of reasonable length I had to chop it up with a lot of ellipses (dot-dot-dots) and add explanatory text and in general it was just messy. I'm not faulting the critics for being long-winded or meandering. I'm sure they see themselves as being thorough in their explanations. I'm just trying to explain why I found it hard to get usable quotes.

Second, many of these criticisms have been used by many different critics. Each states it in his own words, and sometimes varies the details. Which critic should I quote? I felt obligated to quote the person who said it first. But that turned into a lot of research to try to track down just who that was, and the person who said it first didn't necessarily say it best or most clearly.

Third, if I used an exact quote, of course I had to give a source, and naming the critics that I am attempting to rebut could make it sound like a personal attack. My point is not to attack the critic, but to defend the Bible.

In the end, I concluded that using quotes would not really help. Frankly, if I wanted to pick weak arguments that were easy to attack, I could always pick the critic who worded an argument poorly while ignoring one who said it well. I could find some nutcase who makes a weak argument that no serious critic would use. I have tried not to do such things, but to take issues that are widely used by critics or that have been made by well-known critics. There is, of course, no one official source of critical positions, so I had to make judgment calls. But – and here's the point – even if I didn't do that at all, someone on the other side of the argument could claim that I did.

So I gave up on that idea and simply stated the criticisms in my own words in most cases. I used quotes for some where I thought this helped in one way or another, usually when I wanted to emphasize that this is indeed what the critic said.

When I do quote a critic directly, I avoid using the names of critics in the body of the text to avoid sounding like I'm attacking a person rather than an idea. I'm not trying to engage in personal feuds, but intellectual debate.

2. Science - Specific

2.1. Stars

The writers of the Bible believed that the stars were tiny lights attached to a big dome in the sky. Revelation describes a dragon knocking stars down from heaven with its tail. Daniel describes a *goat* knocking stars down from heaven and stomping on them. Revelation says that Jesus held seven stars in his hand. Stars are bigger than the Earth: there's no way a person could hold even one star in his hand, never mind seven. Mark and Revelation talk about stars falling out of heaven and landing on the Earth. It's absurd to talk of stars falling onto the Earth: Again, stars are many times bigger than the Earth. If anything, the Earth would fall onto a star. And if that happened, the entire planet would be instantly burned to a cinder. Genesis casually mentions, "He created the stars also", as if all the trillions of stars were just an afterthought compared to creating the tiny little Earth.

Stars as Symbols

Most of these verses that the critic accuses of demonstrating scientific ignorance about stars are clearly intended to be poetic and metaphorical. Such poetic language should not surprise us. Cultures throughout history, including our own, routinely use stars as symbols for all sorts of things. When Christians say that we take the Bible literally, we don't deny that it uses poetry, metaphor, and figures of speech.

When I was a boy I had many elementary school teachers who said things like, "I will put a gold star on the board whenever you turn in your homework on time." Would a rational person accuse her of scientific ignorance for such a statement? Does she really believe that she has the power to drag a star down out of space and glue it to the wall? If she could somehow do it, the building would instantly be burned to a cinder!

Jesus held seven stars in his hand? The American flag has 50 stars! How do we run a flag up a pole without being burned up?

Yes, Daniel writes in chapter 8 of his book:

> In the third year of the reign of King Belshazzar a vision appeared to me ... [S]uddenly a male goat came from the west, across the surface of the whole earth, without touching the ground; and the goat had a notable horn between his eyes. ... Therefore the male goat grew very great; but when he became strong, the large horn was broken, and in place of it four notable ones came up toward the four winds of heaven. And out of one of them came a little horn which grew exceedingly great toward the south, toward the east, and toward the Glorious Land. And it grew up to the host of heaven; and it cast down some of the host and some of the stars to the ground, and trampled them.
>
> Daniel 8:1, 5, 8-10

Daniel clearly says that this was a "vision", not an actual event. He is not talking about a literal goat with four horns that tramples stars; this is a metaphor. If this is not obvious, the next page clears up the matter:

> And the male goat is the kingdom of Greece. The large horn that is between its eyes is the first king. As for the broken horn and the four that stood up in its place, four kingdoms shall arise out of that nation.
>
> Daniel 8:21-22

Et cetera. He does not explicitly say what the stars symbolize, but he does go on to talk about Greece conquering many other nations, so apparently the goat stomping on stars is a symbol for Greece destroying these nations.

This section is normally understood to be a prophecy about Alexander the Great. Alexander led Greece to conquer territory from Macedonia to Egypt to Persia to parts of India. After his death, his empire was divided into four kingdoms: the one horn is replaced with four.

Revelation's discussion of the dragon knocking stars out of heaven is not explained for us but is likely a similar metaphor.

If the critic insists on taking such poetic and metaphorical language literally, then he still is going to have a problem demonstrating that the Bible contradicts modern astronomy. Modern astronomers routinely talk about stars on a flag or their favorite movie stars. So the statements in the Bible are completely consistent with the statements of modern astronomers!

Asters as Meteoroids

Several places in the Bible talk about stars falling from heaven. For example:

> But in those days, after that tribulation, the sun will be darkened, and the moon will not give its light; the stars of heaven will fall, and the powers in the heavens will be shaken.
>
> Mark 13:24-25

It is not clear, to me at least, if this is intended to be literal or symbolic.

This is from a prophecy. I get into enough controversial topics in this book without taking on interpretation of prophecy, so I am not going to begin to discuss whether this is a prophecy that has already been fulfilled or whether it is still in the future.

Talk of the stars falling from the sky may be, like Daniel, a metaphorical way of saying that nations will fall. It may even be an allusion to Daniel. If the stars falling is symbolic, then the Sun and Moon darkening is probably symbolic also. Perhaps this means that two particularly great empires or some other institutions will be diminished in power or reputation.

These statements might also be literal. The Greek word translated "star" is "aster". "Aster" refers to anything in space. It could be a star, planet, asteroid, comet, meteoroid, etc. Its meaning is closer to the English phrase "heavenly body" than to "star". Modern astronomers sometimes call anything in space an "object". (Personally

I find this a vague and colorless term, but whatever.) The Greek word "aster" is similar in meaning to the modern term "object" when used in this astronomical sense.

(Side note on terminology: In modern astronomical parlance, the word "meteoroid" means an object in space smaller than an asteroid, basically boulder-size or smaller. A "meteor" is the streak of light a meteoroid makes in the sky when it enters our atmosphere and begins to burn up. If a meteoroid reaches the surface of the Earth, it is called a "meteorite".)

The natural reading of this paragraph to any Greek-speaking person would be that meteoroids will fall from the sky. If the statement about meteoroids falling is literal, then the statements about the Sun and Moon probably are too. This might mean that something will happen to the Sun causing it to give off less light or no light. If that happens then the Moon would also be darkened, as its light is a reflection of the Sun. Alternatively this might mean that something will block the light of the Sun, perhaps some object in space or something in the atmosphere like thick dust clouds. Maybe this is all connected: Some object in space blocks the light of the Sun, and then it enters the atmosphere and strikes the Earth as a meteorite. We could speculate endlessly. There just isn't enough information in the Bible verse to be very definitive.

Whether this paragraph is literal or symbolic, it conveys no scientific ignorance about stars, because if it is literal it is not using the word "aster" to mean "star" in the modern English sense of the word. The only way to say that this is an error in the Bible is to insist on not understanding what the Greek word "aster" means.

Similar things could be said about this paragraph:

> And a great star fell from heaven, burning like a torch, and it fell on a third of the rivers and on the springs of water. The name of the star is Wormwood. A third of the waters became wormwood, and many men died from the water, because it was made bitter.

> Revelation 8:10-11

Like the paragraph in Mark, this could be literal or it could be symbolic. The description of it "burning like a torch" sounds like a literal description of a meteoroid. But could a single meteorite contaminate a third of the world's water supply? This sounds unlikely, which makes it more probable that this is either a metaphorical description of something that poisons the water, or that both the star and the poisoned water are symbolic. Or maybe it's a huge meteorite that causes major damage. The fact that it is described as falling on "a third of the rivers and on the springs" may mean that there are many meteorites that strike all over the Earth.

Again, either way, there is no basis to say that this is an error in the Bible. It's not a star; it's a meteorite.

Offhand Creation

It is not surprising that Genesis 1 does not emphasize the creation of the stars. It is clearly written for an audience of people who live on Earth. Thus, it concentrates on the creation of the Earth. This tells us nothing about the relative size or importance of the stars compared to the Earth. If I am reading a book about the history of the United States, I am not surprised if all discussion of foreign countries is limited to how they interacted with the United States. If someone insisted that this short treatment of other countries proved that the author thought that the United States was the biggest country in the world and that all the other countries were just tiny islands around the border of the U.S., we would surely question his logic.

Genesis is not quite as offhand about the creation of the stars as the critics make out. The creation of the Sun, Moon, and stars are told together. This takes one of the six days of creation. The discussion of that day occupies six verses. Five of those verses discuss Sun, Moon, and stars as a group; one verse distinguishes them. In a discussion centered on the Earth, nevertheless almost 1/6 of the text is devoted to the stars. If a biography of Albert Einstein devoted 1/6 of its text to talking about Isaac Newton, it would be absurd to say that the author dismissed the importance of Newton.

Genesis 1 is intended for people living on Earth, so that's where its emphasis is. This doesn't mean the author doesn't know how big stars are or how many there are. These facts are irrelevant to the discussion.

Counting the Stars

One critic references Psalms 147:4 (he miscites it as 147:7), "[God] counts the number of the stars; He calls them all by name." Then he says, "God knows how many stars there are and knows them all by name. That's pretty impressive since there are 100 billion or so gallaxies [sic], each containing about 100 billion stars." [Wells, Steve.

"Science and History in the Bible". *The Skeptic's Annotated Bible.* http://www.skepticsannotatedbible.com /science/long.html. Retrieved September 2010.]

Yes, that's impressive all right. So what? If God is smart enough and powerful enough to create trillions of stars, it is not shocking to suppose that he is capable of keeping track of them afterwards.

There is one indication in the Bible that the authors knew how many stars there really are. In Genesis, God promises Abraham that he will become the father of a great nation. Then he says:

> I will multiply your descendants as the stars of the heaven
> and as the sand which is on the seashore.

Genesis 22:17

Ancient science could only know about the stars visible to the naked eye. Until the invention of the telescope that is all it could know. Ancient people studied these stars, and they therefore knew that there were about 4000 of them, the number of stars visible from the Northern Hemisphere.

So God promised Abraham that his descendants would become a great nation … of 4,000 people? That's not much of a nation.

God immediately goes on to give a second comparison: they would be as many as the sand on the seashore. Some quick arithmetic: A grain of sand is about 1/10,000 of a cubic inch. Assume a beach one mile long, 100 feet wide, and with sand 1 foot deep. That's a total of 528,000 cubic feet, or about 900 million cubic inches. Divide by 1/10,000 cubic inch gives 9 trillion grains of sand. Of course all my numbers here are approximations. Sand comes in many different sizes. We don't know if God had a specific beach in mind or just how big it was. But 9 trillion is a fair ballpark number for the number of grains of sand on a beach. If God meant all the sand on all the beaches in the world, of course the number would be even larger.

Now 9 trillion would be an awesome nation. That's many times the present population of the world. I don't know if God meant that literally Abraham will someday have trillions of descendants, or simply that it would be a very big number.

But either way, "trillions" and "thousands" are in a whole different league. It would be quite strange to lump the two together like that. But if the author knew that there are hundreds of billions of stars in the galaxy, then it makes sense to put these two numbers together like this. Both are huge numbers, bigger than any nation that Abraham was likely to imagine.

Extent of Inspiration

There is no place in the Bible that says that stars are giant balls of gas or that they are light-years away. There's no evidence that the Bible authors had scientifically accurate knowledge of stars. But nowhere does the Bible say anything inaccurate about stars, either, as long as we don't take poetry literally.

How much did the Bible authors know about stars? This brings up questions about the nature of inspiration. I don't know exactly how inspiration works. But when we say that a Bible writer was "inspired by God" and that what we wrote was "without error", that does not mean that the writer knew everything that God knows. I believe that everything that Daniel and Mark and John wrote in their books was inspired and therefore accurate. But I don't therefore suppose that they knew more about astronomy than modern astronomers, any more than I assume they knew all about the geography of Australia or about Unix shell programming. To say that a writer was inspired by God does not mean that God told him all there is to know, just that he told them or somehow guided them to write accurately on the subject they were writing about.

I don't know if the Bible writers knew all about stars. I doubt they did. But that's not the question. The question is, Is the Bible completely accurate? The answer to that question can clearly be "yes" even if the writers were ignorant about many subjects, as long as they didn't write things about those subjects that got included in the Bible.

Conclusion

There are no statements about stars in the Bible that are scientifically inaccurate. To attack the Bible on this point, the critic must: (a) Not know the definition of the Greek word "aster"; and (b) Not understand the difference between poetry and prose.

2.2. Firmament

The Bible says that the sky is a solid dome over the Earth, and that the stars are tiny lights embedded in this dome. Genesis calls this dome a "firmament", that is, something firm or solid. This was a

common belief in ancient times, but of course today we know that this is nonsense.

The Bible does not say any such thing.

We could discuss the origins and meaning of the word "firmament", but this would be irrelevant: It's an English word chosen to translate the Hebrew word.

Examining Genesis

Here's what Genesis says:

> Then God said, "Let there be a firmament in the midst of the waters, and let it divide the waters from the waters." Thus God made the firmament, and divided the waters which were under the firmament from the waters which were above the firmament; and it was so. And God called the firmament Heaven. So the evening and the morning were the second day. ...
>
> Then God said, "Let there be lights in the firmament of the heavens to divide the day from the night; and let them be for signs and seasons, and for days and years; and let them be for lights in the firmament of the heavens to give light on the earth"; and it was so. Then God made two great lights: the greater light to rule the day, and the lesser light to rule the night. He made the stars also. God set them in the firmament of the heavens to give light on the earth, and to rule over the day and over the night, and to divide the light from the darkness.

> Genesis 1:6-8, 14-18

The Hebrew word translated "firmament" is "raqiya" (pronounced ra-KEE-ah). It is not a general term for a dome or some other solid structure. It is only used to describe the sky or space. The Hebrew interlinear Bible I use translates it "atmosphere". [de Mol, Andre. *ISA basic 2.1.0.* 2009]

The word "raqiya" probably comes from the verb "raqa", meaning to stretch out. It is used to describe hammering out a sheet of metal or stretching out a piece of cloth. This has led some translators to render it as "expanse", or to translate "*raqiya* of heaven" as "stretched-out space".

Read the paragraphs from Genesis with no preconceptions about the meaning of the word "firmament". God created "something". Below it was the surface of the Earth. In this something he placed the

Sun, Moon, and stars. There is nothing to indicate that this something is a solid object. The text is completely consistent with it being the sky or space.

A little later Genesis says that God said, "let birds fly above the earth across the face of the firmament of the heavens." [Genesis 1:20] If the firmament is a solid dome, how do birds fly through it? Perhaps you could interpret these words to mean that they fly under the dome.

Another Firmament in Ezekiel

There is one place in the Bible that uses the word "raqiya" that some say must be referring to a solid dome. The prophet Ezekiel described a vision God sent him of some amazing "living creatures" – maybe angels, maybe something else:

> The likeness of the firmament above the heads of the living creatures was like the color of an awesome crystal, stretched out over their heads. And under the firmament their wings spread out straight, one toward another. ...
> And above the firmament over their heads was the likeness of a throne, in appearance like a sapphire stone; on the likeness of the throne was a likeness with the appearance of a man high above it. ... This was the appearance of the likeness of the glory of the Lord.
>
> Ezekiel 1:22-28

The critics say that this must mean there was a glass dome over the heads of the living creatures, and that there was a throne sitting on top of this dome.

Some Christians reply that the context here is different. In Genesis it is the "firmament of heaven", while here it is simply the "firmament". Thus, they say, we are talking about a different thing, like the difference between "the face of the sky" and simply "the face".

Some Christians also point out that all of this is a vision. It is not at all clear if Ezekiel is being shown actual angels or other supernatural beings, or if this is all just symbolic like the visions of Daniel. (We are clearly told that Daniel's visions are symbolic: he sees a goat and is told that the goat represents Greece; he sees a statue and is told that its head represents Babylon, its legs Rome, etc.)

I think there is a much simpler resolution. Where does anyone get the idea that Ezekiel is talking about a solid dome?

The plain reading here is that the air above the heads of the living creatures had an unusual appearance, like a shimmering in the air or a rainbow effect. The words translated "color of a ... crystal" are more literally "sparkle of ice". (The same word, "koin", is sometimes translated "sparkle" and sometimes "color" in King James.) The natural reading is that he is describing the look of the air over the creatures' heads rather than some sort of solid dome. Then above this sparkle was the image of a throne. Note that Ezekiel very carefully says there was the "likeness of a throne", not "there was a throne". There was a projection or a hologram of a throne above the heads of the living creatures. Even if we insist that a physical throne was actually there, the critic assumes that the throne must rest on a solid object, hence the dome. But then he says that the dome is floating in the air over the heads of the creatures. If the dome can hover in mid-air, why not the throne?

Thus, Ezekiel is not saying that there was a dome with a throne sitting on top of it. He was saying there was some strange effect in the air and some image or projection of a throne above that.

The raqiya is not a solid object. It is the air.

Making Space

Some critics point out that the Bible says that God "made" the firmament. They then claim that this must mean that the Bible writers believed the firmament is a solid object, as you can only "make" a solid object.

This criticism fails on two points.

First, there is nothing absurd about saying, "I made a space between these two things". People talk about "making an empty space" all the time.

Second, in any case, the sky is certainly not empty. Our atmosphere is made up of a mixture of gases: oxygen, nitrogen, carbon dioxide, and so on. Space is not completely empty either, though of course it's much "thinner" than a solid object or air.

Conclusion

The Bible does not give any description of exactly what the "firmament" is. There is nothing in the text to indicate it is a dome or any other solid object. The most natural reading is that the word translated "firmament" means sky or space.

2.3.   Flat Earth

The Bible teaches that the Earth is flat. It says that the Earth stands on pillars: "For the pillars of the earth are the LORD's, and He has set the world upon them." [1 Samuel 2:8] It has corners: "I saw four angels standing at the four corners of the earth." [Revelation 7:1] And that from a high enough mountain one can see the whole world: "The devil took Him up on an exceedingly high mountain, and showed Him all the kingdoms of the world and their glory." [Matthew 4:8]

Corners

"The corners of the Earth" is just a figure of speech. Plenty of people today who are well aware that the Earth is a sphere talk about "the far corners of the Earth" or "the ends of the Earth". The clear meaning is that the writer is saying "all the far places of the Earth", or "the entire Earth".

Some Bible versions translate the Greek word here as "quarters", in the sense of "compass points". That is, the writer may effectively be saying "from north, south, east, and west". Again, this is just a way of saying "many places on Earth" or "the entire Earth".

Pillars

Most likely the mentions of the "pillars of the Earth" and the "foundations of the Earth" are also simply figures of speech. The point is that it is God who created the Earth and who upholds it. It is possible that references to the "foundations" are referring to subterranean granite layers that support the surface. I've seen some arguments in this regard that find literal meaning. But frankly, I doubt it. I think it's just a figure of speech.

Mountains

It is true that seeing all the kingdoms of the world from a high mountain is impossible given that the world is round: You could at most see all the kingdoms in one hemisphere, and that would require a mountain 1600 miles high or more. But even if we suppose that Matthew didn't know the world was round, surely he had climbed mountains at some point in his life, and he was well aware that no mountain was high enough that you could literally see the entire world from it. Even if he thought the world was flat, he would have known that he had never climbed a mountain from which he had been able to see the edges of the world. The critic asks us to believe not only that

Matthew was unaware that the world is round, which at least sounds possible. The critic also asks us to believe that Matthew had never climbed a mountain in his life and never met anyone who had. I once climbed a mountain from which, I was told, I could see Vermont, New Hampshire, and Massachusetts. That seemed quite impressive. But I had no illusions that a slightly higher mountain would literally let me also see Canada and Mexico, let alone France and Argentina. We are asked to believe that Matthew was not just scientifically ignorant, but incredibly gullible.

Most likely Matthew's use of the word "all" is not intended to be literal. When he says "all the kingdoms of the world", he means this in the same sense that someone says "tell me all about it" or "Joe had seen it all". The word "all" in such contexts is not meant literally, every single one, but rather to mean "all kinds" or "many examples".

Read the context:

> Again, the devil took Him up on an exceedingly high mountain, and showed Him all the kingdoms of the world and their glory. And he said to Him, "All these things I will give You if You will fall down and worship me."

Matthew 4:8-9

The point here is that the devil showed Jesus a view of the world and offered to give it to him if Jesus met his conditions. It was not necessary to literally show him every single kingdom in the world to make his point. All he had to do was sweep his arm across a landscape and say "All of this ..."

It is possible that the words really are literal and Matthew is describing something miraculous. Perhaps Satan showed Jesus all the kingdoms, not as a physical view from this mountaintop, but in some supernatural way. Perhaps the mountain he refers to is not on Earth but on the Moon. From there they could see all the kingdoms of the Earth if they waited for the rotation of the Earth to bring them all the way around, that is, about a day.

Figures of Speech

Lest a critic accuse me of weaseling out on "Biblical literalism" here, may I point out that in at least one place the Bible explicitly says that words like "all" are not always to be taken literally. In 1 Corinthians 15:27-28 Paul quotes from Psalms to tell us, "For he [God] 'has put everything under his [Jesus] feet.'" But then he explains,

"Now when it says that 'everything' has been put under him, it is clear that this does not include God himself, who put everything under Christ." (NIV) That is, the word "everything" cannot always be taken absolutely literally. There can be exceptions.

In a more general sense, every language has figures of speech. Sometimes we use them very deliberately. When we say that someone is "killing time" or that a co-worker "dropped the ball", we are quite conscious that we are speaking in metaphors.

When people write poetry or songs they often use very involved figurative language. We have all heard songs and read poems that say things like, "My love is a beautiful rose" or "I give you my heart".

You probably use many figures of speech without even realizing it. Many people say that a rival is trying to "undermine" them without realizing that this is a reference to an ancient military tactic. When an army was attacking a walled city, sometimes they would dig a mine, i.e. a tunnel, under the walls, holding up the roof with wooden beams. Then they would set the beams on fire so that the mine caved in and the wall above it collapsed. To "undermine" someone was to destroy his defenses by stealth. Likewise, people will say "Let's try a different tack" without realizing that "tack" is a nautical term referring to the heading of a sailing ship that is within 90 degrees of the wind. To "try a different tack" is to change the course of a sailing ship.

A common game for critics is to pretend that a Greek or Hebrew figure of speech in the Bible is literal, and then make fun of it for being technically inaccurate. This would be like hearing someone say "Let's try a different tack", and crying out, "What are you talking about? You're not on a boat! Are you having hallucinations about sailing?" Or hearing someone sing, "I give you my heart", and demanding, "Why? Does your girlfriend need an organ transplant?"

Circles and Spheres

There are other Bible verses that imply a modern understanding.

"It is He who sits above the circle of the earth, and its inhabitants are like grasshoppers." [Isaiah 40:22] The Hebrew word translated "circle" is "chug". Some Christians say it means "sphere" here and thus proves that the Bible authors knew that the world was not flat. Unfortunately this is weak, as the Hebrew word can also refer to a flat circle. So this is inconclusive.

Of course a circle doesn't have corners, which makes it difficult to insist that the Bible writers believed the world literally had corners if they thought it was a (flat) circle. But then, I suppose the critic could reply that the Bible contradicts itself, saying that the world is both square and circular, and that both ends of the contradiction are scientifically false.

The verb form of "chug" shows up in Job 26:10, "He drew a circular horizon on the face of the waters, at the boundary of light and darkness." The words "drew a circular horizon" are a translation of the single Hebrew word "chg", meaning "circled" or "made a circle".

From the ground, there is no apparent boundary line between day and night. You look around you and it's either day or it's night. You have to get about 80 miles up before you can see enough of the Earth to see both day and night, and from there the boundary looks like a fuzzy straight line, not a circle. From 15,000 miles or so out in space you can see that the Earth is a globe and the boundary between day and night is, indeed, a circle. Need I point out that Job lived long before people were taking pictures of the Earth from space? Perhaps God revealed to him what it looked like, or maybe he was smart enough to figure it out.

Job 26 makes another interesting statement about the nature of the Earth. Verse 7 says, "He spreads out the northern skies over empty space; he suspends the earth over nothing." Job clearly states that the Earth is not on the back of a giant turtle, nor is it held up by Hercules. It is suspended in empty space.

Conclusion

Nowhere does the Bible say the world is flat.

There is some language, like talk about "corners" and "pillars", which if taken literally would be difficult to reconcile with our modern knowledge of the nature of the Earth. But this language is surely intended figuratively. People today routinely use similar figurative language.

There are a few verses that indicate a sophisticated understanding of the nature of the Earth, most notably Job's statements that the boundary between day and night is a circle on a globe and that God "hangs the Earth over nothing".

2.4. Age of the Earth

The Bible says that the world was created in 4004 BC. Modern science has proven this is impossible. Radiometric dating proves that the world is billions of years old.

Genesis and the Age of the Earth

Some Christians reply that the Bible does not say that the world was created in 4004 BC. This date comes from the book *Annals of the World*, written by the historian James Ussher in 1658.

But if we take the Bible literally, we have to take Ussher seriously. While the Bible does not give a date, Ussher did derive this date from the Bible. He took the genealogies from Genesis, "And Adam lived one hundred and thirty years, and begot a son in his own likeness, after his image, and named him Seth. ... Seth lived one hundred and five years, and begot Enosh. ... Enosh lived ninety years, and begot Cainan ..." etc. He added up all these ages until he came to an event that could be connected to a modern calendar, namely, the fall of Jerusalem to the Babylonians, which has been dated to 588 BC. From this he calculated that the world was created in 4004 BC.

It's possible that the date for the fall of Jerusalem is not quite accurate, and Ussher's date would then be off. This could put Ussher off by a few decades, maybe someone would even argue for a century or two. But not billions of years.

A more serious point is that Hebrew genealogies can skip generations. For example, Matthew begins, "The book of the genealogy of Jesus Christ, the Son of David, the Son of Abraham." [Matthew 1:1] Clearly he has skipped a lot of generations between Jesus and David, and again between David and Abraham. But to insert enough generations to stretch this out to billions of years strains credulity. Besides, evolutionists do not say that human beings have been around for billions of years. They say that most of that time passed before the first humans evolved. Thus, such a technique cannot reconcile Genesis with evolutionary ages. So let's go with 4004.

How Radiometric Dating Works

Some elements are naturally radioactive. They decay from one element to another. For example, Potassium-40 decays into Argon-40, and Uranium-238 decays into Lead-206. One can measure the rate at which this decay occurs in the laboratory. As it decays at a known rate, we should be able to calculate exactly how old any given sample is.

It's like an hourglass. If you measure the rate of flow and find that, say, 20 grams of sand per minute fall from the top of the hourglass to the bottom, and there are now 200 grams of sand in the bottom, then it must have been running for 200 divided by 20 equals 10 minutes.

Radiometric dating is a bit more complicated in that it is not a specific *amount* per unit of time that transforms, but a percentage of the original that remains. The original is called the "parent element" and the thing it turns into is the "daughter element". Physicists normally measure the rate of decay in "half-life", which is usually described as the amount of time it takes for half of the parent element to turn into the daughter element. Suppose we start out with 200 grams of the parent and it has a half-life of 1 year. Then we would expect the quantities to go like this:

Year	Parent	Daughter
0	200	0
1	100	100
2	50	150
3	25	175
4	12.5	187.5

Et cetera.

Side note: Students often asks what happens when you get to the last atom. We can't have half an atom. So does the last atom decay or not, and when? This question arises because of a slight over-simplification in the definition of "half-life". The real definition is: The period of time over which the probability that any given atom will decay is 50%. When you are dealing with any non-microscopic amount of a material, it has sextillions of atoms. (A sextillion is 10^{21} or a thousand billion billion. One gram of Potassium-40 contains about 1.5×10^{23} atoms.) When each of those sextillions of atoms has a 50% chance of decaying, the random variations pretty much cancel out, so it is fair to say that half of them will decay, give or take a paltry few million atoms. When we get down to the last atom, there is a 50% chance that it will decay in one half-life. If it does not, it is 50% that it will decay in the next half-life, etc.

To measure long ages you need an element with a long half-life. Actinium-225 has a half-life of 10 days. So after 10 days, half the original sample would have decayed. 20 days, 75%. 30 days, 87.5%.

After three months less than 1/5 of 1% of the original would be left. After a few years it is unlikely there would be enough left to measure.

Thus to measure long ages people uses elements like Potassium-40, which has a half-life of 1.3 billion years.

Radiometric Dating and Science

That's the theory. It sounds good. But science is about experimentation and observation. There have been many ideas that sound good and plausible, but that don't hold up to scientific investigation, that is, to actual experiments.

If an evolutionary geologist says that a certain rock is 4 billion years old, I think we can be confident that he did not actually witness it form 4 billion years ago. This age is based on radiometric dating or some similar theoretical dating method. Has anyone ever performed an actual experiment that proves that these dating methods are accurate? Clearly in the most literal sense of the question, the answer is no. No one has performed an experiment to prove that a rock dated at 4 billion years is really that old because there is no way to verify that date.

Compare this to real science. Isaac Newton proposed one of the most fundamental theories of physics: F=ma, that is, force equals mass times acceleration. According to this theory, if a given force is applied to an object with mass of 100 grams and it results in an acceleration of 5 meters per second per second, then if the same force is applied to an object with half the mass, or 50 grams, it should give twice the acceleration, or 10 meters per second per second. Double the force will give double the acceleration. Etc.

This theory can be tested in the laboratory. Take two objects and weigh them to find their mass. Apply the same force to each and measure the acceleration. It will either match the value calculated based on the theory or it will not.

The same can be said for many other scientific theories. A theory about what happens when you mix two chemicals, or when you apply an electrical charge to the muscle of an animal, or construct an electronic component of gallium and silicon, can be tested in the laboratory. You will either get the results you predicted or you will not. Your theory will be proven true or false.

Yes, it's not really that simple. Experimental results can be ambiguous or misleading. But you can perform repeated experiments, get other scientists to repeat your experiment, etc., and ultimately come to some fairly reliable conclusions about whether your theory is right or wrong.

Can we do this with radiometric dating? Can we take a sample that we know to be, say, 4 billion years old, perform a radiometric dating test, and see if the results as predicted by the theory are, indeed, correct? Clearly, we cannot, because there is no independent way to know that the sample is 4 billion years old.

Or can we? Some have suggested that a way to verify the theory is to compare dates derived from different dating methods. If they agree, this confirms the theory.

For example, Potassium-Argon tests on lava flows from Rangitoto volcano in New Zealand gave dates ranging from 146,000 465,000 years. Buried in the lava flow are trees trunks, which were carbon-14 dated to 225 years. [Doolan, Robert. "How do you date a volcano?" http://www.creationstudies.org /Education/date_volcano.html, retrieved Aug 21, 2010. Citing McDougall, Ian; Polach, H. A.; and Stipp, J. J. "Excess radiogenic argon in young subaerial basalts from the Auckland volcanic field, New Zealand", *Geochimica et Cosmochimica Acta*, Vol. 33, 1969] This presents a problem. If the tree trunks are buried in the lava flow, they must be the same age as the lava flow. So how can the Carbon-14 date of the tree trunks be so vastly different from the Potassium-Argon date of the lava? The experiment has given inconsistent results.

Lava flows from Hualalai Volcano in Hawaii were dated at 140 million to 2.96 billion years. In fact Hualalai erupted in 1801. [Plaisted, David. "The Radiometric Dating Game". http://trueorigin.org /dating.asp. 1998. Retrieved August 21, 2010]

Five samples from a lava flow in Washington state were dated by Potassium-Argon, giving ages ranging from 340,000 to 2.8 million years. That's quite a range, calling into question the reliability of the method. Another dating method gave an even younger age: Eyewitnesses watched that lava flow being formed when Mt. St. Helens erupted in 1980. [Austin, Dr. Steven. "Excess Argon within Mineral Concentrates from the New Dacite Lava Dome at Mount St. Helens Volcano", *Creation Ex Nihilo Technical Journal*. 1996, Vol. 10, part 3.]

Dr Andrew Snelling lists two dozen such anomalous results. [Snelling, Andrew, PhD. "Excess Argon: The "Achilles' Heel" of Potassium-Argon and Argon-Argon Dating of Volcanic Rocks". http://www.icr.org

/index.php?module=articles&action=view&ID=436. Retrieved August 21, 2010.]

When I've brought up these examples in the past, people will occasionally challenge me on the grounds that the Potassium-Argon age may be the age when the rock was originally formed inside the earth, not the date that the volcano erupted. The problem with that idea is that Potassium-Argon dating is based on measuring the rate of decay of Potassium into Argon. Argon is a gas. As long as the lava is liquid, the Argon will escape as gas bubbles. Therefore, the "clock" does not start until the lava flow solidifies.

In some cases the evolutionists offer explanations of what went wrong. For example, they say the lava from Hualalai was under water for many years, which caused Potassium to leach out and contaminated the sample. Maybe so. But are they then telling us that all the other sites that have been dated to such long ages were never, ever, in all those supposed billions of years, ever under water or otherwise contaminated?

In case after case, when we actually can perform a real scientific experiment to validate radiometric dating, it proves to be wrong.

If when you *can* corroborate the evidence, someone is repeatedly proven to be wrong, perhaps you should be cautious about taking their word for it in cases where there is no way to test their claims.

So what's wrong with the method when the theory sounds so convincing? Many secondary theories have been proposed. The evolutionists usually insist that in each case where the method has been proven to have failed, the sample must have been contaminated or the experimenter must have made a mistake. Maybe so, but that's asking for a lot of gullibility.

A creation-based theory is to question the original state of the system. At the beginning of this section I compared radiometric dating to an hourglass and said that you could determine how long it has been running based on how much sand was at the bottom. But this isn't entirely true. To do this, you must start with the assumption that initially 100% of the sand was in the top and 0% in the bottom, or at least that the amount of sand in the top and bottom was known. Radiometric methods assume that when the clock started ticking, the sample contained 100% parent element and 0% daughter element. If this was not true, if the sample contained, say, 50% parent and 50%

daughter, then using the method we would overestimate the age of the sample by one half-life.

This theory may apply in some cases, but not in all. In the case of lava flows, one of the most common subjects of radiometric tests, we can be fairly confident that the sample is at least generally pure because the liquefaction and solidification of the lava flow would naturally cause this to happen. Also, many of these radiometric decay processes involve multiple steps. It is not a simple A decays into B, but A decays into B which decays into C, etc. This theory would require us to believe that the sample originally contained all of these daughter products. Unless we are going to speculate that God deliberately created rocks with just the right elements to fool us, this makes the theory unlikely. On the other hand, a problem with the evolutionary interpretation is that while the daughter elements are normally all found, they are not found in the correct quantities to fit the theory.

The leading alternative idea in creation theory circles is that decay rates are not constant as the basic theory proposes, but can change depending on environmental factors. Exactly what these factors might be is a subject for further research. But even small variations over time in a consistent direction would radically alter the calculated age.

Other dating methods

Numerous other methods have been proposed for estimating the age of the earth. All give radically smaller ages than we get from the radiometric methods.

For example:

You probably learned about the "hydraulic cycle" or "water cycle" in school: Rain falls, accumulates into rivers, and flows into the ocean. Then the water evaporates, forms clouds, and falls as rain. While most of the rain falls right back into the oceans, some falls on the land, where it again accumulates into rivers and flows back into the ocean. When the water flows into the ocean, it picks up materials from the ground, like salts, which dissolve in the water and thus flow into the oceans. These salts do not evaporate with the water. There are some processes that move salt from the oceans back to the land, like hurricanes, but these are not adequate to balance off the salt flowing into the oceans. Thus the amount of salt in the oceans continually increases. That's why the oceans are salty. If the oceans had started with no salt at all, to get to the present amount of salt at current rates would take 42 million years. If they started with some amount of salt, that would reduce this age. Thus that is the maximum age for the world's oceans. [Humphreys, Dr. Russell, PhD. "Evidence for a Young World". ICR Impact #384, June 2005. Also available at http://www.answersingenesis.org /docs/4005.asp]

The Earth's magnetic field is getting weaker. Scientists have been measuring the strength of the magnetic field for 160 years, and over that time the strength has been steadily declining. Projecting this delcine backwards gives a maximum age of the Earth of about 8,000 years. [Snelling, Andrew. "The Earth's magnetic field and the age of the Earth". *Creation* 13(4):44–48, September 1991. Available at http://www.answersingenesis.org /creation/v13/i4/magnetic.asp.] Evolutionists often attempt to rebut this by claiming that the Earth's magnetic field has reversed polarity in the past, that is, the north and south poles have switched. It is difficult to see how this solves the problem. Energy is being lost over time. Switching the polarity will not make the energy magically come back. If your home is experiencing a power failure, you cannot solve the problem by unplugging all your appliances, rotating the plugs 180 degrees, and plugging them back in.

When Uranium decays into Lead it gives off Alpha particles, which are chemically identical to Helium nuclei. Helium is a gas, and so it slowly leaks out of the rocks containing the Uranium. Experiments on rocks which have been dated by Uranium-Lead decay at 1.5 billion years show too much Helium. At the measured rates, the Helium could only have been leaking for 6,000 years, not 1.5 billion. [Humphreys]

Of course none of these dating methods can be proven experimentally, any more than the radiometric methods. But the basic technique behind them is very similar to that used in radiometric methods: Find some natural process that changes A into B, determine the rate of change, measure the relative amounts of A and B, and then project backwards to calculate an age. If radiometric dating is valid, so are these. There could be technical flaws with any of them. But then there can be technical flaws with radiometric dating.

The Only Scientific Technique

There is only one method for dating the age of any object that can truly be said to be "scientific". That is for a human being to observe it being formed and record the date. Well, it wouldn't have to be a human being, it could be a robot or a Martian, but some qualified observer. This is what science is all about: experimentation and observation. Any method based on speculation about what happened in the past – no matter how reasonable and plausible that speculation sounds – is not "science". It is philosophical speculation.

Fortunately, we have exactly such an observation of when the Earth was created. We have the observations of Adam and Eve, passed down to us through the book of Genesis in the Bible. You may reject this evidence on the grounds that you consider them unreliable observers or that the records are inaccurate. But this is the only truly *scientific* evidence we have for the age of the Earth. And this, of course, is precisely the evidence that the critic rejects on supposedly scientific grounds.

Conclusion

I don't claim that this short section is a complete discussion of the evidence about the age of the Earth. That is a highly technical subject on which many books have been written. My intent here is simply to give a quick view of the state of the subject.

There is no scientific evidence – in the literal sense of experimental evidence – that the Earth is billions of years old. Radiometric dating is an interesting philosophical speculation, not a scientific theory.

There is no scientific reason to doubt that the Earth is thousands, not billions, of years old, consistent with Genesis.

There is more evidence that the Earth is thousands or millions of years old than that it is billions of years old. But to the critic, one anti-Bible argument always trumps 100 pro-Bible arguments.

2.5. Argument from Scale

In ancient times people didn't have any idea how big the universe really was. They thought the Earth was the center of the universe and the biggest thing in the universe and that the stars and planets were tiny objects in the sky. So it made sense to suppose that a God who created the universe would consider Earth the most important thing in it, and that the people who inhabited it would be vitally important to him.

But today we know that the Earth is just one tiny planet orbiting an unremarkable star among billions of other stars in our galaxy, and that our galaxy is just one among many billions of galaxies. With this greater scientific understanding of our position in the universe, it is

obvious that, even if there is a God who created all this, our tiny planet and the people on it would barely be an afterthought to him.

The basic principle behind this argument is that an intelligent being must logically and inevitably assign importance and concern to things in direct proportion to their weight. A moment's thought will show that this is not true.

Suppose that your house was on fire. Which would you save first: A 50-pound pile of bricks left over from some old construction, or a diamond ring weighing a fraction of an ounce? The bricks clearly weigh more. Does that make them more important? The diamond ring is surely worth more.

Scenario two: Your house is on fire. Which would you save first: That 50-pound pile of bricks, or your newborn baby daughter? According to the argument from scale, you would logically and inevitably save the pile of bricks, because they are bigger and heavier than the baby. Would that be your choice?

An intelligent being does not value things based on their weight. He values the rare over the common, the complex over the simple, the living over the inanimate, and things that he has decided he loves over things with no personal significance.

Critics who make this argument routinely frame it in terms of the discoveries of modern astronomy, and how the universe is so much bigger than previously thought. But this is only a difference in degree and not in kind from what people in ancient times knew. Ancient people were well aware that there were animals in the world that were larger than people: elephants and whales and so forth. And they knew of many things that were far bigger than any living creature, like islands and mountains. Nevertheless, the Bible writers saw no need to explain why God cares about people more than he cares about big piles of rocks. Apparently the idea that God would love things in direct proportion to their weight never occurred to them.

If there is a God who created the universe, it is quite rational to suppose that he would value intelligent creatures that he loves over balls of gas, even if the balls of gas are bigger and weigh more.

Unless, of course, you think that it is just logical and inevitable that a man would love his wife more if only she gained a hundred pounds.

2.6. Light Before the Sun

In its discussion of "creation week", the Bible says that light was created on the first day, but the sun was not created until the fourth day. This is impossible. How could there be light when there was no sun?

Light Before the Sun

This criticism reflects a naïve and unscientific understanding of light. Light is made up of sub-atomic particles called "photons". There are various physical phenomena that cause objects to emit photons, that is to say, give off light. But photons exist independently of any given phenomenon that sets them in motion.

The Bible tells us that on the first day, "God said, 'Let there be light'; and there was light." [Genesis 1:3] This must mean that at that time God created photons. Then on the fourth day he created the Sun, which does indeed give off photons. But the photons existed before the Sun. Water may come from a faucet, but that doesn't mean that the faucet created the water or that water cannot exist without a faucet.

Technically, some experiments indicate that light is a particle; other experiments indicate that it is a wave. Physicists have concluded that it is both: basically, that each photon exhibits wave-like properties. This phenomenon is known as "wave-particle duality". But this issue is outside the scope of what is necessary for this discussion, so we will not go into any more detail about it here.

We don't even need to get into a technical discussion of photons to see the problem with this criticism. You demonstrate the fallacy every time you turn on an electric light. The sun is not the only source of light in the universe. There are untold numbers of stars, fire, lightning, hot magma, and bioluminescent fish, to name natural light sources that come to mind. Today there are man-made light sources like electric lights and TV screens.

Day and Night Before the Sun

A slightly more rational criticism is that the Bible refers to day and night before the Sun was created. According to Genesis, the Earth was created on the first day. Light was also created on the first day and the Earth experienced day and night, but the Sun was not created until the fourth day. The language is too explicit to be just a measure of time: "God called the light Day, and the darkness He called Night. So the evening and the morning were the first day." [Genesis 1:5] How, the critic asks, could there be "day" and "night", a "first day", a "second day", and so forth, before the sun was created?

We should note that as an attack on the scientific credibility of the Bible, this objection doesn't hold much water. The essence of such a criticism is that a scientific flaw proves that the Bible was not inspired by God but was written by primitive people who didn't know anything about modern science. With our modern scientific knowledge, we now know that they made mistakes.

But that idea can't reasonably be applied here. Even the most primitive people know that night and day are caused by the rising and setting of the Sun. They may think that the Sun goes around the Earth, they may even think that the Earth is flat, but they know that day and night are caused by the Sun. So even if Genesis was not inspired, but was written by some very ignorant and primitive person, he would have to have been ignorant indeed to have not realized that the Sun gives light and causes day and night. While this is curious, scientific ignorance cannot explain the curiosity.

God created the Earth on day one and set it spinning. Then when he created light, he created a stream of light coming from one direction, so as the Earth turned, it experienced day and night. The Genesis account does not tell us whether God created some temporary light source, or whether he just created a stream of photons. In either case, on the fourth day he created the Sun, thus making the temporary means of providing light no longer necessary. Just as scaffolding may be used to temporarily hold up a building until the permanent supports are complete, so God created a temporary light source until the permanent light source was ready. I would guess that the Earth was motionless in space before the Sun was created, as there would have been nothing for it to orbit. But the text doesn't give us any details on this point.

Conclusion

The Sun is not the only source of light in the universe. The critic who brings up this argument demonstrates his own ignorance of the nature of light. God must have created some temporary light source to give the Earth day and night until he got around to creating the Sun.

2.7.   Plants Before the Sun

The Bible says that plants were created on the third day, but the Sun was not created until the fourth day. How did the plants survive

with no sunlight? If the days of Genesis are really long ages, how did plants survive for millions of years with no sun?

Genesis clearly says that there was light from day one. Apparently there was some source of light before the Sun, or God created light directly without creating a light source. See issue 2.6. This light could have sustained photosynthesis until the Sun was created. For that matter, plants could survive for one day without sunlight.

As to the argument that the days of Genesis must really have been millions of years each, this is a theory proposed by people who reject a literal interpretation of Genesis because it is inconsistent with evolutionary theories. I make no claim to defending such theories in this book. I am defending Biblical literalism here. Any liberal Christian who wants to reinterpret Genesis to accommodate evolution can write his own book.

2.8.   Purpose of Distant Planets

Recent discoveries in astronomy prove that there are planets orbiting stars many light years away. If the universe was really created by God for the benefit of human beings, why would he create these distant planets? People will never live there. What purpose do they serve? But if the universe really evolved, then we would expect to see other solar systems much like our own throughout the universe.

Every now and then an atheist demands that the Christian explain God's purpose in creating something that the atheist considers useless. The idea, of course, is that the Christian has no answer, and so this proves that the universe has no purpose, and so it could not have been created by any "God". The evolutionist doesn't have to worry about such questions, because he claims that the universe doesn't have any "purpose", it just is.

This argument has been made about everything from distant planets to mosquitos to, well, I once saw a cartoon where a little boy asks, "How could a loving God have created big brothers?"

Sometimes a perfectly valid answer is, "I don't know, but perhaps with further scientific discoveries we will learn the answer."

If you asked someone 200 years ago why God created Uranium, the best they could come up with might be, "Umm, well, it can be used to make yellow paint." Today we know that it can be used to fuel nuclear reactors.

If you asked someone 200 years ago why God created the asteroids, they might well have had no idea. But now we know that they were put there for us to mine when we begin to colonize the Solar System. If you want to build a space station with materials from Earth, there is a huge cost for the energy to get those materials out of the Earth's gravitational field. If you discovered a way to turn lead into gold that would only work in space, it would be useless: It costs more to lift a pound of lead into space than the value of a pound of gold. But the asteroids are relatively small and so have only weak gravitational fields. Many are big enough to be worth mining for minerals, but small enough that the cost of lifting minerals off their surfaces to send where you want to do the construction is modest.

In the case of planets around distant stars, the answer is obvious to any science fiction fan: Someday we will travel to these stars and we will use these planets to live on, and/or as sources of raw materials.

I'm not going to get into discussions of prophecy and the second coming here. This book is controversial enough without getting into that. But regardless of when Jesus will return or exactly what will happen when he does, I think we will continue to live in the same universe, and our population will continue to grow. Adam and Eve were told to "be fruitful and multiply" before the Fall, so it is likely that this command will still apply after we are restored to paradise. If our population continues to grow forever, sooner or later we will literally fill the Earth. Then we'll need to colonize other planets. It will likely take centuries to colonize the Solar System, and centuries more before we can begin to explore and colonize other star systems. But we'll get there eventually. As we will live forever, the "interstellar speed limit" of 186,000 miles per second will just be an inconvenience.

Of course, we should always be cautious about saying why God created any given thing. I wonder if sometimes God doesn't look down from Heaven in exasperation and say, "You weren't supposed to drink that stuff! I created that for you to fuel your cars."

2.9. Prayer Experiments

There have been some experiments done to test prayer scientifically. In these experiments, the scientists will take a group of patients and divide them into two groups: people will pray for members

of one group, while no one will pray for members of the other group. Both receive the same level of treatment.

These experiments have given very inconsistent results. Some find that the people who were prayed for were more likely to get well, but none found a dramatic difference. The effect is at best a few percentage points. Thus, prayer doesn't work.

These results don't surprise me at all. You cannot study prayer in the laboratory like you can study physics or chemistry.

How could you study prayer "scientifically"? Science is the study of the forces of nature, of mindless, mechanical forces. Prayer is a request made to God. Prayer is not a blind act of nature, but an appeal for action by an intelligent being. This makes prayer virtually impossible to study in a controlled experiment.

Let's consider a simple analogy. Suppose you told me that your Uncle Henry is very generous. You tell me how he is always ready to help any person in need who comes to him. I decide to test your claims about Uncle Henry scientifically. I get fifty people to go to your Uncle Henry's door. My plan is that they will stand in line, and the first person will ring the doorbell and tell your uncle some tale of hardship. I will stand by with a video camera filming your uncle's response, so that I can document whether he offers help. When this person is finished, and your uncle either has or has not given him some assistance, the next person will step up and give his tale of hardship. Et cetera. Then I will conduct a similar experiment where this same group of beggars knock on the doors of randomly selected people, as a control. When all are done, I will study the videotapes and see what aid your uncle gave to each, carefully plot this on charts, and compare it against the amount of help the same group received when knocking on the doors of the control group. Then I will be able to precisely and scientifically measure your Uncle Henry's generosity.

Do you think this experiment will give meaningful results? Surely not. The minute Uncle Henry sees the line of people waiting outside his door and me standing there with the video camera, he will know that these are not honest people seeking help. He may not know exactly what we're up to, but it is very unlikely that he will react the same way he would to people who were truly coming to him for help in time of need. He might call the police and have us all dragged away, or he might play along with it for a joke, but the results of such an experiment are not going to be meaningful.

Scientists who attempt to study human behavior have routinely, and not surprisingly, found that people often change their behavior when they know that they are subjects of an experiment.

With human beings you are sometimes able to study them secretly. You can perform experiments without telling the subjects that this is an experiment, and so observe how they behave "naturally". God is generally supposed to be all-knowing, or at least to be able to see a lot more than we can, so it would be unreasonable to expect that you could fool God into not knowing that this is all an experiment.

Even when people don't know they are the subjects of an experiment, there behavior is not consistent. Inanimate objects behave in predictable ways. If a scientist sets up an experiment the same way three times, he expects to get the same results all three times. If he does not, then he concludes that there must be additional relevant factors which he is not controlling. Maybe the experiment is affected by temperature or humidity or cosmic rays. Indeed, perhaps the only serious modification to the scientific method since Roger Bacon first described it in 1267 has been the idea of "repeatability": You must be able to perform the same experiment many times and get the same results, and other scientists must be able to reproduce your results independently. If not, then your results are suspect. (That doesn't necessarily mean that you of lying. While fraud is one possible explanation, especially if you are claiming dramatic, publicity-winning results, more often the explanation is that you have made an honest mistake.)

Intelligent beings are not so predictable. Social scientists routinely attempt to study human behavior experimentally, and routinely get ambiguous results. Give three people the exact same set of circumstances and they may respond differently. For example, I recently read of a social experiment where the researcher left a wallet with cash and credit cards on a park bench where people were likely to find it, and then observed what they did. It's not hard to guess the results: Some people simply ignored the wallet. Others took the money and threw the wallet in the trash. Still others used the IDs in the wallet to contact the "owner" and return it. Indeed, the same person may respond differently on different occasions. We wouldn't be surprised if in an experiment like the above, someone might ignore a found wallet one day but steal it on another day. This is why there is a vast difference between the physical sciences and the social sciences.

God is an intelligent being and not a force of nature. At least, the God of the Bible is. So he cannot be expected to respond to an experiment in a blindly mechanical way.

In these prayer experiments, God would presumably know that the whole thing was an experiment. He might decide to heal those for whom you prayed and not those for whom you did not pray to strengthen the faith of Christians involved in the experiment. He might equally well decide to heal everyone out of mercy, or to choose whom to heal in accordance with his larger plans for their lives. He might decide to heal only those you did *not* pray for just for fun. The experiment is meaningless. The very fact that we are performing an experiment alters the conditions we are trying to test.

If God wanted to give people proof of his existence or his power, he could find more effective ways to do this than to alter the rate of recovery from illness by a few percentage points in a prayer experiment. He could, say, make the sun stand still or turn a river to blood.

I am not surprised when experiments to test prayer give inconclusive results. God is not a vending machine who dispenses favors if you just put the right coin in the slot. He is an intelligent being, who is not obliged to play along with a silly game.

2.10. Miracles Impossible

In ancient times, people believed in miracles. But modern science has proven that miracles are impossible. Pre-scientific people didn't understand this, but now we know better. Stories in the Bible about miracles cannot be true.

Evidence

People who make this criticism often say that Christians only believe in miracles because of blind faith, while the critic is an impartial scientific observer. This is not just wrong, but the exact reverse of reality.

As the British writer G. K. Chesterton put it:

Somehow or other an extraordinary idea has arisen that the disbelievers in miracles consider them coldly and fairly, while believers in miracles accept them only in connection with some dogma. The fact is quite the other way. The believers in miracles accept them (rightly or wrongly) because they have evidence for them. The disbelievers in miracles deny them (rightly or wrongly) because they have a doctrine against them.

Chesterton, G. K. *Orthodoxy*. Garden City, NY: Image Books, 1959. p. 150. (Originally published 1908.)

There are many eyewitness accounts of miracles, from the Bible and throughout history. The witness's testimony may be accurate or they may be lying or mistaken. The person who is willing to accept the possibility of miracles says that the evidence these witnesses present should be considered just as we would consider the testimony of someone describing any event they claim to have witnessed. We should examine the reliability of the witness, whether they corroborate each other, any physical evidence, etc. The critic says that all reports of miracles must be immediately dismissed without examining the evidence, based on his dogmatic belief that miracles are impossible.

How does the critic know that miracles are impossible? He cannot say that it is because no one has ever observed a miracle. Many people claim to have done exactly that. The critic must first dismiss the testimony of people who claim to have observed miracles. He does this on the basis of his dogmatic belief that miracles are impossible. He then explains that only superstitious people and religious fanatics claim to have observed miracles. How does he know that these people are superstitious or religious fanatics? Why, because they claim to have observed miracles. We know miracles are impossible because no reliable observer has ever seen one. Anyone who claims to have seen a miracle is by definition not a reliable observer, because we know that miracles are impossible.

Gullibility

The people of Bible times were not reliable observers because they were gullible when it came to such things. While a modern person seeing an unusual phenomenon would seek a rational, scientific explanation, people in Bible times were quick to believe in a miracle. Right?

Not according to the Bible. When the Bible reports a miracle, it consistently reports skepticism about the miracle.

Suppose that someone went to the president of the United States claiming to be a messenger from God and demanding that the president take some dramatic political action. To prove that he is sent by God, he performs miracles. Would the president just accept these miracles without question? Surely not. My guess is that he would call in his science advisor to seek a rational explanation.

The Bible says that Moses went to Pharaoh claiming to be a messenger from God and demanding that Pharaoh take dramatic political actions. To prove that he was sent by God, he performed miracles. Did Pharaoh just accept these miracles without question? No. "But Pharaoh also called the wise men and the sorcerers; so the magicians of Egypt, they also did in like manner with their enchantments." [Exodus 7:11] When Pharaoh saw that magicians were able to reproduce Moses' miracles through the same sorts of tricks and misdirection that magicians have used for millennia, he concluded Moses was a fraud. Note that Pharaoh didn't call in his engineers or scientists (they would have called them "philosophers" back then). He sent for stage magicians. I once read that a well-known psychic was perfectly willing to perform his feats in front of scientists ... but not in front of magicians. (Sorry, I can't find a citation for this. I read it decades ago.) Pharaoh was smart: he knew that magicians could spot the sort of trick that they would do themselves, while scientists would likely naively take what they observed at face value. It wasn't until Moses was able to do things that the magicians could not that Pharaoh was impressed.

Or take a New Testament example. Jesus reportedly healed a man born blind. If anyone was going to gullibly accept a miracle, surely it would be the religious people, right? So what was the religious leaders' response?

> But the Jews did not believe concerning him, that he had been blind and received his sight, until they called the parents of him who had received his sight. And they asked them, saying, "Is this your son, who you say was born blind? How then does he now see?"

John 6:18-19

After the parents confirmed that this man had been born blind, the religious leaders still didn't believe. They eventually excommunicated the man for his blasphemy in claiming to have experienced a miracle.

When Joseph learned that his fiancée Mary was pregnant, he did not cry, "Hallelujah! A virgin birth!" No, Joseph knew full well the elementary scientific fact that for a woman to become a mother requires that there be a father. As he knew that he was not the father, he decided to break off the engagement. It is not until an angel came to Joseph and he himself witnessed a miracle that he believed Mary's story about a miracle. [Matthew 1:19]

The critic might say that these stories are fiction, and so the skepticism is fiction too, and proves nothing. At the very least it proves that the Bible writers expected the response to miracles to be skepticism. If the story is true, then this is how people actually reacted. If the story is fiction, then it is how the writers thought it would be plausible to say people would react. Either way, it tells us what the attitude of the people of the time toward miracles was. No one expected that someone would see a miracle and automatically believe. They would demand proof that it really happened, and that it was not a trick. They were at least as rational about this as people today.

Experiments

How could science prove that miracles are impossible? "Science" is the process of gaining knowledge through the scientific method of experimentation and observation. For science to prove that miracles are impossible, there would have to be scientific experiments testing miracles.

This immediately presents a problem. How could you construct a scientific experiment to test a miracle? In a classic scientific experiment, you create the desired situation in the laboratory and observe the results. If, for example, you have a theory about what happens when chemicals X and Y are mixed together, then you construct an experiment where you mix them together and you see what happens.

When we talk about a literal "miracle", we presumably mean an interruption in the natural order brought about by God. That is, a miracle is not a blind act of nature, but the act of an intelligent being. This is, of course, the whole reason why the critic does not believe that miracles happen: he claims there is no such being as "God". But this also makes miracles virtually impossible to study in a controlled experiment. Inanimate objects can be relied on to behave consistently and predictably. Intelligent beings cannot.

Miracles are not the only subject which cannot be tested by a classic laboratory experiment. Human behavior is also difficult to test in the laboratory for the same reasons. Other phenomenon cannot be tested in the laboratory because they are beyond human control, at least with our present technology. We cannot create stars and planets in the laboratory to study their behavior. For that matter, many terrestrial phenomena, like volcanoes and hurricanes, are beyond our power to create or control. To study these, we must fall back to "field experiments": waiting for the event we are interested in to occur naturally and then observing it. Because we cannot control such experiments, the scientist must wait patiently for the event to occur so he can observe it. If the event is rare, he may not even realistically hope to observe it himself, but must rely on the observations of others who were fortunate enough to be there.

It might be possible to scientifically study miracles this way. A God powerful enough to perform miracles in the first place might simply not permit you to study them. If you can study them at all, about the most you could hope for would be to collect the observations of people who claimed to have witnessed miracles and carefully review them. Each report could then be evaluated on its own merits. What exactly did the observer see or hear? Is his report corroborated by other observers? Etc.

Circular reasoning

But the critics refuse to examine miracles scientifically. Instead, they simply declare in advance that miracles are impossible, and then dismiss any evidence offered as "obviously" a mistake or a hoax because they know that miracles are impossible. Anyone who claims to have seen a miracle is dismissed as a "religious fanatic".

So the critic claims that science has proven that miracles never happen. How can science conclude this? Because no one has ever seen a miracle happen. But, someone objects, there are many reports throughout history of miracles. Well, the critic replies condescendingly, those reports just come from religious fanatics, you can't take those seriously.

That is, anyone who claims to have seen a miracle is, by definition, not reliable. Then we see that no reliable person has ever seen a miracle. Thus miracles never happen. Theory proved. QED.

Imagine if a scientist tried to use this kind of reasoning on some other scientific theory. For example, suppose Dr. Jones proposes a theory about Saturn's moon Titan that requires that its atmosphere contains no ethylene. (I'm not referring to any real theory -- I'm just making this up for an example.) As support for his theory, he points out that no observations have ever shown the presence of ethylene in Titan's atmosphere. Then a space probe sent to Titan tests the atmosphere and finds measurable amounts of ethylene. Well, Dr. Jones announces, this just proves that the experiment was flawed. As we know, based on my theory, that the atmosphere of Titan contains no ethylene, then if this experiment appeared to detect any, there is obviously something wrong with the experiment. Thus, he says, my theory is confirmed. No reliable experiment has detected any ethylene, thus confirming my theory. Any experiment that claims or appears to have detected ethylene must be a mistake or even a hoax, because we know that there is no ethylene.

Would any honest investigator find such circular reasoning convincing? But that is exactly the logic we are supposed to accept with regards to miracles.

All of them?

Let me clarify that I am not saying that all claims of miracles must be automatically believed. I certainly do not believe them all. What I am saying is that if we are going to examine them scientifically, we must examine each claim on the basis of the quality of the observation, corroborating evidence, etc., and not on the basis of a pre-determined dogma about what is or is not possible.

Ignorance

Critics often say that ancient people believed in miracles because they were ignorant of science. Ignorance of science cannot possibly explain claims of miracles. If the definition of a miracle is that it is an event that violates the laws of science, then no one would recognize a miracle unless they had some understanding of science.

If the people in Jesus' day did not know that it was impossible for water to turn into wine, they wouldn't have called it an amazing miracle. They would have just said, "Oh, how convenient, now we have some extra wine."

If the people of Joshua's day did not know that a day was always 24 hours long, if they thought that a hot day working in the sun not only seemed longer than a pleasant day lounging around the house, but really was longer, then when Joshua made the sun stand still they wouldn't have called it a great miracle. They would have just said, "Wow, this was a really long day."

The only relevant effect of ignorance of science would be to cause someone to fail to recognize a miracle when he saw it. If someone observed an event that was "scientifically impossible" but didn't know enough about science to realize that, he would simply say, "Hmm, I never saw that before" and never describe it as a miracle. The event might well not even make it into the history books or scriptures, as it would not have been viewed as extraordinary.

Conclusion

Science has not proven that miracles are impossible. It is extremely difficult to test miracles scientifically because they are – or are claimed to be – the acts of an intelligent being and not the blind forces of nature. To the extent that they can be tested, all the actual evidence, based on the reported evidence of eye witnesses, is that miracles do happen. The primary reason to disbelieve in miracles is a pre-conceived dogma that miracles are impossible.

2.11. Rational Explanations for Miracles

Many of the supposed miracles in the Bible can be explained rationally.

When the Gospels say that Jesus fed 5000 people with a little boy's five loaves of bread and two fish [John 6:1-10], what probably really happened was that Jesus held up the example of the little boy and others who had brought food were shamed into sharing it.

When Exodus says that God led the people with a "pillar of cloud by day and a pillar of fire by night" [Exodus 13:20 et al], what probably really happened was that the army had ensigns who carried a torch on top of a pole to lead the people at night, and a smoking brazier on top of a pole to lead the people in the daytime.

When Genesis says that God destroyed Sodom and Gomorrah by raining fire and brimstone from the sky, what probably really happened was that the cities were destroyed by a volcano.

Et cetera, for many such stories.

I've grouped these together – and you can add many similar "rational explanations" for Bible miracles – because my response to all of them is the same.

The people of Jesus day did not have the scientific knowledge that we have today. But whatever their scientific ignorance, they knew the difference between people sharing their food and God miraculously creating food. If what had "really happened" was that Jesus shamed people into sharing their food, John could simply have said that Jesus shamed people into sharing their food. He might have described it as a stirring sermon. He would not have described it as a great miracle.

Similarly, the people of Moses day knew the difference between a man carrying a torch and a miraculous manifestation of God. If the army was led by an ensign with a torch, why didn't the writer just say that?

Maybe in a case like the destruction of Sodom and Gomorrah, you could say that the writers of the time didn't understand what had happened, and so they confused a natural disaster for miraculous judgment. Even that is a stretch: We have ancient accounts of volcanoes, like Pliny's description of the eruption of Mount Vesuvius. The people of the time didn't know as much about volcanoes and earthquakes as modern scientists do, but they knew what they were. Pliny relates the story without any reference to the supernatural or the gods. [Pliny the Younger. "Epistle 65." *Epistles*. ca AD 100] So again, if what "really happened" was that there was a volcano, why didn't the writer say that? If it was a volcano but the writer believed that God had caused it to erupt at that time and place to execute his judgment, why didn't he say that?

You could speculate that the Bible writer took a true story and then made up the part about a miracle. But if he was going to make up a story about a miracle, why would he take a real event and lie about it? Anyone who was present at the real event would know that it was a lie. If the writer just made up a story from scratch, it would be harder for someone to say that it never happened. The writer could always reply, "How would you know? You weren't there." To prove that an account of a real event is not true, you need only find a witness who was at the real event. To prove that an account of a totally fictitious event is not true, you would have to know everything that happened anywhere near the supposed place and time.

The critic takes the position that he believes part of the story, but not all of it. He believes that Jesus really fed 5000 people, but not the part about the only source of food being one boy's lunch box. He believes that the Israelis were led through the wilderness by a pillar of fire, but not that the fire was a miraculous appearance of God. He'll believe one verse but not the next. He'll believe the first half of a sentence but not the second half.

I read one critic who didn't believe that Jesus came back from the dead. And so he quoted Matthew 28:5-6, where Mary met a man at the cemetery who says to her, "Do not be afraid, for I know that you seek Jesus who was crucified. He is not here ... Come, see the place where the Lord lay". You see, the critic wrote, they had come to the wrong tomb and the gardener was trying to point them to the correct one. The catch to this is that where the critic put the "...", the words elided are "for He is risen, as He said", and the next sentence the man says is, "And go quickly and tell His disciples that He is risen from the dead."

What's the point? If you don't believe a miracle is possible, why not just declare that the whole story is a lie? What's the point of pasting together parts of sentences and inserting material you just invented to turn a story you can't believe into a story you can believe?

I don't want to put words into other people's mouths, but I suspect that the critic is trying to pay lip service to the Bible to appease the superstitious simpletons, while gutting the whole point of the narrative.

2.12. Miracles Explain Away

The idea of miracles provides an easy out for Christians. Any time we prove that some event the Bible describes is impossible, the Christian just says, "Oh, it was a miracle."

The Bible is about an all-powerful creator God. Of course such a God could and would perform miracles. This is not a convenient out for when the Bible describes impossible events. These events are only included because a miracle-performing God could have and would have done them. If the Bible didn't describe a miracle-performing God, then it wouldn't mention any incredible events that would need to be "explained away" with the idea of miracles.

Suppose an "aviation critic" doesn't believe that Charles Lindbergh really flew across the Atlantic. He looks for flaws in newspaper accounts of Lindbergh's flight. Ah, he says, this story is clearly impossible! It says that Lindbergh crossed the Atlantic in only 34 hours! But that's a 3,500 mile trip, and there isn't a boat in the world that can travel 3,500 miles in only 34 hours. But, you reply puzzled, Lindbergh didn't take a boat, he flew in an airplane. Ohhhh, the critic says, so when I point out an impossibility in the story, you drag in this "airplane" to magically explain it all away.

Of course the story is impossible without bringing in the idea of an airplane. That's because the whole point of the story is that Lindbergh flew an airplane. If Lindbergh had taken a boat, then we wouldn't need to talk about airplanes to explain how it was possible. But if Lindbergh had taken a boat, the story wouldn't be interesting enough to be worth telling.

Likewise, if the story of Moses didn't include the Nile turning to blood and the mysterious deaths of the Egyptians' first born sons, or if the story of Jesus didn't include him coming back from the dead, then we wouldn't need to "drag in" the idea of miracles to explain it. But the whole point of these stories is that they are about amazing, miraculous events. Without the miracles, these would be obscure stories about a slave rebellion that was crushed by the Egyptian army and a religious leader who said some nice words and then died. We do not drag in miracles to explain away impossible events. The whole point of these stories is that they are about seemingly impossible events that can only be explained as miracles.

2.13. Darkness at the Crucifixion

The Bible says that when Jesus died the world suddenly turned dark. There is no astronomical reason for such an event. This could not have ever happened.

An Eclipse, or Not

An interesting insight on this event can be found in the writings of Julius Africanus, a Christian writer and historian.

About AD 221, he wrote:

On the whole world there pressed a most fearful darkness; and the rocks were rent by an earthquake, and many places in Judea and other districts were thrown down. This darkness Thallus, in the third book of his *History*, calls, as appears to me without reason, an eclipse of the sun. For the Hebrews celebrate the Passover on the 14th day according to the moon, and the passion of our Saviour fails on the day before the Passover; but an eclipse of the sun takes place only when the moon comes under the sun. And it cannot happen at any other time but in the interval between the first day of the new moon and the last of the old, that is, at their junction: how then should an eclipse be supposed to happen when the moon is almost diametrically opposite the sun? Let that opinion pass however; let it carry the majority with it; and let this portent of the world be deemed an eclipse of the sun, like others a portent only to the eye. Phlegon records that, in the time of Tiberius Caesar, at full moon, there was a full

eclipse of the sun from the sixth hour to the ninth —
manifestly that one of which we speak. But what has an
eclipse in common with an earthquake, the rending rocks,
and the resurrection of the dead, and so great a
perturbation throughout the universe? Surely no such
event as this is recorded for a long period. But it was a
darkness induced by God, because the Lord happened then
to suffer.

Africanus, Julius. Chronography, ca AD 221

Thallus wrote about AD 52. Unfortunately, most of his work
has not survived the centuries, so we don't have the exact quote from
Thallus that Africanus is replying to. But it is clear from the context
that Thallus was a secular writer attempting to rebut the claims of
Christians that the darkness that came over the land at the time of
Christ's death was something miraculous. It was, he says, simply an
eclipse of the sun. No miracle, but an ordinary astronomical event.

Eclipses and Lunar Cycles

Africanus replies by pointing out some astronomical facts:
Every report of Jesus death said that he was killed the day before
Passover. Passover takes place on a full moon. But a solar eclipse
cannot occur on a full moon. Therefore, the darkness at Jesus death
could not have been a solar eclipse.

Perhaps Africanus's astronomy requires a little explanation.

The Earth circles the Sun, and the Moon circles the Earth.
While the Sun is much larger than the Moon, it is also much farther
away, so that as seen from the Earth, the apparent size of the Moon is
just about the same as the apparent size of the Sun. When the Moon
passes between the Sun and the Earth in just the right position, it
blocks out the sun, causing a solar eclipse. (Whether this is a
coincidence or whether the Solar System was deliberately created that
way for some purpose is another subject.) But for this to happen, the
Moon must be between the Earth and the Sun.

Furthermore, the Moon does not produce light on its own, but
only reflects the light of the Sun. Thus, only the side of the Moon
facing the Sun appears bright; the side facing away from the Sun is
dark. As the Moon travels around the Earth, sometimes we see the side
that is lit up: that's what we call a full moon. Sometimes we see it at an
angle, half lit up and half dark: what we call a half moon. Sometimes

we just see the dark side, in which case it is invisible to us: what we call a new moon.

A little thought will show that for us to see a full moon, the moon must be on the opposite side of the Earth from the Sun.

When the Moon is "behind" us as viewed from the Sun, then we see the whole face of the Moon lit up. Even though the Moon is behind us, usually we are not positioned to block the light of the Sun. It's not *exactly* behind us. When it is blocked, we have a lunar eclipse. If this is not clear, imagine that you are looking at two friends, Al and Bob. Both are standing to the west of you. Just because both are west doesn't necessarily mean that Al must be hidden behind Bob. He could be just a couple of feet to the left or right.

To have a half moon, the Moon must be beside us. The Earth, Moon, and Sun must form a sort of L-shape.

To have a new moon, the Moon must be on the same side of the Earth as the Sun. Again, just because the Moon is between us and the Sun, it doesn't normally block out the Sun. That requires very precise positioning. But clearly the only time that the Moon can block the Sun is when the Moon and the Sun are on the same side of the Earth.

Thus, the only time we can have a full moon is when the Moon is on the opposite side of the Earth from the Sun, and the only time we can have a solar eclipse is when the Moon is between the Earth and the Sun. We cannot possibly have a solar eclipse when there is a full moon. This was Africanus's point. (As a side note, the fact that Africanus understood this, and expected his readers to understand this, indicates that the people of the time knew a whole lot more about astronomy than people today generally assume ancients were capable of.)

The Implication

So okay, if there was darkness at the time of Jesus death, it could not have been an eclipse. Surely the critic would reply, Big deal. So there must not have been any darkness at all.

But think about the debate. Thallus, writing less than 20 years after the event, tried to explain away the darkness as an eclipse. If there was no darkness at all, if the whole event claimed in the Bible never happened, Thallus would not have had to come up with a "scientific explanation". There would have been tens of thousands of people who were there at the time. Only a tiny percentage of them would have been Christians. Most were Jews, pagans, and secularists who were anxious to refute a Christian story. If the darkness had never happened, Thallus could easily have produced hundreds of witnesses who would testify that it never happened. But he didn't do that. Instead, he had to explain it away.

A Second Source

Africanus goes on to mention a second source: Phlegon. Phlegon was a Greek who wrote a history book called *The Olympiades* about AD 137. The complete book does not survive, but we do have the fragment that Africanus is apparently referring to:

> In the 4th year of the 202nd Olympiad, there was a great eclipse of the Sun, greater than had ever been known before, for at the 6th hour the day was changed into night and the stars were seen in the heavens. An earthquake occurred in Bythinia and overthrew a great part of the city of Nicæa.

Phlegon, Olympiades, ca AD 137

There is no reason to believe Phlegon was a Christian. As far as we know he made only one brief reference to Jesus, and that is disputed.

But Phlegon also reports a great darkness, occurring in about the right year -- the 4th year of the 202nd Olympiad would correspond to our year AD 33 – and also noted to begin at "the 6th hour", that is, noon. There is no indication that Phlegon considered it a miracle, just a big eclipse. (Apparently he didn't think through the astronomy either.) The surviving fragment does not mention this supposed eclipse lasting three hours or occurring during a new moon as Africanus says Phlegon wrote, but then we don't have the full quote.

Africanus goes on to say that even if we conceded that it was an eclipse, that wouldn't explain the earthquake and other events, as there is no way an eclipse is going to cause an earthquake. Personally I find this point rather weak: Who said the darkness caused the earthquake? They could have been unrelated, coincidental events.

Calculated Eclipses

The motions of the Earth and Moon are very regular and predictable, so modern astronomers can calculate when eclipses occurred in the past.

According to NASA, there were two solar eclipses in AD 33. One was on March 19, moving across the Indian Ocean with its maximum south-east of the southern tip of Africa. The other was on September 12, visible from Russia and China with its maximum in Kazakhstan.

There was no total eclipse for ten years in either direction that was visible from Israel. The closest I could find was one on Nov 24, AD 29, that was visible in Syria for 1½ minutes.

[National Aeronautics and Space Administration. "NASA Eclipse Web Site". http://eclipse.gsfc.nasa.gov /SEcat5/SE0001-0100.html. July 21, 2010. Retrieved November 26, 2010.]

The darkness Thallus and Phlegon reported was not an eclipse.

No Connection

In researching this, I came across several critics who pointed out that Phlegon makes no connection between the darkness and Jesus, and so, they say, Phlegon's testimony proves nothing. How so? The point is not to say that a secular writer agreed that this darkness had anything to do with Jesus, but simply that he recorded that it happened.

Suppose an inventor claims that he can make it rain, and he offers to prove that his invention works by making it rain at a particular place on a particular day. A few days later you get a newspaper with a weather report showing it did indeed rain exactly where and when this man said. The fact that the newspaper does not mention the inventor's claims would not make the weather report any less reliable or any less evidence in his favor.

Conclusion

So here we have two non-Christian sources, one apparently uninterested in Christianity, the other actively hostile, both of whom say that there was, in fact, darkness in the right place on the right date and time. The explanation that this darkness was caused by an eclipse does not hold water, as proven either by considering the phase of the moon or by calculating dates of eclipses. So we are left with … a miracle?

2.14. Sun Standing Still

Let's not think of the great results of Earth's suddenly stopping its rotation when Joshua commanded the sun to stand still. (Not only would Joshua's soldiers all have fallen down and rolled for a thousand

miles, but the energy of rotation would have been converted into heat and have melted the Earth's crust.)

Asimov, Isaac. *The Stars in Their Courses.* New York: 1971. p 52

Scenarios

> So the sun stood still, and the moon stopped, till the people had revenge upon their enemies. Is this not written in the Book of Jasher? So the sun stood still in the midst of heaven, and did not hasten to go down for about a whole day. And there has been no day like that, before it or after it.
>
> Joshua 10:13-14

The most straightforward reading is that God slowed or stopped the Earth's rotation so that the Sun and Moon stood still in the sky.

Some people theorize that the day was not really any longer than a normal day. It just seemed long because the soldiers were fighting a difficult battle. I'd discount this theory pretty quickly. The book of Joshua describes many battles that must have seemed long to the soldiers, some that were much harder than this one, but this is the only one where we're told the sun stood still. The text specifically says that "there has been no day like that, before it or after it". There were many days before and after that seemed long to people. Clearly the writer intended us to understand that this was a unique event, not just one of those days that seem long.

It is possible that God did not really stop the Earth from spinning, but only created the illusion that the Sun had stood still for people in this vicinity. Perhaps God refracted the light rays to produce the desired effect. Or perhaps he created a fake light in the sky. If that is the case, then there is no need to account for the physical effects of stopping the Earth's rotation.

I think that God really did stop the Earth's rotation. That's the plain reading of the text. There is corroborating historical evidence for a long day in this period. The Greek historian Herodotus records that when he visited Egypt, the Egyptians told him of a day that lasted twice as long as a normal day. There is a Chinese legend of a long day during the reign of the Emperor Yeo. Several New World tribes have legends of a long night, such as the Mexican Annals of Cuauhtitlan. Note that if there was a long day in Israel, America, on the opposite

- 54 -

side of the world, would have to experience a long night. [Martin, John. "The Day the Sun Stood Still: Joshua's Long Day". http://www.s8int.com/page35.html. Retrieved Nov 9, 2010.] (Disclaimer: I've found many references to these and similar corroborating stories, but I have not been able to track any of them back to primary sources. Perhaps these should be taken with a grain of salt.)

Momentum

So let's work on the assumption that God really did stop the Earth's rotation. Would this have sent Joshua and his soldiers "roll[ing] for a thousand miles"?

An easy reply would be to say that if God had the power to stop the Earth's rotation, he also had the power to prevent any such undesired side effects. However, we do not need to postulate any such "follow-up miracle" to explain the Biblical account.

At the equator, the Earth is spinning at about 1000 miles per hour. The circumference of the Earth is 24,000 miles, and it makes one full circle every 24 hours. 24,000 miles divided by 24 hours equals 1000 miles per hour. Technically, the Earth makes one full rotation every 23 hours and 56 minutes. If we were motionless in space relative to the Sun, a day would only be 23 hours and 56 minutes long. But because we are moving around the Sun, by the time we've made that full rotation we have moved a little further in our orbit, and so to get to the point where the Sun is in the same position in the sky, we have to turn a little further. That takes another 4 minutes, which is why a day is 24 hours long.

As you move toward the poles, the speed goes down. At 60 degrees north or south latitude, the circumference of the Earth is only 12,000 miles, so the speed is only 500 miles per hour. At 90 degrees – the poles – it is zero. Israel is at around 30 degrees north latitude, so at that point the circumference of the Earth is about 21,000 miles (24000 x cos 30 = 24000 x .87 ~= 21000), so the rotation speed is about 21000 / 24 ~= 875 miles per hour.

According to Boeing, the cruising speed of a 747 is 565 miles per hour, which is in the same ballpark as the speed of the Earth's rotation. Military jets routinely fly at two to three times this speed. That is, they travel faster than the Earth is spinning: a military jet can outrun the sun across the sky. As of this writing, the record speed for an aircraft is 4,750 mph by NASA's experimental X-43 Hyper-X.

And yet, every day tens of thousands of military and civilian aircraft manage to come to a stop from these high speeds without killing everyone on-board, or the energy of their motion being converted into heat and melting the aircraft into a lump of slag. How is this possible?

It happens because the aircraft do not go from 500 or 1000 mph to zero in an instant. Rather, they slow down gradually over several minutes.

How fast could the Earth have slowed down without causing any harm? Of course we can't give a specific number, like say losing X miles per hour per minute is completely safe but X+1 would destroy all life on Earth. Still, a ballpark might be to discuss speeds at which one can feel a sensation of deceleration.

A jet approaching its destination airport slows from cruising speed to landing speed at a rate of about 40 miles per hour per minute. I'm not talking about when it hits the runway and slams on the brakes or reverses the engine. That deceleration is much more rapid. Rather, I'm talking about the slowing down as it approaches the airport. Personally, I don't feel any sensation of deceleration during this approach. To go from 1000 mph to 0 at this rate would take 25 minutes.

I did some simple experiments with my car, decelerating at various rates. (On an empty stretch of road. I wasn't going to risk an accident just to fill out a chapter in a book.) I found that I had no sensation of deceleration when braking at 2 miles per hour per second. I began to feel it somewhere between 2 and 3 miles per hour per second. Of course this statement is subjective. Others might feel it at higher or lower speeds, but it should be in the ballpark. At 3 miles per hour per second it would take 333 seconds, or 5 ½ minutes, to come to a stop from 1000 mph.

So if God brought the Earth to a stop in a period of as little as ten minutes, no one would have been thrown to the ground or sent rolling anywhere. They might not have even felt it. There may be more fragile things in the world that would have been affected. If he had slowed the Earth over a period of half an hour or so, it is unlikely that there would have been any noticeable effect.

Heat

What about the claim that the energy of the motion of the Earth would have been converted into heat and melted the crust?

We could again look to aircraft decelerating. Airplanes do not normally melt as they approach the airport. The critic could reply that the energy of the airplane's motion is indeed converted to heat, but that heat is then lost to the surrounding atmosphere. If the entire Earth was decelerating, the air would not be able to absorb all of that heat. That is, the volume of air surrounding an airplane per pound of airplane is much higher than the volume of air per pound of Earth. Maybe there's no practical way to do an experiment on this scale, and we must rely on theoretical calculations.

A big fallacy in the critic's reasoning is that he assumes that all the energy of motion must be converted to heat. But this is not true. It depends on the mechanism of deceleration. In a conventional automobile, when you put on the brakes most of the energy of motion is converted into heat in the brake pads, which then dissipates into the atmosphere. But in a hybrid automobile, a large percentage of this energy is captured and converted into electricity to recharge the battery.

We do not know what mechanism God used to stop the Earth from spinning, If God stopped the world by sending a great fist down from the sky to press against the surface, the friction would have converted kinetic energy to heat. It would also have gouged a huge canyon across the surface of the earth and done incredible damage. I think it unlikely God used such a crude method. How did he do it? Perhaps he temporarily altered the Earth's orbit, converting the kinetic energy of rotation into potential (gravitational) energy. Perhaps the energy was converted into magnetism, altering the Earth's magnetic field. Perhaps he stopped the Earth by miraculously draining off the kinetic energy. We just don't know.

Let's consider the extreme case. Suppose *all* the kinetic energy was converted to heat. (If you find the math and physics here a little complicated, feel free to skip to the end of the paragraph for the final number.) The kinetic energy of a moving object is given by the equation $E = \frac{1}{2} mv^2$, where m is the mass and v is the velocity. Let's calculate using the median velocity, i.e. at 45 degrees north or south. This is about 1000 x cos 45 $\sim= 700$ miles per hour, or 300 meters per second. This gives $E = \frac{1}{2} \times 300^2 = 45,000$ Joules/kilogram. It takes about 4,200 Joules to increase the temperature of 1 kilogram of water by 1 degree Celsius. It takes 850 joules to increase the temperature of dirt by 1 degree. (It depends on the exact composition of the dirt, of course, but that's a typical number.) The surface of the Earth is ¾ water, so this averages out to .75 x 4200 + .25 x 850 ~= 3360 J/kg/°C. The temperature increase at the surface would then be 45,000 J/kg divided by 3360 J/kg/°C ~= 13°C, or 23°F.

This heat would immediately begin to leak out into space. In the summer we routinely lose 10 to 15 degrees C overnight. The higher the temperature, the faster it leaks. According to Newton's Law of Cooling, an object loses heat in proportion to the difference between its temperature and the temperature of the surrounding environment.

Most of the heat would be manifested deep beneath the surface, where the temperatures are already very high, so that as a percentage it would have been minimal. The Earth's core is generally estimated to be 3000 to 5000 degrees C. A change in the double-digit range would be lost in the rounding errors.

Thus, in the worst-case scenario, if all the energy of motion was converted into heat and none of this heat escaped into space, the surface would increase in temperature by about 13°C. That's nowhere near enough to melt the crust as the critic claims or to cause the oceans to boil or vegetation to burst into flames. It's enough to turn a typical fall day into a typical summer day.

The global warming folks talk about disastrous effects from a temperature increase of just one or two degrees. Computer models indicate that a 10 degree increase in ocean temperatures would have dangerous effects on the weather, including huge hurricanes. A 10 degree increase would melt the ice caps and glaciers. (Though the momentum at the poles is zero, so the immediate temperature increase there would also be zero.) Etc.

Even if correct, these predictions are based on a prolonged temperature increase. What if the increase only lasted for one day? Temperatures often change by more than 13° in a single day without destroying the world. Temperatures routinely vary by several times this amount between summer and winter every year.

Conclusion

To avoid destroying the Earth when he stopped its spinning, God just had to take two simple steps: Take at least half an hour to slow it down, and perhaps he would have to do it in a way that did not result in all the energy of motion being rapidly converted to heat. Neither of these things seems inordinately difficult for a being capable of stopping the rotation of a planet to begin with.

2.15. Creating Life

What will Christians say when scientists create life in the laboratory? That will prove that God is not the (unique) creator of life, and prove the Bible wrong.

Sometimes you hear this criticism as "Now that scientists have created life in the laboratory ..." Every now and then you see some story in the news about a scientist having created life. As of this writing, such claims have all been exaggerations to say the least. Usually the reality is that the scientist has synthesized a chemical that previously was only created by living cells, or has transplanted material from one living cell to another. Some of these results have been quite impressive, manipulating living things at the cellular level. But they are a far cry from creating life from scratch. If someone takes an alternator out of one car, installs it in a different model car, and gets it to work, that certainly demonstrates a significant skill at mechanics. But it would be quite a stretch to describe such an operation as "inventing the automobile".

But that said:

What Would it Prove?

If someday scientists do succeed in truly creating life in the laboratory, it is difficult to see how this would prove that life was not originally created by God. If I succeeded in building an airplane, that would not prove that the Wright brothers did not build the first airplane.

It would certainly not prove evolution. If life is ever created in the laboratory, it will likely be the result of years of work by brilliant scientists using the most advanced technology available. It will more likely be evidence that creating life takes a great deal of intelligence and skill then proving that it can happen by blind chance.

I don't know if people will ever succeed in creating artificial life. In order to do it, we will have to learn a great deal more about how living things work than we know today. But it will certainly not prove that God didn't do it the first time. It is more likely that we will gain a new appreciation of how clever God had to be to pull this off.

Not-so-Hidden Assumption

From a different point of view, this challenge demands that the Christian concede the argument based on hypothetical evidence that might be discovered some day. Even if it was true that the creation of artificial life would somehow disprove the Bible, this hasn't happened. The critic assumes that he is right and the Christian is wrong, he assumes that someday he will get evidence to back up this claim, and then he demands that the Christian concede based on these unproven assumptions. You could prove anything with this sort of "logic". Imagine trying this in court: "Ladies and gentlemen of the jury, the prosecutor claims that my client is guilty. But someday the person who really committed the crime may come forward and confess, and that will prove that my client is innocent. So you must acquit him." This is a classic logic error known as "assuming what you are trying to prove" or "begging the question".

2.16. Cain's Wife

The Bible says that the first two people were Adam and Eve, and that they had only two children, Cain and Abel, both boys. And then Cain killed Abel, leaving just one boy. But then we are blithely told, "And Cain knew his wife." Where did she come from? Where did Cain get his wife?

I often see this criticism stated as I quote it above: Adam and Eve had just two sons. Apparently the critics who say this didn't read far enough to get to the part about Adam and Eve's third son, Seth. If they had, they might have read the next sentence, which clears up any mystery. Genesis 5:3-4 says that after Cain and Able, Adam "had a son … and he named him Seth. After Seth was born, Adam … had other sons and daughters" [NIV]

Genesis quite plainly tells us that Adam and Eve had more than two sons. It doesn't tell us exactly how many children they had. The fact that "daughters" is plural implies at least two girls. Combined with three named sons makes at least five children. Also note that it says sons were born "after Seth". Maybe the sons here are Cain and Abel, but they were born before Seth, so the fact that it says these sons came after Seth probably means at least two more sons. So we're up to at least seven children.

The three sons are named in the context of the story of the first murder: Cain killed Abel, and then when Eve had another son, Seth, she considered him something of a replacement for the dead son. As their other children were not involved in any stories included in the Bible, we are never told their names.

There is no mystery how this family populated the world: The brothers and sisters must have married each other.

Some critics discount this obvious explanation by pointing out that this would have been incest. But so what? There is no mention in the Bible that incest was prohibited until thousands of years later.

An important reason why incest is a bad idea today is because it gives a high probability of birth defects: Most genetic defects are recessive, so if you marry someone who does not have the defect, your children will be all right. But if you marry someone else who does have the defect, then your children are at risk, as your brothers and sisters have inherited the same genetic defects that you have. Adam and Eve's children would presumably have had few if any genetic defects. If Adam and Eve were created genetically flawless, there was no time for mutations to accumulate.

Of course there are also social problems arising from incest that might or might not be applicable. But faced with a choice between marrying siblings and the immediate extinction of the human race, incest would be the lesser evil.

According to Genesis, Adam lived to be 930 years old and many other people before the Flood had similarly long lives. I'm sure the critic doubts that too (see issue 2.17), but if it was true, consider: Modern women are fertile for about 40 years, or half their lives. If Eve lived 900 years and was fertile for half that time, that would be 450 years.

A human woman is born with all the eggs she will ever have. She does not produce more during her lifetime. A woman releases one or two eggs each month, so over 40 years she might drop 1000 tops. But she is born with over one million. If she was fertile for 450 years, she could drop over 10,000. This would seem a much more realistic surplus ratio.

Eve might have given birth to dozens of children, possibly even over a hundred. (And none of them ever called.)

2.17. Longevity of Patriarchs

The Bible describes people living absurdly long lives, like Methuselah living to be 969 years old. There is no way a human being could live that long, certainly not in ancient times without the benefits of modern medicine and nutrition.

Begats and Life-Spans

When you think of boring parts of the Bible, the first thing that comes to mind is the "begats": "Cainan begat Mahalel, and Mahalel begat Jared, and Jared begat Enoch ..."

The book of Genesis has several sequences of such names. These are generally referred to as "the patriarchs". In each case it tells us the name of a man in the line, the age at which he had the son who carries on the sequence, and the age at which he died. The son is not necessarily the first son: The very first name on the list is Adam and the son named is Seth. Elsewhere we are told that Adam had at least two sons before Seth.

This chart shows the lifespans of the patriarchs as given in the Bible.

Adam	930
Seth	912
Enosh	905
Cainan	910
Mahalel	895
Jared	962
Enoch	365
Methuselah	969
Lamech	777
Noah	950 (350 after flood)
Shem	600 (500 after flood)
Arphaxad	438
Salah	433
Eber	464
Peleg	239
Reu	239
Serug	230
Nahor	148
Terah	205
Abram (Abraham)	175
Isaac	180
Jacob	147
Joseph	110

Notice that the first few patriarchs all lived to be about 900. The only exception is Enoch. But then after Noah, the ages start a steady downward slide.

Joseph is the end of the begat lists, so we don't have a clear line of life spans after that. But occasionally the Bible does mention someone's age at death, and the ages given are consistent with life spans as we know them today. Moses, several hundred years after Joseph, writes, "The days of our lives are seventy years; And if by reason of strength they are eighty years." [Psalm 90:10] So apparently by Moses time, life spans were about the same as they are today.

Translation Problem

Some have suggested that this is translation problem, that the word translated "year" really means a shorter period of time, perhaps "month". That would give much more plausible ages: Adam's age becomes 77, Seth's 76, Methuselah's 80, etc.

There are two big problems with this theory.

First, Genesis also gives the age at which each person had the son who carries on the line. We are told Adam had Seth when he was 130 years old. If that really means 130 months old, then he had Seth when he was only 10. And he had at least two sons before Seth. Seth has a son at 105. If that's months, that means 8 years old. Mahalel and Enoch have sons at 65, which would mean a mere 5 years old. The idea that a 5 year old could father a child is almost as amazing as the idea of someone living to be 900 years old.

Second, it doesn't explain the fall in lifespan after Noah. If the word translated "years" really means months, then sure, Adam's age becomes reasonable. But that means Abraham only lived to be 14 and Joseph only 9. We are told that Joseph was sold as a slave, thrown in prison after refusing to be seduced by his boss's wife, spent years in prison before being released, became an advisor to the pharaoh, rose to become prime minister, organized a project to build huge storehouses and stock up food against a time of famine, got married and had two sons. Quite a full life for a 9-year-old!

You could suppose that the time period is neither a month nor a year but something in between. But any time period you choose that is short enough to get the ages at death down to a "reasonable" number is going to give these same problems with the ages of other events in the person's life. So if we want to defend the Bible, a translation problem won't get us out of this. We are stuck with defending literal long ages.

Why We Get Old

Are such long ages possible? To answer that, we would have to know what causes people to age. Unfortunately, no one knows for sure. There are two main theories: environmental and genetic. Note I am not talking here about "Christian theories", but about theories that are discussed in the secular scientific community.

Environmental Theory

The environmental theory says that aging is caused by slow, accumulated damage to the body by various factors in the environment, like disease, toxic chemicals, and harmful radiation.

Some creationists see an explanation of the long lives of the patriarchs in the environmental theory. Note that the decline in life span begins right after Noah's Flood. The Flood would have had radical effects on the environment. Most particularly, creationists theorized that before the flood there was a "vapor canopy" around the Earth, that is, a cloud layer. This idea was inspired by the statement in Genesis 1:6-7: "Then God said, 'Let there be a firmament in the midst of the waters, and let it divide the waters from the waters.' Thus God made the firmament, and divided the waters which were under the firmament from the waters which were above the firmament; and it was so." They interpret this to mean that God created the seas and oceans below the sky and a vapor canopy above. This theory explained several things. The vapor canopy could have been a source of much of the water of the Flood. It would also have shielded the Earth from cosmic rays. If cosmic rays are a major source of environmental damage to the human body, this could explain the long ages. In the course of the Flood the vapor canopy would have fallen to the Earth as rain, and so ceased to provide such protection.

But in more recent years, creationists are moving away from this theory. It has two big problems.

One is that computer models indicate that a vapor canopy thick enough to provide any appreciable percentage of the water in the Flood would also have trapped too much heat in the Earth's atmosphere. This is called the "greenhouse effect": the energy of sunlight can pass through clouds and reach the Earth, but it loses energy along the way, and so it cannot escape. This is how a greenhouse maintains temperatures higher than the surrounding air: glass traps heat more effectively than clouds. A vapor canopy thick enough to make a difference would have made the Earth a stifling hothouse.

Second, the theory requires that the vapor canopy completely collapse during the Flood. So before the Flood there was a vapor canopy; after the Flood there was not. The transition would have been very abrupt. But look at how the ages of the patriarchs changed. They don't suddenly drop from 900 for the last man before the flood to 70 or 80 for the first man after. They fall off gradually. Furthermore, there are two men listed who lived in both the pre-Flood and post-Flood worlds. Noah lived 350 years after the Flood, and Shem lived 500. If an environmental factor that enabled people to live long lives disappeared suddenly during the Flood, than however long Noah and Shem lived before the Flood, their life spans after would be at most 70 or 80 years. That doesn't match what the Bible says.

Thus, current creation theory is that while there may have been a cloud layer that helped produce a more moderate climate worldwide, it wasn't thick enough either to supply 40 days of rain or to appreciably block cosmic radiation. There is continuing work on the vapor canopy theory so it isn't dead, but it is no longer the preferred theory.

There were other environmental changes after the Flood. This was a dramatic event. Huge numbers of plants and animals had been wiped out. The landscape was drastically changed. Weather patterns were different. There could be changes that shortened life spans, but which took some time to fully develop. But to the best of my knowledge, this theory remains vague. I don't know of anyone who has identified specific environmental changes that could have reduced life span, and that would have gotten gradually more severe after the Flood. Most of the damage would have been catastrophic, followed by gradual recovery, rather than the other way around.

Genetic Theory

The genetic theory proposes that there is something built into our genes that causes us to age. The most recent incarnation of this theory centers on "telomeres".

Your body is made up of cells. These cells reproduce by dividing in two. You are able to grow from a baby to an adult because your cells continue to divide and grow. But even after you are an adult, this cell division is important. When cells are damaged by disease or injury, healthy cells divide to replace them.

So why can't your cells just continue to divide indefinitely, constantly replacing damaged cells, so you could live forever? There's a catch to cell division. The genetic information in your cells comes in long strands called DNA. When a cell duplicates a DNA strand, there's a problem when it gets to the end. A loose end cannot be copied properly. So there's a kind of cap at the end called a "telomere". When the DNA is duplicated, this cap allows the last piece of "real" DNA to be copied. But a piece of the telomere is used up in the process. After enough divisions, the entire telomere is used up, and the cell cannot divide any more. In humans, the typical telomere is long enough to allow 40 to 60 cell divisions. This is called the "Hayflick limit", after the biologist who discovered it in 1961.

Some specialized cells produce an enzyme called "telomerase" that can rebuild telomeres, and so these cells can apparently continue to divide indefinitely. It appears that cancer cells produce telomerase, and thus can reproduce out of control.

Some medical researchers theorize that if a way could be found to make telomeres longer or to produce telomerase in a controlled way, human lifespan might be greatly extended. So far (as of this writing) no one has succeeded in doing this or proving that it would work, but many believe it is plausible.

There are some diseases that result in rapid, premature aging that are associated with unusually short telomeres. At least one such disease, Hutchinson-Gilford Progeria Syndrome (HGPS), is apparently caused by one wrong base pair in the patient's DNA, that is, a small but devastating mutation. HGPS results in the patient aging at five times the normal rate. People with this disease typically die of old age at about 13 years old.

Perhaps before the Flood, human telomeres were longer -- maybe nine times longer. Or perhaps there was some mechanism to rebuild telomeres, involving telomerase or something else. The Flood reduced the human population to a mere eight people. A recessive gene or mutation that might otherwise have rapidly died out could instead have become established as the new norm.

Conclusion

We should not be dogmatic about any theory of aging. The scientific jury is still out.

As the life spans start falling off rapidly after the Flood, the change was almost surely related to that event. The environment was certainly changed dramatically by the Flood. The reduction of the human population to just eight people reduced the gene pool, enabling a mutation or other recessive gene to become the prevailing norm.

As we don't know what causes aging, the Christian cannot say with any great confidence how it might have been slower before the Flood. But likewise, the critic cannot say that there is no way.

At present the most plausible theory is that before the Flood human telomeres were longer or were able to regenerate, and that a genetic defect impaired this and thus shortened human lifespans. But we should be cautious about investing too much in this theory as it is far from proven.

2.18. Where Did Flood Waters Go?

The Bible says that during Noah's flood it rained for 40 days and 40 nights and the water covered all the mountains. That would have been a huge amount of water. Then it tells us that the rain stopped and Noah and the animals left the ark. How did all the water disappear overnight? Where did it all go? There isn't enough water in the world today to cover all the mountains.

Time to Recede

The Bible does not say that the water disappeared overnight. According to Genesis 7 and 8, it took 150 days for the water to recede far enough for Noah to see any land visible above the water. Genesis says they boarded the ark on the 17th day of the 2nd month, and they didn't get off the ark until the 27th day of the 2nd month of the following year. They were on the ark for over a year. Even after the first land was visible, it was months more before the waters had dried up enough for them to get off the boat. We don't know what calendar is used here so we can't say exactly how long their year was, but assuming it was 365 days give or take, then we have 375 days on the ark minus 40 days of rain leaves 335 days for the water to recede. That seems like plenty of time.

Where the Water Went

Of course most of the water is now in the oceans. It is estimated that 97% of the Earth's water is in the oceans. Another 2% is in the ice caps and glaciers. 1% is in underground rivers and lakes. Only about .02% is in above-ground fresh-water rivers and lakes.

Enough Water

If the Earth was a perfect sphere, the water would cover the surface to a depth of about 1.7 miles. The Earth is not all under water today because it is not a perfect sphere. Mountains rise up and valleys and oceans trenches plunge down. The deepest point in the oceans is the Mariana Trench, 7 miles (36,000 feet) deep. The highest point is Mount Everest, 6 miles (29,000 feet) high.

Before the Flood, the world was different.

There was more water vapor in the atmosphere. There was probably a thick cloud layer, which helped to create a greenhouse effect and thus produce a more temperate climate worldwide. (But see issue 2.17 for some caveats on the vapor canopy.)

The Flood was not simply a long rain shower. The Bible says that "the fountains of the great deep were broken up" [Genesis 7:11]. Reservoirs of water under the sea floors and/or underground erupted.

When the world was originally created, it was flatter than it is today. Not flat as in a flat earth, but more nearly spherical. The highest mountains were about one-fourth as high as the highest mountains of today, and the oceans similarly shallower. Less of the world's water was in the oceans and more was in underground reservoirs and a thick cloud layer.

During the Flood the water in the atmosphere came down as rain and the water underground came up as geysers. If before the flood the highest mountains were only 1½ miles high, then the amount of water known to exist in the world today would have been enough to cover them. It is also possible that there is more water underground than we know about.

After the Flood

God promised in Genesis 9:11 that he would never again destroy the entire world with a Flood. We see the physical manifestations of this promise in two ways.

First, he depleted the vapor canopy. There is not enough water in the atmosphere today to sustain such a long rainfall. (Some creationist scientists say there couldn't have been enough to sustain 40 days of rain back then, either, but that the water must have been replenished in some way. But we need not get into that here.)

Second, he radically altered the landscape. The Flood was the most dramatic geological event in the history of the world. Between huge quantities of water gouging out the landscape and tectonic activity, there would have been major changes to the shape of the land. There would have been large-scale geological events that created mountains, valleys, and ocean rifts.

The Flood involved huge geological activity, earthquakes and volcanoes and shifting tectonic plates, causing violent upheavals in the land. Mountains were thrust up and valleys formed between them. This led to the higher mountains and deeper oceans depths of today. As the mountains rose, the water ran off into the lowlands, forming our modern oceans.

Conclusion

Critics who fault the Bible for saying that the water of the Flood disappeared overnight haven't read the Bible. It says it took almost a year.

The waters of the Flood were able to cover the mountains because the mountains were smaller then. Our present mountains were formed by geological activity during and after the Flood.

2.19. The Overloaded Ark

According to the Bible, Noah carried two of every animal in the world on board the ark. If there really was a flood that covered the entire world, than any animals not on board the ark would have been drowned, so every animal in the world today must be descended from animals that were on board the ark. But there are ten million species in the world. The size of the ark as given in the Bible would have made it a big boat, but nowhere near big enough to hold twenty million (two each of ten million species) animals.

The number of species of animals in the world can only be estimated. About 1.4 million have been identified and cataloged by biologists. There are surely others that have not been identified and cataloged, but no one knows how many. How could anyone know how many unknown, undiscovered species are out there? It sounds like a riddle. On the flip side, among the 1.4 million, duplicates turn up fairly often. It's hard to manage a list of 1.4 million of anything. Duplicates creep in. Ever get duplicate mailings from a business or a charity? It's hard to prune duplicates from so simple a thing as a list of names. So estimates of the total number of species range from less than 2 million to 100 million or more.

Either way, that's a lot of creatures to fit on the ark. Or is it?

The vast majority of species are microscopic. These wouldn't take up any measurable amount of space on the ark. The International Union for Conservation of Nature counts 1.3 million non-microscopic animal species in the world. That's still a lot. But 1,000,000 of those are insects and another 102,000 are arachnids (spiders, scorpions, and the like). These wouldn't take much space either. 31,000 are fish. The salt-water fish, at least, would not have been bothered by a flood. Noah did not need to have fish tanks on board the ark to save the fish from the waters of the flood. Ditto the 85,000 mollusks, most of which are marine creatures.

What would require space on the ark are what's left after excluding the above. The IUCN counts 5,490 species of mammals, 9,998 birds, 9,084 reptiles, and 6,433 amphibians. Some of the amphibians could have survived outside the ark, but let's be conservative. This makes 31,005 species or 62,010 animals. [International Union for Conservation of Nature. *IUCN Red List.* Gland, Switzerland: 2010. Table 1.]

But even that is an upper limit. The Bible doesn't say that Noah took "two of each species", but "two of each kind". A created kind, or "baramin" in creation theory, is defined as a set of creatures capable of interbreeding, which would generally make it larger than a species.

Most estimates I've seen of the number of animals on the ark put it in the 30,000 range. A very meticulous study on this is found in the book, *Noah's Ark: A Feasibility Study*, by John Woodmorape. [El Cajon, California: 1996.] He calculates that the ark would have had to carry 15,754 animals, including 7,428 mammals, 4,602 birds, and 3,724 reptiles. This includes all living animals and known extinct animals. While some of these are quite large – moose and elephants and the larger dinosaurs -- over half weigh less than one kilogram. The average animal would have weighed about 100 grams, "about the size of a small rat". [Woodmorape, p. 13]

How much space would these animals take? Woodmorape estimates this making two key assumptions: (a) Noah gave an amount of space to each animal comparable to the amount of space used to keep animals in laboratories and factory farms. This is more than is given when transporting animals on trucks or railroad cars and less than modern zoos. That makes it a plausible "middle-ground number". The animals were on the ark for a little over a year, so the space given in a truck would be unrealistically low. But for such temporary accommodations, they didn't need the space given in zoos today, where, after all, creating an interesting environment for the human visitors to see is almost as big a concern as the health and safety of the animals. The animals had to be kept alive and healthy, but this wasn't a pleasure cruise. (b) For the larger animals, Noah didn't bring full-grown adults, but was smart enough to bring younger, smaller individuals. This would not only alleviate space problems but also mean that when they left the ark, they'd have a young and healthy specimen and not a worn-out old man like your present author.

Given these assumptions, he calculated the total floor space required for all the animals as 4,300 square meters. This is less than half of the floor space on the ark. In real life Noah could have stacked the cages of the smaller animals, so this is a high estimate.

He goes on to calculate that the food would have taken about 6 to 12% of the space on the ark. If Noah had to bring along enough fresh water for the entire voyage, that would have taken another 9%. This number is likely high as they could have collected rain water for at least some of their requirements.

So all the animals, plus sufficient food and water, would have taken up about two of the ark's three decks. That would have left the entire third deck for extinct animals unknown to us today, quarters for Noah and his family, the dance floor, movie theater, and karaoke bar.

2.20. A Whale is not a Fish

The book of Jonah says that Jonah was swallowed by a "great fish", but according to Matthew Jesus said that Jonah was swallowed by a whale. A whale is not a fish, but a mammal. The Bible writers didn't know the difference between a fish and a mammal.

Words

The English word "fish" is defined as an aquatic, cold-blooded vertebrate, typically having fins and breathing by gills. A whale has lungs rather than gills, and so is not a fish. If the Bible referred to a whale as a fish, this would be a scientific error.

But the Bible does not use either the word "fish" or the word "whale" when describing the creature that swallowed Jonah, for the simple reason that the Bible was not written in English, and so it does not use English words.

The book of Jonah was written in Hebrew. Matthew was written in Greek. The Hebrew word translated "fish" in Jonah is "dagh". The Greek word translated "whale" in Matthew is "ketos".

Both dagh and ketos mean "large sea creature", with no reference to whether it breathes by gills or lungs. Both words were understood to include creatures like whales and sharks.

Any time you translate from one language to another, you are going to run into this sort of problem. It is not always possible to find a word in the target language that has exactly the same definition as the word in the original language and that reads naturally. So the translator must pick a word that is close in meaning based on the context.

This objection amounts to criticizing the Bible for not being written in English. The critic is saying that for the Bible to be accurate, it must use words which have exactly the same definition at all places and all times -- even after being translated from one language to another. He might as well say that when the Bible uses the word "Egypt", that this is an error because the ancient country of that name did not have exactly the same borders as the modern country. Or that when the Bible talks about "David", this is clearly an error, because his friend David Jones did none of the things that the Bible says David did.

Classification

At this point critics sometimes reply that this is not a question of language but of biology. The Bible is flawed because it uses unscientific biological terminology. If the Bible was really inspired by an all-knowing God, he would have used a word that matches the modern technical definition of the English word "fish". (I've never gotten far enough in this conversation to point out that ancient Hebrew has no such word. I suppose the critic might reply that an all-powerful God could have caused such a word to be added to the Hebrew language so he could use it.)

This argument demonstrates lack of understanding of science. Yes, whether a particular creature has lungs or gills and whether it reproduces by laying eggs or live birth is a scientific fact. If the Bible said that whales have gills, this would be a scientific error. But how you classify creatures is not a scientific fact. It is a way or organizing scientific facts. Modern biologists divide creatures into classes based on a variety of criteria, including means of reproduction (born alive versus hatched from eggs), respiration (lungs versus gills), temperature regulation (warm-blooded versus cold-blooded), and skeletal structure (vertebrate versus invertebrate). But there are creatures that do not fit neatly into this classification scheme. Why do biologists call the platypus a mammal even though it lays eggs, when part of the definition of mammal is giving birth to live young? Instead of calling it a mammal that lays eggs, why not call it a reptile that has fur? (When the platypus was first discovered, many biologists were sure it was a hoax.) Why choose these criteria at all, instead of, say, number of limbs or type of vision or number of chromosomes or hundreds of other possible criteria? The answer is that any classification system is inherently arbitrary.

Suppose you are classifying motor vehicles. If you are trying to organize the want-ads in a newspaper, you would probably classify them by things likely to matter most to the potential buyer, like car versus truck versus motorcycle. If you are a government official responsible for import tariffs, your top-level classification would likely be domestic (not subject to import taxes) versus foreign (subject to import taxes), and within the foreign-made vehicles you would further classify by country of origin. If you are in the business of selling tires, you would classify them by size of wheel, and would happily lump an electric motorcycle together with a diesel truck if they take the same size tires. Etc.

Would you say that one of these classification schemes is "right" and the others are "wrong"? That would be, well, wrong. A classification scheme is not right or wrong. It is useful or not useful for a particular purpose.

Thus, a word that groups together creatures based on the fact that they live in the water is not "wrong" simply because it does not match the modern system of classifying living creatures. To call it "unscientific" would be highly unscientific. It is highly practical for many day-to-day uses.

Conclusion

The Bible was not written in English. The fact that the technical, modern definition of the English word used to translate a Hebrew word does not match the technical, modern definition of the English word used to translate a Greek word is not an error in the original text. At most it is an error in translation. More realistically, it is an example of the problems that translators have to struggle with.

The fact that the ancient Greeks and Hebrews used a different system for classifying living creatures is not an error in science. There is no one, correct classification system. People routinely use different classification systems depending on the context.

Both the Greek and the Hebrew words used in the originals have similar meanings. The fact that different English words were used to translate them is not significant.

Based purely on the text, there is no way for us to know today whether the "great fish" of Jonah was what an English-speaking person would call a fish or if it was a whale or some other sea creature.

2.21. Jonah Could Not Live in a Whale

Whether Jonah was swallowed by a whale or big fish, there is no way that any such creature could swallow a human being whole, and even if somehow it did, there is no way he could survive inside its stomach for days.

The Bible says that God "prepared" the great fish. This could mean that the event was a miracle. In that case, it is no argument to say that it was impossible in the normal cycle of events. That is the definition of a miracle: that it is something impossible without divine intervention. (See issues 2.10 and 2.11.)

On the other hand, we cannot rule out the possibility that this could be explainable naturalistically.

Some have suggested the sperm whale and the white shark are likely candidates for the "great fish" that swallowed Jonah. Both these creatures can have mouths and throats large enough to swallow a man whole. There have been many reported cases of creatures as big as a man being found intact inside the stomachs of sperm whales and white sharks. The real question is not whether they could swallow a man, but whether he could survive the experience. How long would it take for a man to be killed by the creature's digestives juices? (The very thought certainly conjures up images of a horrible way to die.) How would he breathe inside the creature's stomach? Could there be a trapped air bubble?

There have been a handful of reported cases in relatively modern times of people being swallowed by whales and surviving to tell the tale. For example, James Bartley was reportedly swallowed by a whale near the Falkland Islands in February 1891, and living long enough for his shipmates to kill the whale and cut it open. (See issue 2.22.) Marshall Jenkins was reported to be swallowed by a whale in the South Seas in 1771 and survived. And an unnamed sailor was supposedly swallowed by a carcharodon ("sea dog") in the Mediterranean in 1758 and survived. [Riss, Richard. "Jonah".

Christian   *Evidences.*   http://www.grmi.org /renewal/Richard_Riss/evidences/8jonah.html. 1996. Retrieved April 4, 2010.]

These stories have been challenged, so I wouldn't point to them as proof. Claims like this are difficult to prove. But they are interesting. What is the evidence on each side? On the one hand we have the eye-witness testimony of people who said they were there. On the other hand, the critic says it's impossible, mostly because if it was true, it would tend to validate the Bible, and such a result is unacceptable. Is there any other real evidence against these reports?

If a few dozen people in history have been swallowed by large sea creatures and survived, then Jonah is one of a very select group. The event would then be possible even without a miracle, though it would still be a miracle in the sense that God arranged an otherwise extremely unlikely event to serve his purpose. Of course at that point it is no rebuttal to say that it couldn't have happened to Jonah because such an event is extremely rare. No one is claiming that humans are routinely swallowed by whales or sharks and survive. If Jonah had never been swallowed by a large sea creature, or if he had died, the story wouldn't have made it to the history books. History records the extraordinary, not the commonplace.

If all the claims of similar events prove to be exaggerations or mistakes or hoaxes, then Jonah's experience is a miracle in the purest sense. Either way, it's a miracle. I suppose you could say the question is how big a miracle.

But pointing out that something would have to be a miracle doesn't prove that it didn't happen. Not unless you start with the assumption that miracles are impossible. But that's the question being debated.

2.22. A (Relatively) Modern Jonah

Newspapers reported in 1891 that a man named James Bartley was swallowed by a whale and survived for about a day before being rescued. Ever since, Christians have seized on this story as validation of the story of Jonah. Recent scholarly investigation has proven that the Bartley story was just a publicity stunt.

The Context

Before we get into this story, let me point out that Christianity does not stand or fall on the story of James Bartley. If the Bartley story is true, then the Biblical account of Jonah may be explainable without recourse to a miracle. Even if every word of Bartley is true, the story of Jonah is extraordinary. If the Bartley story is total fiction and nothing of the kind is scientifically possible, then Jonah is a pure miracle. So what? Christians believe that lots of amazing events in the Bible are miracles. Proving Bartley false would not prove Jonah false.

The New York Times printed an article about Bartley in 1896. A few days later they printed this follow-up, discussing letters to the editor received on the subject:

> Several of these correspondents seem to be in doubt as to how the story should be taken ... More than one writer intimates that if the reality of Mr. Bartley's alleged experience could be proved, it would tend to dispel such doubts as may exist in regard to the recorded history of Jonah. Maturer reflection may convince correspondents now holding this view that evidence tending to show that all the details of a miracle are explicable, and that they have been more or less nearly duplicated without any exercise of supernatural power, constitutes the severest possible attack on that miracle as a miracle. Therefore, persons who are wise, as well as orthodox, will not insist that the case of James Bartley, if there is or ever was a James Bartley, gives the slightest added credibility to the case of Jonah.
>
> "Topics of the Times". *New York Times*. Nov 25, 1896.

Frankly, I included this discussion in this book, not because it is important, but simply because I found it interesting.

The Story

That said, let's look at the details of the story.

In 1891, a British newspaper, the Greater Yarmouth Mercury, printed the fascinating story of James Bartley. They reported that Bartley was a member of the crew of a whaling ship, the *Star of the East*. They harpooned a whale near the Falkland Islands, and the whale fought back and sank one of the boats. One of the men drowned and Bartley disappeared and could not be found. He was presumed dead.

In the end the whale lost the fight and was killed. The next day, 36 hours later, as the crew was cutting up the carcass:

The vast [stomach] pouch was hoisted to the deck and cut open, and inside was found the missing sailor doubled up and unconscious. He was laid out on the deck and treated to a bath of sea water, which soon revived him; but his mind was not clear, and he was placed in the captain's quarters, where he remained for a fortnight a raving lunatic. He was carefully treated by the captain and officers of the ship, and he finally began to get possession of his senses.

At the end of the third week he had entirely recovered from the shock and resumed his duties. During the brief sojourn in the whale Bartley's skin, where it was exposed to the action of the gastric juices, underwent a striking change. His face and hands were bleached to a deathly whiteness and the skin was wrinkled, giving the man the appearance of having been parboiled. Bartley affirms that he would probably have lived inside his house of flesh until he starved, for he lost his senses through fright and not through lack of air. He says that he remembers the sensation of being lifted into the air by the nose of the whale and of falling into the water; then there was a fearful rushing sound, which he believed to be the beating of the water by the whale's tail; then he was encompassed by a fearful darkness, and he felt himself slipping along a smooth passage of some sort that seemed to move and carry him forward. This sensation lasted but an instant, then he felt that he had more room.

He felt about him, and his hands came in contact with a yielding slimy substance that seemed to shrink from his touch. It finally dawned upon him that he had been swallowed by the whale, and he was overcome with horror at the situation. He could breathe easily, but the heat was terrible. ... [H]e must have fainted, for the next he remembered was being in the captain's cabin.

... The skin on his face and hands has never recovered its natural appearance.

"A Modern Jonah". *Indiana Progress*. March 16, 1892. p. 6 (Reprinting the story from the Greater Yarmouth Mercury)

The Rebuttal

In 1991 the American Scientific Affiliation published an article that is widely quoted and appears to have become the definitive rebuttal of this story: "A Whale of a Tale: Fundamentalist Fish Stories", by Edward B. Davis. (ASA in an organization whose stated goal is "to investigate any area relating Christian faith and science". In practice this appears to primarily mean advocating theistic evolution. See www.asa3.org.)

Prof. Davis went to a great deal of effort to track down the origins of this story. Basically, the results of his research are:

- The Greater Yarmouth Mercury did indeed print this news story in 1891. (Verifying this took more work than one might at first think, as his sources for the story gave the wrong name for the newspaper and had conflicting dates.)
- Another version of the Bartley story was printed in 1896. This gave a different date for the incident – August, 1895 – and included first-person quotes from Bartley instead of being entirely third person, but otherwise had essentially the same information.
- Another "Jonah" story was printed in a 1927 book. It told of a man being swallowed by a rhinodon in the English Channel. (The rhinodon is also called the "whale shark". It is not a whale but a type of shark, and is the world's largest fish.) His crewmates chased down the rhinodon the next day to kill it and recover the body for a dignified burial. To their surprise, when they cut open the creature they found their friend unconscious but still alive. His skin was hairless and covered with yellowish-brown blotches. The critic was unable to find the original source for this story, and the book did not give the man's name, calling him only "A Jonah for the Twentieth Century".
- Lloyd's Register lists three ships in operation in 1891 named *Star of the East*. None were whaling ships. Davis further investigated the largest of the three and found a list of crew members which did not include any "James Bartley". The ship's route would likely have taken it past the Falklands at the right time, but it was based in Yarmouth, Nova Scotia, not Great Yarmouth, England.
- A man named Williams wrote a letter to the editor of the magazine *Expository Times* in 1907, in which he quoted a correspondence he claimed to have had with the widow of the captain of the *Star of the East*, a Mrs. Kellam, in which she said that no such event had ever happened on her husband's ship.

From the above research, the critic came to the following conclusion:

Suppose there was at that time an imaginative young man, let's call him James Bartley ... Having been graced by nature with an unusual complexion, he might easily pass for Jonah himself, so much so that he becomes a circus side show ... billing himself as "The Jonah of the Twentieth Century." He also spins a yarn, complete with a real ship that really was in the South Atlantic in February 1891 in case anyone should make inquiries, that is printed by at least one provincial newspaper ...

Never mind that the ship he chose wasn't a whaler, and that British whalers didn't fish off the Falklands in 1891. Only a suspicious person would ask those sorts of questions, and a suspicious person wouldn't believe the story anyway. ...

Perhaps ... Bartley changed his story after Mrs. Kellam's denial. This time the animal was a whale shark slain by a deck gun from a trawler in the English Channel ..., not a sperm whale harpooned by men from a whaling ship off the Falkland Islands. To be sure, these are not insignificant differences. But otherwise the stories are so much alike that I am convinced they represent variants of the same original fish story ...

Davis, Edward B. "A Whale of a Tale:
Fundamentalist Fish Stories" http://www.asa3.org
/ASA/PSCF/1991/PSCF12-91Davis.html. 1991.
Retrieved April, 2010.

The Counter-Rebuttal

Davis clearly did a lot of research. I've made only a brief effort to substantiate his claimed discoveries. It's not necessary, because even if we accept all of his assertions, his conclusions are quite a stretch from the facts.

The identity and nature of the ship *Star of the East* is certainly a problem for anyone who wants to defend the accuracy of this story. But the critic's explanation explains nothing. If Bartley was going to invent a story and he decided it would be a good idea to get the name of a real ship, wouldn't it have been elementary intelligence to get the name of a *whaling* ship, and not just any random ship? Why bother to go to the trouble of looking up a real ship, and then pick one that doesn't fit the story for the most obvious of possible reasons? If I was going to make up a hoax centering around an oil tanker, I might just make up the name of a ship and hope nobody ever checked. If I looked up the name of a real ship, surely I would pick an oil tanker and not a fishing boat.

If Bartley was a hoaxster who picked this ship without regard to the fact that it was not a whaler, why would he then carefully select one that had indeed been in the vicinity of the Falklands at the right time? The critic points out that British ships did not normally go whaling in the Falklands in the 1890s. If someone was going to spin a hoax, wouldn't he claim the ship went whaling in a place where ships did, indeed, routinely go whaling? Why invent details that make your story harder to believe and carefully choose a ship that fits this "bad" detail, but not bother to pick a ship that would fit details that would make your story easier to believe? Again, if I was going to invent a hoax involving an oil tanker, surely I would say that it was loaded with oil in the Persian Gulf and not in Chesapeake Bay.

If I was going to seriously try to prove that the story is true, my next step would be to research the Lloyd's listing further. It's possible that the ship was not registered with Lloyd's. Since 1880, Lloyd's has attempted to list "all sea-going, self-propelled merchant ships of 100 gross tonnes or greater". [Lloyd's Register. *Infosheet #44*. London: 2007. p. 1] Of course they are not 100% successful: they miss ships now and then, especially those which did not contract with them for their other services. More likely, the newspaper got the name of the ship wrong. This would not be an unlikely error; newspapers do it all the time. Personally, I used to live on a road named "South Street". At one point one of my neighbors got involved in a shoot-out with the police. (It seemed like a nice neighborhood when we bought the place …) The local newspaper covered the story, except that they gave the name of the road as "Smith Street". The name of the ship may have been changed and the newspaper gave a later or earlier name. Ship's names change often enough that Lloyd's has been cross-indexing ship names by previous names since 1886. [Lloyd's. p. 1]

The critic takes the letter to *The Expository Times* as conclusive. After subjecting all the evidence in defense of Bartley to the most minute scrutiny, he accepts this letter without question. Who is this "Williams" person who wrote the letter? Perhaps Williams is an atheist spinning a hoax of his own to shoot down the Bartley story and never talked to Mrs. Kellam. Or as I suggested above, maybe this is the wrong ship, and so of course Mrs. Kellam cannot corroborate the story.

The critic offers no evidence that Bartley had an "unusual complexion" to capitalize on. This is pure speculation.

He offers no evidence that Bartley made himself a "circus side show" or did anything else to make money off his claims. This is an invention by the critic to bolster his theory that it was a hoax. In my (admittedly limited) research I was unable to find anything else in the newspapers of the time concerning Bartley besides debate about the original story. After telling his story to the newspaper, it seems he quietly went back to his life. Bartley did not call himself "A Jonah for the Twentieth Century". For one thing, he told his story in 1891, which was in the nineteenth century. The "twentieth century" title was applied to the man in the shark story, which, by the critic's own research, does not even appear until 1927, 36 years later.

So how does the critic conclude that Bartley "changed his story" from a whale in the Falklands to a shark in the English Channel? The only evidence to connect Bartley to the shark story 36 years later is the critic's unsubstantiated speculation.

The critic makes much of the similarities between the two stories. Both are about a man being swallowed by a large sea creature and surviving. In both, the digestive juices have affected his skin. Yet even here there's an important difference. The critic starts out by theorizing that part of Bartley's inspiration for a hoax was that he had an "unusual complexion". But if the 1891 whale story was his hoax, then his "unusual complexion" was white and wrinkly; while if the 1927 shark story was his hoax, it was hairless and yellow-brown.

A hoaxster making up two stories might recycle details. But if it's not a hoax and the stories are true, one would expect many details to match. The criticism is like saying that the fact that two accounts of automobile accidents both described the victims as being knocked unconscious and having broken bones proves that one story must be copied from the other. The critic is playing a classic "heads I win, tails you lose" game: He says that because the claimed physical effects of being swallowed by a sea creature in two stories are the same, they must both be fictions invented by the same person. But if the claimed physical effects had been different, he would surely have pointed to these as contradictions that prove the stories are false.

There is absolutely no reason to believe that Bartley had anything to do with the shark story. First the critic tosses out his totally fanciful theory that Bartley used this as his "backup" story, and then he uses the "fact" that Bartley changed his story as proof that the original story is a hoax.

Conclusion

The ASA rebuttal to the Bartley story doesn't hold water. The critic "proves" the Bartley story false by simply inventing evidence. He has a good point when he shows that the existence of the ship cannot be corroborated, though his theory about how and why Bartley picked this ship to spin his supposed hoax around is implausible. The rest of his evidence, that Bartley had an unusual complexion, Bartley used his story as a publicity and money-making scheme, Bartley changed his story, etc., all have no basis in fact. The critic just made all this up. Then he calls his made-up "facts" evidence.

Critics have seized on this rebuttal for the same reason that many Christians seized on the original Bartley story: because it supports their preconceptions.

Of course that doesn't prove that the original Bartley story is true. Frankly, I don't know.

2.23. A Bat is not a Bird

Leviticus refers to the bat as a "bird". But the bat is not a bird: it is a mammal.

This objection refers to Leviticus 11, which gives lists of animals that the Jews were and were not allowed to eat.

> And these you shall regard as an abomination among the birds; they shall not be eaten, they are an abomination: the eagle, the vulture, the buzzard ... the stork, the heron after its kind, the hoopoe, and the bat.
>
> Leviticus 11:13, 19

The critic's objection is that a bat is a mammal, and birds are not mammals. Birds have feathers and lay eggs, which bats do not. Therefore it is scientifically inaccurate to include the bat on a list of birds.

The issue here is essentially the same as with Jonah and the whale versus fish. See the discussion in issue 2.20. The essence of the criticism is that the Bible was not written in English and thus fails to use English words.

The Hebrew word translated "bird" here is "eouph", which more strictly means "flying creature". The Hebrew lexicon I use translates it "flyer". [de Mol, Andre. "Interlinear Scripture Analyzer" version 2.1.0. 2009.] It is broader than the English word "bird".

A word that groups together creatures based on the fact that they fly is not "wrong" simply because it does not match the modern system of classifying living creatures. To call it "unscientific" would be highly unscientific. It is highly practical for many day-to-day uses.

As with fish and whales, it is not an error to use a different classification system than the one popular with biologists today. Classification is not fact.

2.24. Labor Pains

The Bible says that human women have labor pains as part of the curse that God put on people for their sins. In reality, women have labor pains because the human pelvis and birth canal are narrow compared to the size of a baby. It has nothing to do with any supposed supernatural curse.

This criticism confuses the *motive* that an intelligent being – in this case, God -- has for doing something with the *mechanism* he uses to do it.

Suppose an auto manufacturer put on a TV commercial where they said, "Because we care about our customers and their children, we have dramatically improved the safety of our cars, so today your chance of surviving an accident is three times what it was twenty years ago."

A critic of the car company might rationally reply that they had improved the safety of their cars, not because they love their customers, but because they were losing business to competitors who made safer vehicles, or because they were forced to do so by government regulations.

But what if a critic said, "Their cars aren't safer today because they lover their customers or care about people. Their cars are safer because they now have airbags, anti-lock brakes, and improved bumpers."

Such a criticism would make no sense. If the company wanted to make their cars safer, they couldn't accomplish this simply by wishing for it. They would have to take practical steps to make it happen. "Our cars are safer today because we care about our customers" and "Our cars are safer today because we include air bags on every model" are not contradictory statements; they are complementary.

Likewise, to say that women experience labor pains because it is part of God's punishment for sin, and to say that women experience labor pains because of the size and shape of the birth canal, are not contradictory statements; they are complementary. Presumably when God performs a miracle, there must be *some* physical manifestation.

2.25. Mustard Seeds

Jesus said that the mustard seed was the smallest of all seeds, and that it grows into a huge tree. This is wrong on two counts. One: The mustard seed is small, but it is not the smallest seed in the world. And two: The mustard seed does not grow into a tree, but a small bush.

Seeds

Here's what the Bible quotes Jesus as saying. These verses are quoted from the New King James Version:

> Another parable He put forth to them, saying: "The kingdom of heaven is like a mustard seed, which a man took and sowed in his field, which indeed is the least of all the seeds; but when it is grown it is greater than the herbs and becomes a tree, so that the birds of the air come and nest in its branches."
>
> Matthew 13:31-32

> It is like a mustard seed which, when it is sown on the ground, is smaller than all the seeds on earth; but when it is sown, it grows up and becomes greater than all herbs, and shoots out large branches, so that the birds of the air may nest under its shade.
>
> Mark 4:31-32

> It is like a mustard seed, which a man took and put in his garden; and it grew and became a large tree, and the birds of the air nested in its branches.
>
> Luke 13:19

In Mark, the word translated "earth" is "ges", the same word translated "ground" in the first part of the same sentence. Thus, the real sense of the Greek may be better reflected as it is translated in the New

International Version: "It is like a mustard seed, which is the smallest seed you plant in the ground." That is, the mustard seed is not necessarily the smallest seed in the world, but it is the smallest seed that the people in his audience planted.

Likewise, Matthew may mean "the least of all the seeds which a man sowed in his field". The New International Version translates Matthew 13:32 as, "Though it is the smallest of all your seeds ..." Again, not the smallest seed in the universe, but the smallest of *your* seeds, the smallest that the Jews of Palestine in the first century planted.

The people of that time were well aware of smaller seeds. They knew of the black orchid, for example. But they didn't cultivate black orchids, so it wasn't relevant.

Bushes and Trees

As Jesus was telling a parable and not giving a lecture on botany, he was not specific about exactly what plant he was referring to. Christian botanists generally conclude that he probably had the black mustard plant in mind, today technically called the Brassica Nigra. Wild black mustards along the Jordan River often grow to ten feet or more. Note that, technically, Jesus does not say that the mustard grows into something very large for a tree, but rather that it grows into something larger than a normal herb. [Medema, Henk P. and Musselman, Lytton John. "Bible Plants: Mustard". http://www.odu.edu /~lmusselm/plant/bible/mustard.php. Old Dominion University: 2006. Retrieved Oct 30, 2010.] Indeed, the phrase "large tree" in Luke is simply "tree" in many manuscripts. The word "large" may have been added through a copying error. In any case he's contrasting a tree to a bush, not a tree to other trees. It is a bush that is big enough for birds to perch on the branches.

Conclusion

Jesus' point was that something small can grow into something very large. (I'm not going to go into an in-depth interpretation of the parable here. I just want to talk about challenges to the scientific accuracy of the Bible.) The mustard plant was an example that his audience could understand: It came from the smallest seed that they normally planted, and it grew into a sizable plant.

The people of Jesus' time knew that smaller seeds existed in the world, and they were aware that there were bigger trees than mustard plants. This could not possibly be an example of scientific ignorance on the part of Jesus or of his audience. Jesus was not trying to convince people that there was some amazing new fact about mustard plants that they did not previously know. He was using what they already knew about mustard plants as an analogy for a point that he was trying to make. If his audience did not accept what he said about mustard plants as established, routine fact, then his story would have made no sense. Even without any investigation into the scientific facts, it should be apparent that his audience must have understood his words in a way that was not only technically accurate, but obviously so.

This is a modern criticism. The people at the time had all the same facts available to them that the critic does today, and yet no one then saw a problem. There is no question here of new discoveries or theories proving that the Bible writers were the victims of the ignorance of their own age. If the mustard seed had been the smallest seed known to people in first century Palestine, but in recent years smaller seeds were discovered in some other part of the world, there might be some grounds for a criticism here. But there are no relevant new discoveries. The critic is so anxious to find scientific errors in the Bible that he doesn't think through the scenario. In order to find an error here, he has to assume that for almost two thousand years, everyone who read Jesus' words, supporters and opponents alike, not only misunderstood what Jesus meant, but misunderstood it in a way that turned an error into truth. And now suddenly the critic comes along and for the first time understands what Jesus really meant, and that what he meant was a mistake.

2.26. The Soul

The human mind is purely a function of the electrical and chemical processes in the brain. Primitive people didn't understand the brain, and so invented a supernatural soul. Today we know that the idea of a soul is unnecessary and false.

Modern science is a long way from understanding the mind, consciousness, and personality.

Let us call the physical organ in the body the "brain", our sense of consciousness the "mind", and the part of us that is alleged to live on after death the "soul".

There is no experimental evidence that proves that brain and mind are the same thing, or that the mind can be completely explained in terms of the chemistry of the brain.

It is clearly true that there is a relationship between the brain and the mind. Physical damage to the brain can result in memory loss or erratic behavior. Drugs – both the legal and illegal varieties – can affect the mind. On the one hand they can cause disorientation and hallucinations; on the other hand they can treat depression and schizophrenia.

But it's a long way from saying that the brain and mind are connected to saying that they are the same thing.

Are the mind and the soul the same thing? Again, we just don't have any serious evidence one way or the other.

How could science study the soul? We don't know how to even begin such an investigation. This could mean that the soul is a fairy tale, and of course science cannot investigate fairy tales. Or it could mean that science has just not progressed to the point of understanding this particular phenomenon. Three hundred years ago electricity was a barely-understood phenomenon. It was a mysterious, inexplicable force, known only by its effects. Two hundred years ago radiation was a mysterious, inexplicable force. Et cetera. Perhaps someday science will be able to detect and measure a soul, and the soul will be no more mysterious than electricity. Or perhaps the soul will always be something beyond scientific study.

Weighing the Evidence

Or, incredible as it may sound, perhaps science has already detected and measured the soul.

In 1907, the New York Times reported on an unusual series of experiments:

> That the human soul has a definite weight, which can be determined when it passes from the body, is the belief of Dr. Duncan Macdougall, a reputable physician of Haverhill.
> ...
> Dr. Macdougall told of the results of his experiments as follows:
> "Four other physicians under my direction made the first test upon a patient dying with tuberculosis ... We placed him, a few hours preceding death, upon a scale platform, which I had constructed and which was

accurately balanced. Four hours later with five doctors in attendance he died.

"The instant life ceased the opposite scale pan fell with a suddenness that was astonishing – as if something had been suddenly lifted from the body. Immediately all the usual deductions were made for physical loss of weight, and it was discovered that there was still a full ounce of weight unaccounted for."

"Soul Has Weight, Physician Thinks". *New York Times.* March 11, 1907.

MacDougall (the NY Times spelled his name with a small "D", but in his own writing he used a capital) and his team went on to repeat the experiment with five other patients, for a total of five men and one woman. Four died of extrapulmonary tuberculosis, one of pulmonary tuberculosis, and one (the woman) of diabetes. In each case, the body showed a loss in weight of between ½ ounce and 1¼ ounces. He chose tuberculosis because this disease causes the patient to slowly waste away. Not to be morbid, but from a practical point of view, someone dying a violent, painful death would be thrashing around on the scale, which would make it difficult to weigh them accurately.

They performed the same experiment on dogs and found no measurable loss of weight.

Almost every discussion I've seen of this experiment ridicules it as not just flawed, but absurd. I've seen four serious technical objections:

1. MacDougall failed to account for the fact that when a person dies, their bowels often release. MacDougall replied that this is irrelevant because the urine and feces were still on the scale and so their weight would still be accounted for.

2. He didn't account for the weight of the air in the patient's lungs. When the dying person releases his last breath, some amount of air is expelled. This accounts for the missing ounce. MacDougall considered this, too. He had several healthy people (including himself, in one test) lie on the scale, inhale as deeply as they could, and then force the air out as hard as they could. His scale was accurate to 1/5 of an ounce, and it did not register any change during this procedure.

To do it by the textbook: Adult humans have a lung capacity of 4 to 6 liters, that is, about 0.2 cubic feet. Air weighs 1.2 ounces per cubic foot at sea level and room temperature. This gives a total weight of the air in a person's lungs as about 0.24 ounces. That's right at the minimum resolution of his scale. When a person dies he doesn't completely empty his lungs, so we would not expect a last breath to register on MacDougall's scale.

Throughout his experiments he carefully tracked changes in the patients' weight. Most of his patients slowly lost weight, typically at rates of an ounce or so per hour. He attributed this to body fluids evaporating from the patient's skin and similar causes.

3. The unexplained weight loss varied by a large percentage range, so the results cannot be meaningful. MacDougall did not address this, but I can offer what seems to me an obvious reply: We do not all have the same size ears or fingers or kidneys. Why would you assume we must all have the same size souls?

4. His sample size was very small: six patients, and he acknowledged that the results from two of them were unreliable due to technical difficulties. MacDougall acknowledged this and called for further experiments by other researchers to validate his results. I have been unable to find any record of anyone attempting to repeat the experiment. (Not to say that no one has done it, but my brief Internet search didn't turn anything up.)

[MacDougall, Duncan, MD. "Hypothesis Concerning Soul Substance Together with Experimental Evidence of the Existence of Such Substance". *Journal of the American Society for Psychical Research*. May, 1907. pp 239-264]

Why do so many people write off this experiment as absurd? Is it because the experiment is technically flawed? Or is it because they have preconceived ideas about the soul that are inconsistent with the results? The fact that MacDougall printed his results in a publication generally devoted to clairvoyance and telekinesis detracts from his credibility. I do not think that this experiment proves the existence of the soul. It may well turn out in the end that the results are not repeatable or have a more mundane explanation. But it is interesting. I'd like to see someone attempt to repeat it.

Conservation of Energy

Suppose that there is a form of energy not presently understood by science, and that the soul is made up of this energy. This energy field would have to interact with the brain to allow the soul to control the body. It is clear that brain chemistry can affect one's personality, so the relationship would have to be two-way. By the law of

Conservation of Energy, this energy would continue to exist after the death of the body.

While postulating a new form of energy is a stretch, it's not unreasonable. All the forms of energy that we know about had to be discovered at some point. Gravity was discovered in the 17th century, electricity was only vaguely understood before the 18th century, the nuclear strong force (the force that holds the nucleus of an atom together) was not even postulated until the 1930s. It does not seem unbelievable that there might be other forms of energy discovered in the future.

Can I prove any of this? No. I can't prove that from Scripture and I certainly can't prove it scientifically. But it's an amusing speculation.

Conclusion

Science has not proven that the soul does not exist. We just don't know enough about the brain to do more than speculate on this subject. Perhaps at some time in the future science will have advanced to the point that we can seriously study the question.

2.27. Life after Death

The Bible says that you have a "soul" that continues to live after your body has died. This is impossible: there's no way that your consciousness can survive your physical death. When you're dead, you're dead.

Untestable

There are many ideas or theories that are difficult or impossible to test scientifically. I don't claim that I can prove that there is life after death. But then, I have never seen any evidence that there is no life after death either. The position of the critic here seems to be: You think one thing and I think another. There is no solid evidence one way or the other. Therefore, we must conclude that I am right and you are wrong.

Let's try this reasoning on other theories that are difficult or impossible to test. Like, there is no solid evidence for or against the existence of life on other planets. Therefore, we must conclude that there is such life. Or, therefore we must conclude that there is not any such life. Either way, the conclusion does not follow at all. We don't know means we don't know, not, therefore we must assume that my guesses are correct and yours are wrong.

Eyewitness Testimony

That said, there clearly is evidence for life after death.

You have probably heard of "near death experiences", or NDEs. In 1975 Dr. Raymond Moody published his groundbreaking book, *Life after Life*. Moody interviewed hundreds of people who were clinically dead, and after they were resuscitated said that they had strange experiences while "dead". Others collected similar reports – Dr. Elizabeth Kubler-Ross was doing similar research at the same time, and many others have followed.

These researchers found that the patients' experiences were remarkably similar. They had many common elements. Their subjects typically reported that when they reached the point of death from illness or injury that they heard a loud and annoying noise, found themselves moving rapidly through a dark tunnel or void, and then were outside of their bodies. They could see the doctors working on their body or the people gathered around the accident scene, but they could not communicate with them in any way. They became aware of people they had known who had died before, who were now gathered around them. Many reported meeting a "being of light". This being would show them their whole lives in an instant and encourage them to consider what they had accomplished in life. Then they encountered a boundary or barrier of some kind, and they understood that they must decide whether to cross this, or to go back. They decided to go back, and suddenly found themselves back in their bodies.

Moody used 150 case studies for his book. Other researchers have added thousands to that list. Surveys indicate that there may be millions of people with similar experiences.

Critics often dismiss these reports as obviously hallucinations. There are two problems with this explanation.

First, hallucinations, like dreams, may seem real while a person is experiencing them. But once the hallucination or dream is over, people normally have no problem distinguishing them from reality. People who have had near death experiences routinely say that they were not dreams, but were objectively real events.

Second, near death experiences have many similarities and do not particularly resemble popular ideas about an afterlife. If people reported visions of angels in white robes with wings and halos and playing harps, we might reasonably wonder if they were having a dream or hallucination based on popular culture. But actual NDE experience has only marginal resemblance to such popular ideas. At the time Moody and Kubler-Ross were doing their research, the "story line" of an NDE was not widely known. How would all these thousands of people have had the *same* hallucination, with no knowledge of each other? If we learned that millions of people all had the same dream last night, that would be a profound mystery itself.

Some have tried to attribute NDEs to the effects of drugs given dying people. But this doesn't fit the facts: There is no single set of drugs or kind of drugs given to people who have had NDEs, and many had no drugs at all. People have had NDEs before they reached the hospital or received any medical treatment, like while they were in the wreckage of automobiles waiting for the ambulance to arrive. The experiences of people who had no drugs show no pattern of differences from those who were given drugs. Indeed, statistically people who were given sedatives or pain killers are *less* likely to experience an NDE.

Some have tried to make a case that the nature of the hallucination derives from the physiological nature of death. There is certainly validity to this approach. If you could show that something that happens to the brain or the nervous system would cause hallucinations of the sort reported for NDEs, this would be interesting. But no one has offered a convincing argument in this direction. One critic proposed that as the brain dies, it dies from the outside in, and so the patient would see a constricting tunnel of vision, thus explaining the tunnel of the NDEs. But this theory assumes that a person's field of vision will take the shape of the working part of his brain, like if you burned a section of his brain with a branding iron in the shape of a letter "W" he would then see a letter "W" floating in front of his eyes. That is just not the way the eye and brain work.

The real evidence for saying that NDEs are hallucinations is the conviction that life after death is impossible, so anyone who claims to be an eyewitness to life after death must be lying or hallucinating. Of course if you accept this argument, then you can easily dismiss any theory that you don't like. Imagine someone offering this sort of argument in court: Ten eyewitnesses claim to have seen the defendant stab the victim. But your honor, we just know that a nice man like the defendant could never hurt anyone, so these people must all have been hallucinating.

So evidence on the side that there is life after death: Thousands, maybe millions, of eyewitness reports. Evidence on the side that there isn't life after death: The certainty of atheists that it is impossible. The evidence is all on the "pro" life-after-death side. On the "anti" side is just dogma.

What Does It Prove?

> Abraham said to him, "They have Moses and the prophets; let them hear them." And he said, "No, father Abraham; but if one goes to them from the dead, they will repent." But he said to him, "If they do not hear Moses and the prophets, neither will they be persuaded though one rise from the dead."

> Luke 16:29-31

When I read this Bible story many years ago I thought, "How could that be true? Surely if someone came back from the dead and said, 'I've been there, and I can tell you what I saw', people would have to believe". Then reports of NDEs began to come out. People said that they had, in fact, come back from the dead. Did this lead all the atheists to believe? No. They simply dismissed these reports as lies, hallucinations, or otherwise proving nothing.

Frankly, I'm a Christian, I believe in life after death, and I'm not sure what to make of NDEs.

To call them hallucinations is too simplistic a dismissal to take seriously. For them to be lies would require a massive conspiracy, involving many thousands of people, with no apparent motive. But I'm just too skeptical to accept them uncritically.

The thing I find most persuasive about claims of NDEs is that they do not match either the popular-culture idea of an after life, nor what serious theologians have theorized, but they are generally consistent with what the Bible says.

This isn't "proof" of life after death. But it is certainly an important and persuasive piece of evidence.

3. Science - General

3.1. Christianity is Closed-Minded

Science is inherently open-minded and progressive. Religion is inherently closed-minded and stagnant. Scientifically-minded people follow the facts wherever they lead. Religious people think they know all the answers already because they are written in their precious scriptures, so they are uninterested in looking at the facts.

Atheists like to think of themselves as "scientific", as opposed to Christians who are "unscientific" or even "antiscientific". They are atheists because they studied the evidence, while Christians don't care about evidence.

People who say this apparently don't know any real scientists or real Christians, and they have a rosy view of atheists.

I don't doubt that many people are Christians, not because they have carefully studied the facts and logic for themselves and concluded that Christianity is true, but because that is what their parents or Sunday School teachers told them and they simply believe it, or because they find the idea of eternal life in paradise pleasant to believe. But then by the same token, many people are atheists not because they have carefully studied the facts and logic for themselves and concluded that atheism is true, but because that is what their college professors or TV shows told them and they simply believe it, or because they find the idea that they are not answerable to any "supreme being" pleasant to believe.

Neither group tells us anything about the truth of Christianity or of atheism. You can't judge the validity of an idea based on the weakest arguments given in its favor. The fact that an ignorant person believes something doesn't prove that it's true, but it certainly doesn't prove that it's false, either.

It is true that Christians do not often abandon their beliefs and become atheists because of logical arguments. But then, atheists don't often abandon their beliefs and become Christians because of logical arguments either. I have had many conversations with atheists where I have presented them with evidence that they could not rebut, and their last word is that they can't answer the argument, but they know that it must be flawed, because they just can't believe that there is a God or angels or demons. Sometimes I think they don't care about the evidence. They came to their conclusions before they looked at the evidence, and any arguments are just after-the-fact attempts to validate what they've already decided.

Of course, it's also happened that I've had conversations with atheists where they have presented an argument that I can't rebut. Do I immediately convert to atheism? Of course not. I've been studying the evidence on both sides for decades and I've come to the conclusion that, while there are some things I can't explain, the weight of evidence points to Christianity. One argument that I can't rebut does not outweigh all the evidence on the other side.

Likewise, I'm sure an atheist would say that he's studied the issues for years and concluded that the evidence favors atheism, and one odd argument that seems to point the other way isn't going to change his mind.

There is no objective reason to believe that atheists are any more open-minded than Christians. People on both sides have come to their conclusions for a variety of reasons, some valid and some not.

I've heard this argument most often with regard to evolution versus creation. Atheists say that Christians reject evolution purely for religious reasons. They, as atheists, are not committed to any religious dogma, and so are free to follow the evidence wherever it leads. A moment's thought will show that this is the opposite of the truth. Someone can believe in God and the Bible and also believe evolution. (They have to give up a belief in the literal inspiration of the Bible, but many Christians believe this way.) On the other hand, it is difficult to

- 95 -

imagine how someone could be an atheist and believe in creation. Thus, the Christian is free to follow the evidence wherever it leads, to creation or to evolution, without having to abandon his Christianity. The atheist is not free to follow the evidence wherever it leads. To remain an atheist, he must believe in evolution. Only the Christian can afford to be open-minded on this issue.

3.2.   The Bible is Unscientific

Most claims of the Bible cannot be proven scientifically. There is no way to prove scientifically that people have immortal souls, that Jesus came back from the dead, or that there are such places as Heaven and Hell. Therefore, the Bible is unscientific.

This is absolutely true. So what? These are not scientific claims. The opposite of "scientific" is not necessarily "false". Often it is simply "not scientific".

There is no scientific experiment we could perform to prove that Jesus came back from the dead. That is because this is not a scientific question. It is an historical question. There is no scientific experiment we could perform to prove that Julius Caesar conquered Gaul, or that Columbus discovered America. Science can only study things that exist in the present, and these things happened in the past. Science can sometimes give us clues about historical events. Archaeologists might dig up an artifact related to a past event, and it could be studied to see if it was consistent with the claims of the history books. But ultimately, science cannot now and never will be able to prove that a claimed past event did or did not happen or that it happened one way or another. Not unless someone invents a time machine.

Some say that the soul is "supernatural", and thus outside of any possible study by science. I tend to disagree, though I readily admit I am now entering into a highly speculative area. In many ways, "supernatural" is just a word for things beyond our present scientific knowledge. To the ancient Greeks, large sea creatures like the giant squid were beyond their ability to study scientifically, so they called them monsters and made them the subject of myths. Lands outside the vicinity of the Mediterranean Sea were beyond their ability to study scientifically, so they made them the subject of myths. Today our science has progressed, so such creatures and places are now the subjects of scientific study. Likewise, today we do not know any way to study whether there is such thing as a soul, so we call it "supernatural". Perhaps someday our science and technology will advance to the point where we can identify, study, and measure a soul. Or perhaps not; it may be fundamentally unknowable to science.

None of this proves the Bible to be somehow flawed. There are many aspects of reality that cannot be studied by science. I've already mentioned historical questions. Science cannot tell us what political system is best, or resolve arguments about morality. Science can sometimes contribute relevant information, but it cannot answer the question. There is no experiment you can perform to tell whether marijuana use should be legal or generally accepted by society. Science could tell you exactly what the medical effects are. But it cannot answer questions that include the word "should".

Science cannot tell us whether a poem is moving or trite, or whether a painting is beautiful or amateurish. I freely admit that I have no talent as an artist. I can barely draw a recognizable stick figure. Any objective observer would say that my attempts at drawing are pathetic while the works of Da Vinci and Michelangelo are great art. But there is no way we could prove such statements scientifically. There is no relevant scientific experiment that we could perform. Statements about art and beauty can be clearly, obviously true, but science can contribute nothing to the discussion.

It is questionable whether science will ever prove or disprove the existence of Heaven and Hell. It is not clear from the Bible if these places are in -- or "supposed to be in" if you prefer -- the universe that we know, or if they are in some alternate plane of existence. If, say, Heaven and Hell are on other planets, then they are not fundamentally unknowable to science, they are just beyond our present science. If they are not in the universe we are familiar with, then our present science has no tools to investigate them. Either way, it is like ancient Greeks talking about mysterious lands across the Atlantic Ocean. They could not build ships capable of making the trip, so they had no way to study such places. That doesn't mean the Americas did not exist or where somehow less real than Europe.

Conclusion

It is true that many statements in the Bible cannot be proven scientifically. That is because these are not scientific statements. Statements about history generally cannot be proven scientifically.

Statements about morals or politics or art can never be proven scientifically.

3.3.   The Bible is Anti-Science
There is a fundamental conflict between science and religion.

Science and religion are two different ways of gaining knowledge. Science gains knowledge through experimentation and observation. Religion – or at least, western religion: Judaism, Christianity, and Islam – claim to gain knowledge by revelation from God.

Some scientific theories conflict with some religious doctrines. Not only does this prove a lot less than people who talk about the "conflict between religion and science" say, it happens a lot less than they imply.

Some newspaper stories conflict with what is in some textbooks. For example, you could easily find a newspaper story that assumes economic theories that are inconsistent with what is taught in a particular economics textbook. Would you therefore say that there is a fundamental conflict between journalism and education?

What, exactly, are the issues on which religion and science conflict? Critics have come up with a handful of supposed scientific errors in the Bible. We discussed some of them in the last chapter. Even if valid, none of them are fundamental to Christianity. If someone absolutely proved that the Bible was wrong on some technical point, it would shoot down the idea of Biblical inerrancy, but it would not therefore demolish all religion. I would have to seriously revise my beliefs, but I would not have to abandon all forms of Christianity. (Not that I'm saying that I expect this to happen.)

Usually when people say there is a conflict between religion and science, what they really mean is that there is a conflict between evolution and Christianity. Despite the claims of evolutionists, evolution has not only never been proven, but they do not even attempt to prove it scientifically. "Science" means experimentation and observation. No one has ever observed evolution happening. No one has ever performed an experiment in which they tested evolution. Evolutionists are quick to reply that of course no one has ever observed evolution: It happens too slowly. But that's the point. Evolution cannot be tested experimentally. Rather, evolution is a philosophical conjecture. They look at living creatures and speculate about how they might have come into existence. We could debate whether the speculations of evolutionists fit the facts better than the Biblical account of creation or not. I'm not going to go into that here; people have written many books on both sides of the subject and I'm not going to recap it all in a couple of pages. But regardless of your opinion of the validity of the claims of evolution, it is not "science" by a strict definition of the word.

Evolutionists will sometimes admit this, though usually indirectly. For example, the National Center for Science Education, a pro-evolution lobby group, says on their web site:

> The failure of many students to understand and accept the fact of evolution is often a consequence of the naïve views they hold of the nature of science ... According to this naïve view, the key to the unique success of science at producing true knowledge is 'The Scientific Method', which, on the standard account, involves formulating hypotheses, making predictions, and then going into the laboratory to perform the crucial experiment. In this parody of scientific methods, if a hypothesis passes the test set up by the crucial experiment, that is, if it is confirmed by direct observation, then it is "proven" and it is considered a fact or a law and it is true for all time. In contrast, the work of many evolutionary biologists involves the reconstruction of the past. The methods they use do not conform to the standard view of 'The Scientific Method'."

> Cooper, Robert A. "The Goal of Evolution Instruction: Belief or Literacy?" *National Center for Science Education.* http://ncse.com /rncse/21/1-2/goal-evolution-instruction-belief-literacy (retrieved Apr 19, 2010)

That is, the writer here clearly admits that evolution cannot be demonstrated by the scientific method, and so he ridicules the very idea that the scientific method has anything to do with science. To suggest that we use experiments and observation to test and confirm a scientific theory is "naïve" and "a parody". For hundreds of years scientists thought that the scientific method was what science was all about. Apparently not.

Evolution is a philosophical speculation. If you want to say that there is a fundamental conflict between some philosophical speculations and some religious beliefs, well, yeah, of course. But there is no conflict between Christianity and science.

3.4. Christianity Inhibits Scientific Progress

Christian belief is incompatible with scientific inquiry. To the extent that Christians dominate a society, that society will see scientific progress grind to a halt. Science can only progress in a culture free of religious dogmatism.

The people who make this objection think of themselves as scientific. And yet, I have never seen someone present a scientific argument to back up this claim. It is always presented on purely dogmatic, philosophical grounds.

By testing it scientifically, I mean performing an actual experiment and observing the results. Ideally, we would create several societies, one Christian, one atheist, maybe one Buddhist, Moslem, etc. We would make these societies otherwise initially identical. Then we would sit back and observe which shows the greatest scientific and technological progress.

I'm sure just reading that description you see that such an experiment would be difficult on both practical and ethical grounds. To make the experiment valid we would have to someone isolate these societies from each other. It would take decades to get measurable results. What are we going to do, put a wall around each of three cities and lock the people in there while we observe them?

But we can do an indirect experiment. Let's review societies that have actually existed.

Make a list of the societies in history that have shown the greatest scientific and technological progress. We could debate just how to measure this, but surely any such list would include ancient Greece, ancient Rome, Victorian Britain, 20th century United States, maybe Renaissance Europe. Make a list of societies where Christianity has been strongest. Surely any such list would include ancient Rome, Medieval and Renaissance Europe, Victorian Britain, and 20th century United States. You might say that by the time Rome became Christian it was living off the glories of its pagan ancestors. Medieval Europe is often described as a "dark age" but the High Middle Ages and the Renaissance saw great advances in astronomy and laid the groundwork for modern physics. Britain and the U.S. clearly achieved their scientific heights at the same time that Christianity was at its strongest.

Make a list of atheist-dominated societies. There have been relatively few in history, but they would include revolutionary France, the Soviet Union, Maoist China, North Korea, Cambodia, and

Vietnam. Of these, only the Soviet Union could make any serious claim to being scientifically advanced, and that's a maybe. They had advanced military technology, but besides that they were virtually a Third World country. In fairness, small countries like North Korea can't be expected to compete with great powers like the U.S. But North Korea is comparable to, say, South Korea, a country where Christianity is active and growing. Which shows greater technological prowess: atheist North Korea or semi-Christian South Korea?

Many of the best-known scientists of all time have been Christians. Isaac Newton (gravity, calculus), Louis Pasteur (biogenesis, pasteurization), and Robert Boyle (gas laws) actively opposed anti-Christian ideas of their own time. Johannes Kepler (planetary motions), Gregor Mendel (genetics), Nicholas Copernicus (heliocentric universe), and Michael Faraday (electromagnetism) were all Christians. In more modern times, how about Edward Morley (first to measure the speed of light), Arthur Eddington (relativity, measuring temperature of stars), and Werner von Braun (rocketry)? Indeed, Roger Bacon is generally credited with being the first person to clearly formulate the scientific method. In the same book in which he described the scientific method, *Opus Majus*, he also said that all science is ultimately based on the Bible, and he called for education reforms that included more Bible study in the original languages. If anyone can be said to have "invented science", it was Roger Bacon – a Christian.

Conclusion

There is no evidence that Christianity inhibits scientific progress. Quite the contrary, the times and places where scientific progress has been greatest are often places where Christianity is strong. There is certainly no evidence that atheist societies are unusually scientifically advanced. Many of the greatest scientists of all time – including the man who could be said to have invented science itself – were Christians.

3.5. Science Explains It All

Science has proven to be incredibly powerful. No one can deny that science works. Every time you turn on an electric light or fly in an airplane you see that science works. There is, therefore, no longer any need to resort to the supernatural to explain the universe. Ancient people who didn't know much about science used the supernatural to

explain the unexplained. But today we know that science explains it all. Belief in the supernatural is outdated and unnecessary.

I certainly do not deny the power and success of science. I'm a software engineer by profession. I work with the products of advanced science and technology every day.

But it is quite a leap from saying "science explains many things" to saying "science explains everything". Science is a tool for gaining knowledge. It is a very effective tool. But that doesn't make it the only legitimate tool.

A screwdriver is a very useful tool. It can put in screws, pry things apart, in an emergency it can be used as a weapon. But that doesn't mean you should throw away all your other tools. It is not irrational to say that one tool is good for one job and a different tool is good for another job.

The belief that everything can be explained by science is called "materialism". Not materialism in the sense of "greed", but materialism in the sense that everything in the universe can be explained in material terms. Some now use the term "scientism" as essentially a synonym for "materialism" and avoiding the ambiguity. (I'm sure that there are professors of philosophy who will point out technical distinctions between materialism and scientism.)

Materialism doesn't just exclude God from the universe: It excludes any actual human beings. According to materialism, the mind, all human thoughts and feelings, can be completely explained in terms of electrical and chemical activity in the brain. The materialist doesn't claim that he actually can explain all human thoughts and feelings in electro-chemical terms. But he insists that this is just because science has not progressed far enough. He is convinced that someday scientists will fully understand exactly what causes all human emotions: fear, anger, love, patriotism, smug satisfaction, everything. The scientist could then induce these emotions in you through the appropriate electrical stimulation, drugs, or whatever. Such induced emotions would not only be indistinguishable from the real thing; they would be the real thing. Someday, the materialist is sure, science will find all the answers.

People who believe in materialism think of themselves as very scientific. All questions can be answered by scientific experimentation and observation.

So what experiments have been done that prove that materialism is true? What scientific evidence is there to prove that everything in the universe can be explained by science?

The answer, of course, is: None. Materialists do not believe in materialism because they have been convinced it is true by scientific evidence. It is hard to imagine what scientific evidence could be offered. How do you perform an experiment to prove that experiments are valid? That's like trying to give a logical argument to prove that logical arguments are valid. If the other person doesn't already agree that logical arguments are valid, how would he be convinced by a logical argument that logical arguments are valid?

It's even harder to imagine an experiment to prove that *only* experiments are valid. Can you even suggest what such an experiment would be like?

There is no scientific evidence to support materialism. Materialists believe in materialism purely on philosophical grounds, without evidence.

Take the example I gave above. The materialist cannot actually explain the human mind completely in electro-chemical terms. He just has faith that science will eventually progress to the point where it can. His only evidence that this is true is his gut feel. If I expressed such blind faith in the Bible, he would laugh at me as naïve and gullible.

The materialist defends his science with dogma. I prefer to defend my dogma with science.

3.6. God of the Gaps

Religion originated when pre-scientific people tried to explain natural phenomena that they did not understand. Anything that science can't explain, religion declares must have been done by God or the gods. As our scientific knowledge grows, there are fewer mysteries to explain and the area available to religion shrinks. Religion is based on embracing ignorance. Modern Christians continue this sorry tradition of using religion as an easy answer to every hard question. When all else fails, they say "God did it."

The critic describes this as a general principle of religion in general and of Christianity in particular.

A common theory among atheists is that religion originated as an attempt by pre-scientific people to understand the universe. These ignorant people saw natural phenomena that they did not understand, like lightning or the passage of the sun across the sky. They asked who was responsible for these things. They could see that they and the fellow members of their tribe did not do them, so they imagined gods as responsible.

This explains nothing about the origin of religion. Where did the idea of gods capable of performing such things come from? Why would primitive people suppose that these things were done by anyone, in the sense of human-life beings? Why did they suppose that the gods had human hands and faces and were capable of rational thought and experienced love and happiness and anger? To go from, "I wonder what causes lightning?" to "Zeus lives on Mount Olympus where he dines on nectar and ambrosia and is married to Hera but he has numerous affairs with mortal women and he loves eagles and the oak tree is his symbol and he uses lightning bolts as a weapon" is quite a leap.

I don't believe in Greek and Roman polytheism, but even I can see that it is not just a slander, but a silly one, to say that their religion was just a lame attempt to explain natural phenomena without recourse to science. Attributing natural phenomena to the gods was a tiny part of their religion. You could cut all that out and what is left would stand on its own.

Such a charge has even less to do with Christianity. I am hard pressed to think of any Christian doctrine that is explained as, "No one knows what causes X, so it must be God". You might find some Christians who say things like that about isolated issues, but it is certainly not what Christianity is all about.

Consider the key doctrines of Christianity:

"All human beings sin, that is, do evil things." This is not a statement of ignorance but of positive knowledge: We look around and observe the behavior of human beings, and we note that while people sometimes do good, they also routinely do evil.

"Jesus Christ was God come to Earth in human form." Christians make this statement based on the eye-witness testimony of people who were there at the time. You may find their testimony unconvincing, but this statement is not an attempt to explain something in the absence of scientific knowledge. If Christians did not believe in Jesus Christ, we would not be left with an unexplained mystery. There would be nothing to explain.

"Human beings have an immortal soul." Again, this is not a statement desperately seeking an explanation of some phenomenon beyond the scientific knowledge of the observers. It is based on claimed revelations from God. The theory of the soul does not explain a mystery. It creates a mystery.

Most Christian doctrines are based on what someone claimed God miraculously revealed to him, or some event that he observed. I'm hard pressed to think of any Christian doctrines that are based on ignorance in the sense that this criticism implies, that is, someone saying, "I can't think of any scientific explanation for this natural phenomenon, therefore, it must be a miracle."

Perhaps you could say that (claimed) miracles fall into this category. When Jesus turned water into wine, was that really a "miracle"? Or are there some circumstances under which water naturally turns into wine, and if we just had more scientific knowledge, we would understand it?

But you almost never hear the critics make such an argument. They generally agree that the miracles described in the Bible would indeed be miracle if they conceded that they actually happened, which they don't, because they insist that miracles are impossible. Occasionally someone comes along offering naturalistic explanations of Biblical miracles. Velikovski wrote several books claiming that all the miracles of Exodus were the result of a giant comet passing by the Earth. Von Daniken claimed that stories of angels and demons were really inspired by aliens from other planets. Atheists are as quick to challenge such people as Christians. Christians say they are wrong because they are claiming that events that the Bible calls miracles really have a naturalistic explanation. Atheists say they are wrong because they are claiming that events that never happened did happen.

Critics often point to the Biblical account of creation as a prime example. Christians say that evolution is impossible because all the amazing complexity of living things could not have come into existence by chance, and so life must have been created by God. The critic says that this is an argument from ignorance: The Christian cannot imagine how this could happen by natural processes, therefore it must have been done by a supernatural God.

As I said in the introduction, I'm not going to get into the subject of evolution in this book. I'm not going to get into all the details of the scientific evidence. So let me just briefly discuss this philosophical question. Namely, there is a vast difference between saying, "I can't think of a way to do this", and "This is physically impossible."

It is impossible to add two even numbers together and get an odd number as the result. This can easily be proven mathematically. I am quite confident that advancing scientific knowledge will never find a way to add two even numbers and get an odd result. I am quite confident that you will not achieve this by using a more powerful computer, or getting a very strong man to attempt it, or big enough power tools. No brilliant new invention will make it possible. (If this was a riddle, you might solve the problem by redefining the terms somehow. But you haven't really solved the problem then: you've just played a word game to pretend it was a different problem.)

Compare this to a statement like, "It is impossible to build an electric car that can travel more than 500 miles without recharging." It may be that the laws of physics make this impossible. But it is more likely that no one has accomplished this yet just because no one has been clever enough to find the solution. With advancing science and technology, perhaps this will be accomplished.

When creationists say that it is impossible for something as complex as a living creature to come into existence by chance, naturalistic processes, they are saying it is impossible in the first sense. The objection is not in the form, "I can't think of a way to do that", but rather, "Let me demonstrate why that is mathematically impossible and violates known laws of physics, chemistry, and biology". It is conceivable that the science, math, and logic being offered are in error. Someone might find a flaw in the argument. But the argument is not an argument from ignorance. It is an argument from positive knowledge.

An ironic side note here is that the same critics who attack Christianity for resorting to a God of the Gaps, often themselves use a "Godless of the Gap" argument. They will say, "I just don't see how miracles can happen, therefore miracles are impossible." Or, "I can't imagine where God came from, therefore there is no God." Their arguments against the supernatural generally come in the form, "I can't imagine how the supernatural could be possible, therefore there must be a scientific (i.e. a naturalistic) explanation."

Conclusion

Christianity is not based on a "God of the Gaps" argument. One is hard-pressed to find a Christian doctrine or theory that is based on the idea that because we cannot explain some phenomenon, it must have been done by God. Rather, Christian doctrines are based on an affirmative believe in eyewitness testimony of miracles, revelation from God, and observations about human nature and the universe. We could certainly debate whether Christian claims are true. The fact that someone claims to have witnessed an event does not prove that he really did. But it is an affirmative argument, not an argument from ignorance.

4. Inspiration and Authorship

4.1. Q the Mystery Writer

Literary analysis proves that much of the material of the "Gospel of Matthew" and the "Gospel of Luke" was not really written by Matthew and Luke, but by somebody else. There are large chunks of Matthew and Luke that are clearly copied from Mark, and other chunks that are copied from some other unknown source. This seriously undermines the credibility of these books.

Parallels

Of the 661 verses in Mark, 606 appear to have been copied – sometimes directly, sometimes paraphrased – in Matthew, and 380 in Luke. Furthermore, there are about 250 verses that are common to Matthew and Luke but which are not found in Mark.

For example, compare these:

Matthew 8:14-15: "Now when Jesus had come into Peter's house, He saw his wife's mother lying sick with a fever. So He touched her hand, and the fever left her. And she arose and served them."

Mark 1:29-31: "Now as soon as they had come out of the synagogue, they entered the house of Simon and Andrew with James and John. But Simon's wife's mother lay sick with a fever, and they told Him about her at once. So He came and took her by the hand and lifted her up, and immediately the fever left her. And she served them."

Luke 4:38-39: "Now He arose from the synagogue and entered Simon's house. But Simon's wife's mother was sick with a high fever, and they made request of Him concerning her. So He stood over her and rebuked the fever, and it left her. And immediately she arose and served them."

Not only do all three tell the same story, but they use many of the same words, like "sick with a fever" and "arose and served them". If there were just one or two cases of such similar wording, it might be coincidence. But there are hundreds of examples.

Critics often state this like they think it will be a stunning revelation to Christians. But this fact does not come as a surprise to serious Bible students. Many Bibles and Bible study books include a section with a title like "Gospel Parallels", in which they chart out the common text.

Matthew and Luke must have copied this common material from Mark.

Similarly, when we see that Matthew and Luke have common material that is not in Mark, the most logical explanation is that they both copied from some other source. This hypothetical source has come to be called "Q", from the German word "quellen", meaning "source".

Thus, most of the books of Matthew and Luke could not have been written by Matthew or Luke.

Research

Critics often present this as an anti-Christian argument. I accept all the claimed facts. I just don't see how this is an argument against the Bible.

It is common when writing historical or biographical books to consult books written earlier. This is called "scholarship" and "research". Only when it comes to the Bible does an author doing research before writing a book suddenly become some sort of ethical violation or deceit. I've consulted many sources when writing this book. It never occurred to me that this was something to be ashamed of.

True, Matthew and Luke do not include any footnotes citing Mark or Q. But they wrote almost 2000 before the *MLA Style Handbook* was published: You can hardly fault them for not following conventions invented long after they wrote.

Mark

A common criticism of the reliability of the Gospels is the claim that they were written long after the events they describe happened. But scholars generally agree that Mark was written about AD 50-65. There are many quotes from Mark in writings of early Christians starting at least AD 130, so that is the absolute latest possible date. Assuming a reasonable "compromise" date of AD 65, that is just 30 years after Jesus death. There would have been plenty of people still around who had seen and heard Jesus.

Who was Mark, anyway? According to Papias, a Christian historian who lived circa AD 130:

> Mark having become the interpreter of Peter, wrote down accurately whatsoever he remembered. It was not, however, in exact order that he related the sayings or deeds of Christ. For he neither heard the Lord nor accompanied Him. But afterwards, as I said, he accompanied Peter ... For of one thing he took special care, not to omit anything he had heard, and not to put anything fictitious into the statements.
>
> > Papias, as quoted in Eusebius, *History of the Church*, ca. AD 324. (Papias's books do not survive today. We know his writing only from quotes in other writers.)

So Mark was an interpreter for Peter, translating from Peter's Hebrew and Aramaic into Greek and maybe other languages. He wrote his biography of Jesus based on what he translated for Peter and other things Peter told him in the course of their association. As Papias notes, Mark was not an eyewitness, but he got his information from an eyewitness.

Q

What about the mysterious Q?

Most of the Q information consists of teachings and sayings of Jesus. It appears then that someone compiled a collection of quotes from Jesus some time before Matthew and Luke were written. Again, looking at the dates shows this must have been done within the lifetime of people who had heard Jesus speak. It may even be that someone took notes on Jesus' sermons as he was speaking or shortly thereafter. The sources for the Gospels are pushed back even further.

We don't know who wrote the original Q. But here's a tantalizing possibility. Papias tells us that Matthew put together notes from Jesus' sermons:

> Matthew put together the *Sayings* in the Hebrew language, and each one interpreted them as best he could.
>
> <div align="right">Papias, as quoted in Eusebius, <i>History of the Church</i>, ca. AD 324</div>

Language scholars say that Q was probably originally written in Aramaic, because the Greek shows signs of Aramaic grammar and idioms. Aramaic and Hebrew are closely related. Matthew may have written a book of Jesus' sayings in Hebrew which was later translated into Greek and incorporated into Matthew and Luke.

Was Matthew the author of the mysterious Q? The evidence is slim, but it's intriguing.

Conclusion

Does textual analysis of the Gospels cast doubt on their authorship and reliability? No, just the opposite. It reveals that the Gospels writers researched their subject and used sources that must have been written within the lifetime of eyewitnesses.

4.2. Gospel Language

The four Gospels were all written in Greek. But the supposed authors, Matthew, Mark, Luke, and John, were Jews. They didn't speak Greek, they spoke Hebrew. They could not have been the authors of these books.

This criticism is based on the assumption that it is impossible for a human being to learn a foreign language.

In the 21st century, English is the language of international communication. Many people around the world speak English in addition to their native language. It is *the* official language or *an* official language of 63 countries. For example, English is the language of international aviation. An Italian pilot flying an Italian plane into an Italian city will talk to the air traffic controllers in English. Many common people around the world speak English so that they can do business with tourists. Many businessmen around the world speak English so that they can participate in international commerce.

In the time of the Gospel writers, Greek was the international language. The conquests of Alexander the Great had spread Greek from Macedonia to Egypt to Babylonia. Greek was the language of scholarship and international diplomacy.

Did Matthew, Mark, Luke, and John speak Greek?

According to the early church leader Papias, Mark served as Peter's interpreter. (See issue 4.1.) He was "brought in" specifically because of his knowledge of Greek and perhaps other languages.

Luke was a doctor. Paul refers to Luke as the "beloved physician" [Colossians 4:14] Then, like now, a doctor was an educated man. Greece was famous for its medical advances. Ever hear of the Hippocratic Oath? Hippocrates was Greek. We would expect a doctor of the time to know Greek.

Matthew was a tax collector [Matthew 10:3] He had to work with Roman government officials. He would have had to know Latin and probably Greek.

This leaves John as the only claimed Gospel writer who was not an educated man and who we cannot say must have known Greek. Greek scholars say that John's Greek is simpler and more like the Greek of everyday people than the other Bible books. This would be consistent with John being an uneducated man who either learned Greek just to write these books, or at least who had less occasion to use Greek and become proficient at it than the other writers. There is certainly no reason to say that John could not have known Greek.

In any case, if I see a book written in English by someone with a foreign name, my general assumption is that, even though this person lives in another country, he must have learned English somewhere along the line. It would be absurd to claim that an English-language book could not possibly have been written by a German because German's don't speak English. Without specific evidence that this particular German does not speak English, there is no rational base to deny that he could have learned it.

Side Note: Providence

Many Christians theorize that God arranged for there to be just such an international language at this particular time for the purpose of helping to spread the Gospel message. If there was no international language, the Gospel writers would presumably have written in Hebrew or Aramaic. But these were languages spoken by only a small group of people. If people had had to learn Hebrew to read the Bible, this would have been a serious impediment to spreading the news around the world.

4.3.   Author of Pentateuch

The Bible says that the first five books – Genesis, Exodus, Leviticus, Numbers, and Deuteronomy, often called the Pentateuch – were written by Moses. But no serious scholar today believes this. Rather, these books represent a skillful blend of several different documents composed over hundreds of years and put together by a later editor. We can identify these documents by the name used for God and other stylistic differences.

The first document is associated with the use of the name Yahweh or Jehovah for God, and so is called "J". The second uses the name Elohim, and so is called "E". The third is primarily concerned with laws and rituals and other priestly matters, and is called "P". The final document is found only in Deuteronomy, and is called "D".

Documentary Hypothesis

The first five books of the Bible are traditionally called "the books of Moses". Nowhere in the text of these books does the author identify himself, but the Jews traditionally attributed them to Moses, and Jesus refers to them as being written by Moses (Mark 12:26, Luke 24:44), as do Luke (Luke 2:22), John (John 1:17) and Paul (Acts 16:22).

This criticism is called the "Documentary Hypothesis"; or the "JEPD Theory", from the letters of the four supposed sources. Some advocates of this theory break it into more sources. For example some break J into three sources, calling them J1, J2, and J3. Most also add "R" for the "Redactor" who supposedly combined the other sources and had to add some text of his own here and there to tie it all together. But this makes little difference to the fundamental discussion here, so we won't go into this.

For centuries people have pointed out problems with the idea that Moses wrote the entire contents of all five books. Conservative Christian scholars generally do not insist on a "100% Moses" theory. But JEPD is quite different from the Christian theories. We'll get back to Christian theories at the end of this section.

Two Names

The germ of the Documentary Hypothesis came when critics noticed that the Old Testament routinely uses two different words for God.

One of these is the Hebrew word "Elohim", which is normally translated "God" in English Bibles. This is a descriptive word or title, like calling someone "the President".

The other is the Hebrew word "YHWH". Ancient Hebrew was written without vowels and for centuries the Jews believed it was presumptuous to speak the name of God aloud, so no one today knows what the correct vowels are, but the pronunciation was probably something like "Yahweh or "Yahveh". Some English Bibles, especially older ones, translated this word "Jehovah". If you look at just the consonants in Jehovah, you get JHVH, which is an alternative English translation of YHWH. Most modern English Bibles translate it "LORD", in all capitals. (Why they do this is a subject for another day.) This is God's proper name, like calling someone "George".

So the essence of the JEPD Theory is that because some places call this being "God" and others call him "Yahweh", these must have been written by two different people. After all, it is impossible to imagine a single author using both a proper name and a title to describe one individual. Like, you would be hard pressed to find a biography of America's first president in which he is sometimes referred to as "George Washington" and at other times as "the President", unless that book was written by two authors. Right?

Doublets

Defenders of the JEPD Theory explain that the different words for God were just a starting point. The four sources are different in many other ways. They have different styles, display different views of the nature of God, and reflect different political and cultural concerns. For example, they explain, J and E must have been written after the nation of Israel was divided into two kingdoms when Solomon died. J was apparently written by someone from Judah, the Southern Kingdom, because it emphasizes places in the south and shows a political bias toward the south. E was written by someone from the Northern Kingdom because it emphasizes places in the north and shows a political bias toward the north.

What is the evidence for this?

They saw that there were apparently two versions of a large number of biblical stories: two accounts of creation, two accounts of each of several stories about the patriarchs Abraham and Jacob, and so on. Then they noticed that, quite often, one of the two versions of a story would refer to God by one name and the other version would refer to God by a different name ...

Friedman, Richard Elliott. *Who Wrote the Bible?* San Francisco: Harper, 1987. pp. 50-51

This writer goes on to give a number of examples. As stated, this sounds like impressive evidence. There are two complete versions of various stories. JEPD Theorists call them "doublets". In one the deity is *always* called God and in the other he is *always* called Yahweh. The two stories have numerous differences in detail, including some contradictions. These two stories are simply stuck together in the Old Testament. [Friedman, p. 51]

But there's one gigantic catch to this argument. Take the story of Noah, for example. It sounds like they're saying that we find the "God" story in, say, Genesis chapter 6 and the "Yahweh" story in chapter 8. But in fact, when they get to the details, this is not what the JEPD folks claim at all. Rather, they claim the two stories are mixed together. They say that Genesis chapter 6 verses 5 through 8 are from J, while verses 9 through 22 are from P. Then in chapter 7 verses 1-5 are J, 6 is P, 7 is J, 8-9 are P, 10 is J, 11 is P, 12 is J, 13-15 and part of 16 are P, the end of 16 and 17-20 are J, 21 is P, 22 and 23 are J, 24 is P, etc. This is how they actually break out the verses. I am not making up an exaggerated example.

How did they decide which verse goes with which source? Any place that a name for God is used puts it in one or the other. After that, any place that has what the analyst considers a similar "style" or "tone" to a J passages is also assigned to J, and similarly for P.

Verse 7:16 presents a particular challenge, as it reads, "So those that entered, male and female of all flesh, went in as God had commanded him; and the LORD shut him in." Note this verse uses the word "God" (Elohim) in the first part and "LORD" (Yahweh) in the second part, so the JEPD theorists are forced to split a single sentence to accommodate their theory. They must insist that one author wrote the first half of the sentence, and then another author, living hundreds of miles away and decades or even centuries apart, wrote the second half.

Their dissection of the text is simply an exercise in circular reasoning. The critic divides the text up into four piles depending on which word for God it uses and certain other differences in style. Then they claim to be impressed that all the material in each pile uses the same word for God and shows these same peculiarities in style.

You could prove anything this way. Like: I claim that Martians are invading the Earth. I can identify the Martian spies: Martians all paint their mailboxes red. I can prove this theory. If it is not true, how do you explain the fact that all the people I have identified as Martians have red mailboxes? That would be an extraordinary coincidence, that what you claim to be a random group of people all just happen to have red mailboxes, huh?

There might be a semblance of plausibility to this circular reasoning if many stylistic differences converged neatly. If all the places that called God "Elohim" also showed a bias toward the Northern Kingdom and also had an emphasis on religious ritual and also, etc., if there were dozens of common characteristics. But as we can see in the case of the story of Noah, it does not.

The critics repeatedly say that there are "two complete versions" of various stories. Again, look at the Noah example. After slicing up the story, neither version could be said to be "complete". Each takes several odd jumps. For example, in Genesis 7, J is supposed to jump from verses 10 to 12 to 16b. Reading this gives, "[10] And it came to pass after seven days that the waters of the flood were on the earth. [12] And the rain was on the earth forty days and forty nights. [16b] [A]nd the LORD shut him in." Shut who in where? It is the P verses that supposedly come from a different story that state that Noah and the animals entered the ark. You could, of course, suppose that redundant verses were dropped. But the key evidence for the JEPD Theory is supposed to be that there are all these "doublets", i.e. complete, redundant stories. Without redundant stories, the theory falls apart.

Then there are the supposed contradictions between the J and P sources. In the stories of Noah's ark they identify two:

First, the P verses say Noah brought two of each animal, while the J verses say that he brought seven pairs of some animals. (There is some dispute about the translation: it may be just seven or it may be seven pairs.) But the command to bring two of each animal is given early on, in a summary of the instructions. Later more details are given, and at that time we are told that Noah was to bring seven pairs of some animals. So this is only a contradiction if you assume that God could not have given Noah an overview of the instructions and then later filled in details, or that the narrator might not have skipped details when introducing the story. Later P tells us the animals entered the ark in pairs, but "entered in pairs" does not necessarily mean only one pair of each.

Second, P says that Noah sent a raven to look for dry land, while J says that he sent a dove. Thus the critic says that they contradict on what kind of bird it was. If you read it as a single story, most readers understand there to be two birds: First Noah sends out the raven, then later he sends out the dove. There is nothing mysterious about this. Noah sends out the birds to find out if the land is dry yet. When the raven returns, Noah concludes it could not find any dry land. So he waits a few days and then sends out another bird to try again. The only reason for supposing that there is only one bird is because the JEPD theory claims the two accounts of sending out a bird come from different versions of the story. Again, we have circular reasoning: The critic claims the two discussions of sending out a bird come from separate sources. He concludes this must mean there were not two birds but only one, and the differences in the discussion of each bird are then "contradictions". Then he uses the conclusion that there are contradictions to prove that there must have been two separate stories. But there is no contradiction if we accept the plain reading that there is only one story that involves two birds.

In other cases, the critics' "doublets" really are two complete, separate stories. Many of their "conflicting" stories would appear to the casual reader to be describing different incidents, and not two versions of the same incident.

As an example of this, the JEPD theory says that J and E have two different versions of how Israel came to own the city of Shechem, the E story in Genesis 33:19 and the J story in Genesis 34: "How did Israel acquire Shechem? The E author says they bought it. The J author says they massacred it." [Friedman, p 63]

The "E story" is short and simple. It is a single sentence, saying that Jacob bought a piece of land from a man who lived in Shechem for 100 pieces of silver. [Genesis 33:19]

The "J story" which immediately follows takes all of chapter 34. Dinah, Jacob's daughter, goes to visit some women friends in the city. While she is there she is raped by the prince. In retaliation her brothers go to the city and, with the aid of a little trickery, kill a bunch of the men, including the king and the prince, and free their sister.

Neither story is about how Israel "acquired Shechem". All of this happened almost 300 years before Israel was a nation that controlled any territory. The E story says that Jacob bought some land from a person who lived in Shechem. If I say, "I bought a house from a man who lives in Chicago", would you understand that to mean that I now own and rule the city of Chicago? The J story says that Simeon and Levi killed a bunch of people in Shechem and left. There is no mention of them taking over the city.

But to the important point: Before the sophisticated JEPD analysis came along, people read this as not two contradictory stories, but as a continuous narrative. The "E story" leads quite naturally into the "J story". Genesis 33 says that Jacob and his family bought some land from a person who lived in Shechem. Apparently this land was near Shechem. Genesis 34 says that some time later Dinah went to visit some women in the city, where she was attacked and raped. Chapter 33 is not a competing story that contradicts Chapter 34. Chapter 33 is a brief introduction that explains how Jacob's family came to be living near Shechem, thus setting the stage for Chapter 34.

Stretching the Rules

The Yahweh versus Elohim parsing runs into trouble in numerous places, and the critics are forced to adapt the theory:

> I have pointed out two places where the name Yahweh occurs in E stories. Until now, I have said that the name of God was a key distinction between J and E. Now let me be more specific. In J, the deity is called Yahweh from beginning to end. The J writer never refers to him as Elohim in narration. In E, the deity is called Elohim until the arrival of Moses.
>
> Friedman, p 81

> Individual persons in J stories use the word Elohim, but the narrator does not.
>
> Friedman, p 265 (footnote)

So the JEPD theorist tells us that the different authors can be identified by which word they use for God: J uses "Yahweh" while E and P use "Elohim". But then he is "more specific": sometimes they do and sometimes they don't.

The theory is that there are other differences between J, E, P, and D, like J is pro-southern and E is pro-northern. Except some places that use the word "Yahweh" appear to be pro-northern, or in some other way are inconsistent with the other characteristics the critics want to attach to J. Ditto for the other supposed sources. No problem, they just declare that in this case J decided to call God by the E name or the other way around. Even though the whole theory was founded on the idea that the use of different names for God proves multiple authors and we can distinguish these authors by which name a given verse uses, in fact this leads to inconsistent results. When it does, this rule is promptly abandoned.

Occasionally a critic admits just how much this theory stretches the actual evidence.

> The question remains as to why so many similarities exist between J and E. They often tell similar stories. They deal largely with the same characters. They share much terminology. *Their styles are sufficiently similar that is has never been possible to separate them on stylistic grounds alone.* [emphasis mine]
>
> Friedman, pp. 83-84

> I was able to establish this picture of [the Redactor's] work by isolating the lines that he added to these archive texts. It is only possible to find them in the puzzle now by careful examination of wording, grammar, syntax, theme, and literary structure. I refer here only to those lines about which there is a relatively high degree of certainty. As a general rule we do not rush to call a line an insertion unless two or more of these clues are present.
>
> Friedman, p. 130

That is, assignment of text to one source or another was at best guesswork and at worst stretching the facts to fit a preconceived theory. The highly speculative and arbitrary nature of this analysis does not stop the JEPD theorists from identifying the gender of the writers, the city each lived in, the year, and in some cases, picking an historical figure who they claim must have been the anonymous writer. Yes, from such vague facts as "uses a title rather than a proper name" and "seems to be sympathetic to the concerns of priests", they claim to be able to identify the specific writer.

Preconceptions

An important factor behind JEPD was the belief on the part of many liberal scholars that Judaism could not have come into existence "full grown" at the time of Moses as the Bible claims. Rather, it must have evolved slowly over many centuries. It had to begin as a set of primitive fertility rites and worship of nature, and then gradually over time become more sophisticated, acquiring ethical teachings, then rituals, then laws, and finally in the latest stages developing into monotheism. Thus, the Books of Moses must have been written after this long evolution had taken place, and then the writers put the later ideas into the mouths of the earlier figures.

The text of Genesis and Exodus says exactly the opposite: that the essentials of Judaism – belief in one God, the Ten Commandments and the rest of the law, the rituals, etc. – were all given to people by God in the space of a few months.

The critics started out with a theory about religion based on their "gut feel" of how religions must evolve. Then they looked at the documentary evidence, and discovered that it did not fit the theory. So they concluded that the documentary evidence must be a fraud, and must be reinterpreted in light of their preconceived theories.

Legitimate Challenges to Moses

Are there legitimate arguments against Mosaic authorship, and how do Christians respond to them?

The most obvious argument against Moses as the author of the entire text of all five books is that Deuteronomy ends with an account of the death of Moses. Perhaps Moses could have described his own death through divine inspiration, but this section is not presented as a prophecy but rather in the past tense. (Or more technically, in the Hebrew perfect tense.) It goes on to say "But since then there has not arisen in Israel a prophet like Moses" [Deuteronomy 34:10]. This statement implies that many years had passed since the time of Moses.

This is only a minor challenge to Mosaic authorship. Traditionally Jews have said that the last chapter or two of Deuteronomy were written by Joshua. Most conservative Christian scholars agree that they were a postscript to the original book written by someone other than Moses, maybe Joshua and maybe someone else.

There are a few other places scattered through the books that seem unlikely to be written by Moses. One that critics love to bring up is Numbers 12:3, "Now the man Moses was very humble, more than all men who were on the face of the earth." It would seem like something of a paradox for the most humble man on earth to boast that he was the most humble man on earth.

It is possible that Moses wrote this without intending to boast. In context, it helps to make sense of the story: It explains why Moses did not defend himself against charges of arrogance, which led God to take action to defend him.

More concretely, Genesis 14:14 refers to the city of "Dan". But Judges 18:29 tells how the city came to be called Dan in the time of the judges, after the death of Moses, and that before that it was called Laish. So in the lifetime of Moses, the city would have been called Laish, not Dan.

Thus, it seems likely that an editor or editors some time after Moses made some minor additions and updates. It is common when an old book is republished today that an editor will add footnotes giving modern names for places, identifying people mentioned, explaining cultural or historical references, etc. Footnotes are a fairly recent idea. An editor living before footnotes were invented simply updated the text.

Toledoth Colophons

Four of the five books of Moses – Exodus, Leviticus, Numbers, and most of Deuteronomy -- describe events that occurred during the lifetime of Moses and where he was present or was in contact with people who were present. Moses could easily have written this history.

But the book of Genesis all occurred before the life of Moses. How did Moses know what happened hundreds or thousands of years before he was born? It is possible that God miraculously revealed this information to him. But a far more mundane explanation is likely: that Moses used written records left by earlier writers. Moses would not be the first writer to consult older works when writing a history book: this is called "research". Throughout the book of Genesis we find what may be citations to these older sources: the repeating phrase "these are the generations of ..." or "this is the genealogy of ..." or "this is the account of ..." All of these are translations of the Hebrew word "toledoth", which means an account of a family history.

Bible scholars traditionally took these toledoths to be headers over the following text, like someone writing in modern English puts headings or titles in front of sections of a book. But in the 1930's archaeologist P. J. Wiseman discovered that ancient clay tablets of this period routinely *ended* with a signature line, or "colophon", giving the name of the author, the subject, and sometimes some identification of when it was written. The toledoth phrases in Genesis are in this same format. [Sewell, Curt. "The Tablet Theory of Genesis Authorship". http://ldolphin.org /tablethy.html. July 5, 2000. Retrieved Nov 29, 2009]

Note that the Bible wasn't divided into chapters and verses until the 13th century. The fact that these toledoths often occur at the beginning of a chapter tell us nothing about the intent of the writers.

Trying to understand the toledoths as headers leads to many curious anomalies. For example, Gen 37:2 says, "This is the history [toledoth] of Jacob", but the following material is all about Joseph, with just a few brief mentions of Jacob. But if we interpret the toledoths as footers, they almost always follow sections that would quite plausibly have been written by the person whose name is given.

There are twelve of these toledoths in Genesis. From the New King James Version, where the italicized word in each verse is the translation of "toledoth":

2:4	"This is the *history* of the heavens and the earth when they were created"
5:1	"This is the book of the *genealogy* of Adam."
6:9	"This is the *genealogy* of Noah."
10:1	"Now this is the *genealogy* of the sons of Noah: Shem, Ham, and Japheth."
10:32	"These were the families of the sons of Noah, according to their *generations*, in their nations."
11:10	"This is the *genealogy* of Shem"
11:27	"This is the *genealogy* of Terah"
25:12	"Now this is the *genealogy* of Ishmael, Abraham's son, whom Hagar the Egyptian, Sarah's maidservant, bore to Abraham."
25:19	"This is the *genealogy* of Isaac, Abraham's son."
36:1	"Now this is the *genealogy* of Esau, who is Edom."

| 36:9 | "And this is the *genealogy* of Esau the father of the Edomites in Mount Seir." |
| 37:2 | "This is the *history* of Jacob." |

The New International Version translates each of these as "account", as in "This is the account of Noah," etc.

Note that the first toledoth, the "*toledoth* of the heavens and the earth when they were created" is the only one that does not have the name of a person. It follows an account of creation, at which there were no witnesses other than God. This makes a lot of sense in light of the footer theory: This section might have been written by God himself.

A problem with the footer theory is that the toledoths of Ishmael and Esau follow a lot of material unlikely to have been written by those men, and leave only very short sections for Isaac and Jacob. Advocates of the footer theory say that Ishmael's book may have been included within Isaac's and Esau's within Jacob's. That is, the book of Isaac may be Genesis 11:28 to 25:19, with the book of Ishmael inserted at 25:12 to 25:18. Likewise the book of Jacob may be 25:12 to 37:2, with the book of Esau inserted at 36:2 to 36:43.

All of the other toledoths fit the preceding text quite neatly. The last section of the book, the story of Joseph, does not end with a toledoth colophon. Perhaps it was written in a different literary style.

If the toledoth colophon theory is true, then Genesis was not written by the mysterious J, E, and P of the Documentary Hypothesis, but by Adam, Noah and his sons, Isaac, and Jacob. Moses then collected and edited the documents. Moses and a later editor or editors also added some of the side notes and historical updates, like "and to this day the name of the town has been Beersheba". [Gen 26:33]

Conclusion

The JEPD theory was initially based on the assumption that a single writer could not use two different words for the same person. This would be a thin enough argument if both were personal names. Like, if we read a book where the same person is sometimes called "George" and in other places called "Harold", we might find this puzzling. But it would be quite a leap to say that this proves that the book must originally have been two books by two different authors that have been mashed together. Perhaps one is the person's first name and the other a middle name, or one is a given name and the other a nickname, or any of dozens of other explanations. In the case of "Elohim" and "Yahweh", there is no mystery at all: Elohim is a title and Yahweh is a personal name. It's like sometimes calling a person "Fred" and other times calling him "my boss". Not only is there no error or contradiction in using two different words for the same person, but writers are commonly encouraged to do just that. When I was in school my English teachers often told us to switch between synonyms to avoid making our writing dull and repetitive. Like, we were told not to write, "I drove my car to the car dealer where the car salesman convinced me to buy a new car." It sounds much better to write, "I drove my car to the auto dealer where the Ford salesman convinced me to buy a new vehicle."

From there they go to circular reasoning. They divide the text into these supposed different sources based on use of Elohim versus Yahweh and some other variations in style. Then they claim as proof of their theory that each of the sections is amazingly consistent in the various points of style. Well, duh. They pick out all the verses that use the word Elohim, and then point out the startling fact that these verses all use the word Elohim.

Once they've broken the same story into multiple pieces, they claim that the fact that piece number one mentions a certain event but piece number two does not shows that there are contradictions between the sources, further proof that they were written by different people hundreds of years apart. But the only reason why these contradictions exist is because they've taken what a "naïve" reader would have understood as a single story and insisted on breaking it into pieces.

Much of the evidence for the JEPD theory comes from assuming that the theory is true, and then showing that this assumption leads to the conclusion that it is true.

The primary evidence for the JEPD theory is the conviction that a religion must inevitably begin as nature worship and fertility rites and can only acquire a moral code and evolve into monotheism after centuries of development. As the Pentateuch says that Judaism began with monotheism and a moral code, this must be a fraud. All that remains is to figure out who invented this fraud and when.

Accepting the theory that Moses wrote these books leads to some technical problems, like how Moses could have described his own death or how a humble man could have called himself the most humble man in the world. But the obvious reply is to say that another author added the story of the death of Moses as a postscript, and some

- 124 -

later editor updated place names and added some other explanatory notes for the people of his own time. The JEPD theory involves far more problems and far wilder assumptions to sustain.

4.4. Virgin Births

Christians stole the idea of a "virgin birth" from other religions. There are a number of other people in various ancient mythologies and religions who are said to have been born to a virgin.

Perhaps the best known is Horus, who was reportedly born to the virgin Isis.

Other notable virgin births are:

Zoroaster, also known as Zarathustra, the founder of Zoroastrianism.

Romulus, the legendary founder of Rome, was born to the Vestal Virgin.

Buddha, founder of Buddhism, was born to the virgin Maya, or Mary.

Critics list anywhere from four or five to dozens of pre-Christian stories of virgin births. They are not, of course, saying that all these people really were born to virgins. The claim is that this is a common theme in mythology, and Christians stole the story from pre-Christian sources, either to make their God as good as the pagan gods, or to appeal to pagans.

The existence of a fictional story does not prove that a similar story claimed to be true is in fact a lie. There were many science fiction stories written before 1969 about people traveling to the Moon. Does that prove that the Moon landing was a hoax?

The idea of a virgin birth isn't all that hard to dream up. If you wanted to make up a story about an amazing birth, the idea of the mother being a virgin doesn't seem like an incredible thing for someone to think of. Just like, if you wanted to make up a story about an amazing man, things like being super strong or able to fly seem pretty obvious.

That said, the most surprising thing is that most or all of the supposed pre-Christ virgin birth stories evaporate on investigation.

Some of the lists are so long that discussing the stories of all of the claimed "other virgin births" would take a book all by itself, so here I will concentrate on a few that are typical, where the person is reasonably well known, and that show up frequently and prominently on such lists. The others are similar.

Zarathustra

Zarathustra, also translated Zoroaster, was the founder of Zoroastrianism. The details of his life are sketchy. The year of his birth has been variously given as anywhere from 7000 BC to 600 BC. [Lendering, Jona. "Zarathustra". *Livius*. http://www.livius.org /za-zn/zarathustra/zarathustra.htm. Revised Dec 9, 2006. Retrieved Jan 2, 2010]

The primary Zoroastrian sacred text, the *Gathas*, does not give any real details of his life. The oldest biography of him is probably that found in a much later work, the *Denkard*, which is basically a commentary on his life and work written by his followers.

The account of his birth in the *Denkard* says:

> And he was born of his father Pourushasp -- a descendant of [the Peshdadian King] Jamshed -- and of his mother Dukdaub. Further, when he [the prophet] was born, there was a light like the blaze of fire -- a glare and a twilight -- irradiating from his house in all directions, high in the air, and to great distance on the earth, as a token of his greatness and exaltation.
>
> Denkard, Book 5, Chapter 2. http://www.avesta.org /denkard/dk5s.html. (Retrieved Jan 2, 2009.)

(Note: If you look up that web site, they translate his name as "Zartosht".)

While this clearly indicates some unusual circumstances surrounding his birth, there is no indication that his mother was a virgin. It quite specifically refers to an ordinary human father.

Zoroaster is also reported to be the third of five brothers. [Lendering] This would also argue against his mother being a virgin, unless we are to suppose that his two older brothers (at a minimum) were also virgin births.

Romulus

Many critics include Romulus, the legendary or semi-legendary founder of Rome, as a virgin birth. According to the Roman historian Livy, Romulus and Remus were the twin sons of a woman named Rhea Silvia. Rhea was a "Vestal Virgin", that is, she was a member of a group of women who dedicated their lives to the worship of the goddess Vesta, and as part of this service they took a vow to remain virgins for life. (Note: Some critics refer to her as "the Vestal Virgin" in a way that implies she was the only one. Roman historians record four to seven Vestals at any given time, and the order lasted for centuries.) As the story goes:

> The Vestal Virgin was raped and gave birth to twin boys. Mars, she declared, was their father — perhaps she believed it, perhaps she was merely hoping by the pretense to palliate her guilt.
>
> Livy (Titus Livius), "Book 1". *The Early History of Rome*, tr. Aubrey de Sélincourt (Harmondsworth: Penguin Books, 1960) Available on-line at http://www.nyu.edu /classes/reichert/sem/city/livy.html

The reference to "her guilt" is apparently an attempt by Livy to imply that she may not have been raped at all but simply broke her vow of virginity.

"Vestal Virgin" was a religious title. As the quote from Livy makes clear, no one thought this woman was a virgin when Romulus and Remus were conceived. If a nun becomes pregnant, the fact that she took a vow of chastity at one time does not mean that this is a "virgin birth".

Horus

Almost every discussion of pre-Christian virgin births that I have seen uses as its prime example the Egyptian god Horus, born to the "virgin Isis".

Our knowledge of Egyptian mythology comes primarily from the Pyramid Texts, inscriptions found on the walls of pyramids; the Coffin Texts, later inscriptions found on coffins; and the *Book of the Dead*. The story of the birth of Horus is found in the Pyramid Texts. According to the story, the gods Osiris and Set fight and Osiris is killed. His sisters Isis and Nephthys find the body and Isis uses her magic powers to restore him to life. Then Osiris makes Isis pregnant and she gives birth to Horus.

The Egyptian text is quite blunt and graphic in its description of how Isis becomes pregnant. I give the translation of the Egyptian text below.

WARNING: GRAPHIC LANGUAGE

If you are concerned that you will be offended by graphic language, you may want to skip this page. The gist of it is that it explicitly describes a sex act between Isis and Osiris.

Here's how the Egyptian texts describe the conception of Hours:

> Isis comes to thee rejoicing for love of thee; thy semen goes into her, while it is pointed like Sothis. Horus the pointed has come forth from thee, in his name of "Horus who was in Sothis."

> Samuel A. B. Mercer (translator). "Utterance 593".
> *The Pyramid Texts*. 1952. Available on-line at
> http://www.sacred-texts.com /egy/pyt/pyt43.htm

There is another version of the birth of Horus that is even more explicit:

> Thy sister comes to thee, rejoicing for love of thee. Thou hast placed her on thy phallus, that thy seed may go into her, (while) it is pointed like Sothis. Horus the pointed has come forth from thee as Horus who was in Sothis.

> Samuel A. B. Mercer (translator). "Utterance 366".
> *The Pyramid Texts*. 1952. Available on-line at
> http://www.sacred-texts.com /egy/pyt/pyt19.htm

It is difficult to see how one can read the Egyptian version of the story and say that the Egyptians believed Isis was a virgin. Indeed, suppose you wanted to say that a certain woman was not a virgin. How much more clearly could you say it than this?

According to James Breasted, "At Abydos and Philae the incident is graphically depicted on the wall in relief." [Breasted, James Henry. *Development of Religion and Thought in Ancient Egypt*. 1912. http://www.sacred-texts.com /egy/rtae/rtae05.htm (Retrieved Dec 31, 2009)]

Egyptian mythology makes quite clear that Isis was not a virgin and that Horus was conceived in the normal way.

Many critics go on to find numerous other parallels between the New Testament account of Jesus and the Egyptian stories about Horus. Some of these get quite elaborate. One source I found on the Internet -- http://www.near-death.com /experiences/origen046.html (retrieved Jan 1, 2010) -- finds over 20 parallels.

Some of these are:

Horus [was] the rising sun. Jesus is the rising Son.

This only sounds like a parallel when you translate the words into English. The original story of Horus was written in Egyptian and the story of Jesus was written in Greek. As neither was written in English, the fact that our word for the big yellow thing in the sky sounds like our word for a male child is not particularly relevant. This similarity might be turned into an amusing joke, but that's about the most that can be said for it.

Horus was born of the virgin Isis on December 25th in a cave/manger.

As noted above, the Egyptian stories make it quite clear that Isis was not a virgin. There is no mention in the Pyramid Texts, the Coffin Texts, or the Book of the Dead of the date of Horus birth – neither December 25 nor any other date. The Egyptian calendar was not 365 ¼ days like our own, so any given Egyptian date would correspond to different Gregorian dates from year to year.

[He] was baptized by "Anup the Baptizer" when he was thirty years old.

There is no one called "Anup the Baptizer" in any ancient Egyptian text. "Anup" may be a misspelling of "Anpu", the god of the dead. This name is more commonly translated into English as "Anubis". But Anpu/Anubis is never said to have baptized anyone.

Nor is there any mention of Horus being baptized, at age thirty or any other time.

He raised a man named El-Azar-us, from the dead.

There is no mention in the Egyptian texts of Horus raising anyone from the dead, nor do they include anyone named "El-Azar-us". The Pyramid Texts do say that Horus's father, Osiris, was raised from the dead – but by Isis, not by Horus. Perhaps "Azar-us" is supposed to be an alternate spelling of "Osiris", but Osiris is never called "El-Osiris" or anything of the sort.

One critic explained that the Greek name "Lazarus" was derived from the Egyptian name Osiris by adding the Hebrew prefix "El", changing the "s" to a "z", and changing the ending to the Latin "us". He doesn't mention that you would also have to change the "i"s to "a"s. Similarities between names in different languages can be interesting, but you can't just add, change, and subtract letters as many letters as you want. Before the fanciful changes, the only similarity between "Lazarus" and "Osiris" is that both include the letters "r" and "s". By that reasoning, we could much more easily prove that Harry Truman was a myth borrowed from Horus. Just change the "o" to an "a", double the "r", and change the ending to "y".

Horus was called "KRST," or "Anointed One".

The word "Krst" in Egyptian means "burial", and there is no reason to believe that its resemblance to the Greek word "Christ" is anything but coincidence. It was not a title of Horus, and Horus is never called the "Anointed One".

I'll refrain from going through the remainder of these supposed parallels, as in each case the response is the same: I cannot find any mention of anything of the sort in the Pyramid Texts, the Coffin Texts, or the Book of the Dead, which are our primary sources for Egyptian mythology. I have found many similar lists of parallels between Horus and Jesus on the Internet, and the one I cite above is the only one which gives any sort of reference to an Egyptian source at all. But it simply says, "The Egyptian Book of the Dead", with no mention of any specific chapter or page. I obtained an electronic copy of the Book of the Dead and did text searches on "El-Azur-us" and several variations, "Anpu", and every mention of Horus, and found none of the incidents this critic claims are there.

For a more complete discussion of the supposed parallels, two good Internet sources are http://www.kingdavid8.com /Copycat/JesusHorus.html and http://ct.grenme.com /index.php/Horus-Jesus_Correlations.

Buddha

Buddha is the only claimed pre-Christian virgin birth story for which I have been able to find any support at all in primary sources, and it is a stretch.

If we wanted to be abrupt, we could easily brush this one off as quickly as the others. Buddha's mother was not a virgin. Buddha was the son of Queen Maha Maya, who was married to King Shuddhodana.

According to Dharma Web, a Buddhist web site (Note Buddha is a title; his name was Siddhartha):

> For many years [King Shuddhodana's] chief consort, Queen Maha Maya, had no children. Then, almost twenty years after their marriage, she gave birth to a baby prince whom they named Siddhartha, meaning *wish-fulfilled.* ... The king and queen were very happy for they had no children and were longing for a child.
>
> > Radhika Abeysekera. "Relatives and Disciples of the Buddha". http://www.dharmaweb.org /index.php/Relatives_and_Disciples_of_the_Buddha _By_Radhika_Abeysekera Oct 21, 2005. Retrieved Jan 2, 2010.

If a couple were married for twenty years and "were longing for a child", it seems likely -- to put it mildly -- that they would have had sexual relations. There is nothing in the story that indicates otherwise.

That said, the primary source for the story of the birth of Buddha is the *Buddha-Karita.* It describes Queen Maha Maya as having a dream in which:

> Then falling from the host of beings in the Tushita heaven, and illumining the three worlds, the most excellent of Bodhisattvas [another title for Buddha] suddenly entered at a thought into her womb, like the Naga-king entering the cave of Nanda. Assuming the form of a huge elephant white

like Himalaya, armed with six tusks, with his face perfumed with flowing ichor, he entered the womb of the queen of king Suddhodana, to destroy the evils of the world.

Asvaghosha. Buddha-Karita. Translated by E. B. Cowell, 1894. p 4. Available on the web at http://www.sacred-texts.com /bud/sbe49/sbe4903.htm.

This could be taken to mean that the conception of Buddha was not the result of intercourse with her husband, but was a miraculous event.

But there is another obvious interpretation. This story came out of a Hindu culture, where people believed in reincarnation. They believed that when a person died, his soul would inhabit a new body. So to the Hindu mind, this story would be more likely to make them think of a great soul "moving in" to a baby conceived in the normal way than of a virgin birth.

Furthermore, shortly after Buddha's birth a seer, Asita, comes to the palace to speak to King Shuddhodana. After some introductions and flowery speeches he gets to the point:

But hear now the motive for my coming and rejoice thereat; a heavenly voice has been heard by me in the heavenly path, that thy son has been born for the sake of supreme knowledge.

Asvaghosha, p 11.

He goes on to give a number of prophecies about the child's future. Note that this seer, who we are given to understand knows all the mystical secrets about the baby Buddha, refers to him as "thy son" when speaking to Shuddhodana. Shuddhodana calls him his son. (Evidence again that Maha Maya was not a virgin: If she and Shuddhodana had never had sexual relations, how could he think her child was his son?) Throughout the remainder of the story, Buddha is routinely and frequently referred to as Shuddhodana's son and Shuddhodana is referred to as his father.

The Wikipedia article on Maha Maya says:

Some interpretations of the life story of the Buddha attribute his birth to a virgin birth. This is likely due to a specific interpretation of the prophetic dream Queen Maya is said to have had prior to conception and is not a widely held view amongst Buddhists.

"Maya (mother of Buddha)". http://en.wikipedia.org /wiki/Maya_(mother_of_Buddha) Dec 24, 2009. Retrieved Jan 2, 2010.

Another Buddhist text, the Digha Nikaya, or "Long Discourses", says that Buddha "was well born on both sides, of pure descent through the mother and through the father back through seven generations, with no slur put upon him, and no reproach, in respect of birth". [Digha Nikaya. i, 113] If Buddha was "well-born" for seven generations on his father's side, then he must have had a human father.

The claim that Buddha's mother was named "Mary" just like Jesus' mother is simply wrong. She was named "Maha Maya". Yes, her name shares several letters with "Mary", but you could play this kind of game with many names. It is just a coincidence.

Several critics say that Buddha was born on December 25, thus making another parallel to Jesus. Buddha's birthday is celebrated by Buddhists worldwide as the holiday of Vesak – in May, except on leap years, when it is in June. [BuddhaNet. "Festivals and Special Days". http://www.buddhanet.net /festival.htm. Retrieved November 27, 2010.]

Conclusions

After studying a number of these claimed pre-Christian virgin birth stories, I have not found one where a primary source clearly states "so-and-so was born to a virgin", and some that make quite clear that his mother was not a virgin. In many cases the subject of his mother's sex life never comes up. But if the fact that an account of someone's birth fails to specifically state that his mother had sexual relations is to be understood to mean that she was a virgin, then we would have to conclude that almost everyone recorded in history is a virgin birth. I have never read a biography of George Washington that describes his parents having intercourse. I have never concluded from this that his biographer thought he was an example of a virgin birth, just that they didn't find it necessary to state the obvious.

One critic lists at least 14 supposed virgin birth stories (I can't give an exact count because he includes phrases like "many Egyptian pharaohs"), and then ends with this interesting clarification:

However, there are two types of virgin births found in the world's religions. One type, as in the conception and birth of Jesus and Buddha, involves the Holy Spirit inducing the pregnancy in a virgin without engaging in intercourse. The other type is more common and involves an actual physical God engaging in sexual intercourse or interacting with a virgin in some other way.

Robinson, B. A.. "The virgin birth (conception) of Jesus" http://www.religioustolerance.org /virgin_b1.htm.Apr 5, 2008. Retrieved Jan 2, 2010.

So, a story in which a god engages in sexual intercourse with a woman and she then has a child is a "virgin birth story"? Perhaps before we began the discussion we should have asked for a definition of "virgin". In many pagan religions the gods are described in very human terms and engage in typical human behavior, like eating and sleeping and, well, having sex. They are "man writ large": just like humans except that they have magic powers. The idea of a human woman having sexual relations with such a god is not at all difficult to imagine. It strains any plausible definition of the word to call such a woman a "virgin". It's like saying that a woman is a virgin because she only had sex with rich men and that doesn't count.

As I said, I am not going to go through every claimed virgin birth story. I have found only one claim of a pre-Christian virgin birth story that references a primary source from Egyptian or Greek or any other mythology, and that one turned out not to back up the critic's claims. (The "Book of the Dead" reference I mention above for Horus.) In all cases I have found, the idea that this mythological or legendary character was born to a virgin is simply asserted without any reference to the original myths or any other evidence, or the only citation given is to another source attacking the Bible that asserts it with no evidence. For the cases that I have researched, I had to dig out primary sources for the birth stories of these people myself.

This lack of citation does mean that it is possible that there are alternate versions of the stories in sources other than those that I have been able to find that do describe a virgin birth. I don't claim to have read every word of every sacred writing of every religion in the world. But if someone is going to claim that there are ancient legends that say X, then to be taken seriously they should refer us to some actual text of the ancient legend to back up that claim. You can't just say, "The ancient Egyptians believe X", and then when challenged for evidence reply that you know the evidence is out there but you don't know where, and expect everyone to just take your word for it.

If you think I am just picking those who are easiest to refute and skimming over the "real" cases, I encourage you to visit some web sites that go through many of the reported stories, such as King David 8 [http://kingdavid8.com /Copycat/Home.html] or Divine Evidence [http://www.thedevineevidence.com /pagan_copycat_krishna.html] (Note the deliberate misspelling of "divine" in the URL.)

When I first read claims of parallels between the life of Jesus and the lives of other real, legendary, or mythological figures, I suspected that the parallels were strained. Like, they would find that Buddha was visited when he was a young man by three ambassadors, and Jesus was visited when he was a baby by three magi, so, aha, the story of Jesus must be stolen from the story of Buddha. I would think that with a little effort you could dig up many parallels like this just by coincidence. Take enough incidents from someone's life and you could always find someone, somewhere in history who had something fairly similar happen to him. But when I started to research this, I found that the parallels weren't even that good. A few of the parallels are so vague as to be meaningless. One critic said that Horus had disciples and Jesus had disciples, so, Aha! a parallel. Of course anyone who could be called a "leader" must by definition have followers, and if he's a religious leader you could call them disciples. You might as well claim that the story of Jesus is obviously stolen from the life of Aristotle because the Bible says that Jesus had two hands, and so did Aristotle!

Besides these silly and trivial examples, every claimed parallel that I investigated turned out to have zero evidence to back it up. The critics do not cite any books of history or mythology, they just take an incident from the life of Jesus and claim that this also happened to some other ancient person.

Before you are unduly impressed by some claim that the life of Jesus is stolen from someone else's biography, apply one simple test: Can the person making this claim actually point you to some ancient text telling this story about the other person? Can they actually point to some ancient Egyptian or Greek or Roman or whatever book of mythology? Or is the only place where this story is found on atheist web sites claiming to find parallels between Jesus and other people?

4.5. Nazarene Prophecy

Matthew says that Jesus lived in Nazareth in fulfillment of an Old Testament prophecy, "He shall be called a Nazarene." But there is no such prophecy in the Old Testament. Matthew is either mistaken or he made it up.

The verse in question is:

> And he came and dwelt in a city called Nazareth, that it might be fulfilled which was spoken by the prophets, "He shall be called a Nazarene."

> Matthew 2:23

It is true that there is no verse in the Old Testament that says, "He shall be called a Nazarene", either in a prophecy about the Messiah or in any other context.

Many Christians try to solve this problem by saying that Matthew's quote refers to Isaiah:

> A shoot will come up from the stump of Jesse; from his roots a Branch will bear fruit.

> Isaiah 11:1

Perhaps you see no resemblance at all between this verse and the quote in Matthew. The relationship is that the word "Nazareth" may come from the Hebrew word "nesret", meaning "branch", and this is the same word used in Isaiah.

A fair-minded Christian must admit this is weak. The "quote" has one word in common with the prophecy supposedly being quoted, and even that is just a word derived from the other word.

Compare that to the other prophecies that the New Testament writers quote. In the very same chapter of Matthew he says that Jesus lived for a time in Egypt, "that it might be fulfilled which was spoken by the Lord through the prophet, saying, 'Out of Egypt I called My Son.'" [Matthew 2:16] If we turn to Hosea we find that the prophet wrote, "When Israel was a child, I loved him, and out of Egypt I called my son." [Hosea 11:1]

Or a little later, again in that same chapter of Matthew, "Then was fulfilled what was spoken by Jeremiah the prophet, saying: 'A voice was heard in Ramah / Lamentation, weeping, and great mourning / Rachel weeping for her children / Refusing to be comforted / Because they are no more.'" [Matthew 2:17-18] Turn to Jeremiah and read, "This is what the LORD says: 'A voice is heard in Ramah / mourning and great weeping / Rachel weeping for her children and refusing to be comforted / because her children are no more.'" [Jeremiah 3:16]

The quotes are almost word-for-word. Clearly, Matthew wanted to show that Jesus fulfilled the Old Testament prophecies literally, not in some obscure, "Well, if you look at this way, he sort of, kinda, might have fulfilled the prophecy." So why, when it came to the prophecy about the "stump of Jesse", would he have suddenly completely reworded the prophecy in his quote?

There is a much simpler explanation: Matthew is quoting from some book of prophecy which does not survive today.

There are many books written in ancient times that do not survive. The Bible makes a number of references to ancient books that we do not have today. Joshua 10:13 mentions the "Book of Jasher". Chronicles 9:29 mentions three such books in one sentence: "Records of Nathan the Prophet", "Prophecy of Ahijah the Shilonite", and "Book of Iddo the Seer". Etc.

There are at least three other quotes in the New Testament from books that are not part of the Bible.

Jude 14-15 quotes from the Book of Enoch. "Now Enoch, the seventh from Adam, prophesied about these men also, saying, 'Behold, the Lord comes with ten thousands of His saints, to execute judgment on all, to convict all who are ungodly among them of all their ungodly deeds which they have committed in an ungodly way, and of all the harsh things which ungodly sinners have spoken against Him.'"

Acts 17:28 quotes Paul quoting the Greek poet Epimenides: "For in Him we live and move and have our being, as also some of your own poets have said, 'For we are also His offspring.'"

In Titus 1:12-13 Paul again quotes Epimenides: "One of them, a prophet of their own, said, 'Cretans are always liars, evil beasts, lazy gluttons.'" (Not the nicest quote, but a quote none the less. Epimenides was himself a Cretan, so it's a self-deprecating comment.)

The fact that the Bible mentions or quotes another book does not, of course, mean that the book is also the inspired word of God, but simply that the one statement quoted is accurate or useful to make some point.

So let's get back to the prophecy, "He shall be called a Nazarene". Matthew does not say where this prophecy is found or who made it. If we look at Matthew's other references to prophecy, in some cases he gives a specific source, like "what was spoken by Jeremiah". Other times he does not, like here. There is no reason to claim that Matthew thought this prophecy was found in the Old Testament or that he was trying to imply that it was. He simply says that it was a prophecy that was made and that Jesus fulfilled.

Conclusion

In the context, Matthew is trying to demonstrate that Jesus fulfilled all these ancient prophecies. From the fact that Matthew quotes it, it seems likely that it was at least reasonably well known to people of the time, at least to the religious scholars. There would have been little point in quoting a prophecy about the Messiah that no one had ever heard of and then claiming that it was an amazing miracle that Jesus fulfilled it. If no one knew of the prophecy, they would not have been impressed. But whatever book it was from does not survive today.

4.6.   Translation Error Cop-Out

The claim of Biblical inerrancy puts the Christian in the position of not just claiming that the *original* Bible was free of error (and, remember, none of the original autograph manuscripts exist) but that their modern version of the Bible is the end result of an error-free history of copying and translation beginning with the originals. ... If one is prepared to allow for the possibility of translator or transcriber errors, then the claim of Biblical inerrancy is completely undermined since no originals exist to serve as a benchmark against which to identify the errors. ... You could have the Bible say whatever you want it to say by simply claiming that words to the contrary are the result of copying or translation/interpretation errors, and nothing could prove you wrong.

> Edwards, P. Wesley. "Bible Errors and Contradictions". http://www.freethoughtdebater.com /tenbiblecontradictions.htm Sept 1, 2004. Retrieved Oct 23, 2009.

Few Christians claim that there have been absolutely no errors in copying or translating the Bible. Yes, in theory, this could mean that a Christian could explain away any error found in the Bible by claiming that it must be a translation error.

But to say that therefore to be "fair" the Christian must insist that there are no copying or translation errors is a bizarre demand. This criticism requires that the Christian take a position that he does not really believe, because it is easier to argue against this than his real position. You can't refute his actual position, so you invent a position that will be easier to refute and put it into his mouth.

If I am allowed that sort of reasoning I can rebut any opponent. You claim that you live in Atlanta? While, Atlanta is a big city, that's difficult to prove true or false. There's no way I could visit every home in Atlanta to determine whether or not you live there. No, for your statement to really be testable, I insist that you claim that you live in Atlantis. Then I prove there is no such place, and I have proven you a liar. If you say, "No, no, I didn't say I live in Atlantis, I said I live in Atlanta, in Georgia", I laugh and say, "Oh, so you admit that you can't prove you live in Atlantis! Now you're trying to weasel out!"

This argument assumes that real life must always be clean and neat. But experience shows this is not the case. Science is a powerful tool for gaining knowledge. It would be very convenient if the results of every scientific experiment were 100% reliable. But in real life this just isn't so. Sometimes the scientist's instruments malfunction, or the experiment was inadequately designed so that the results are misleading, or any of dozens of other problems. It would be absurd to insist that the only options are that science is perfect, or that it is all a fraud.

In practice, copying and translation errors can be blamed for only a small subset of possible criticisms of the Bible. There are challenges to the Bible that center on the definition of a single word. These could arguably be translation problems. There are challenges that center on a single number or phrase. These could arguably be problems in copying over the centuries. But for any challenge that depends on a wider context – Did Noah really build an ark? Did Moses really get the Ten Commandments directly from God? etc. – trying to argue that entire chapters of the Bible are one big translation or copying error would be absurd. I cannot imagine anyone seriously suggesting that the original text of the book of Exodus said that the Ten Commandments were written by a committee of lawyers who met to hash out a legal code, and somehow the whole story of Moses climbing Mount Sinai and getting tablets of stone written by God himself was accidentally inserted through a copying mistake.

It is far more likely for a scribe to miscopy a number than to miscopy a word, or to miscopy a word than to miscopy a sentence. Suppose that someone is copying the sentence, "Bob was 18 years old when his family moved to Pennsylvania." If he accidentally left out the letter "f" from the word "family" and wrote, "Bob was 18 years old when his *amily* moved to Pennsylvania", anyone reading the sentence could quickly see that "amily" is not a real word and that something is wrong, and it is likely that they would get the error fixed. But if he dropped the "1" off of 18, we get, "Bob was *8* years old when his family moved to Pennsylvania." There's nothing obviously wrong with that sentence. A copying error on a number is much more likely to pass proof-reading.

The same can be said for a copying error on a list, such as a list of names: Dropping a name or accidentally copying a name from somewhere else does not make the list incoherent.

It is, of course, possible to add or drop a word from a sentence or replace a word with a similar-sounding word and have the result still make sense. But this is much less likely to happen by chance than the dropping of a digit from a number or a name from a list.

So yes, there are a few criticisms of the Bible that Christians blame on translation or copying errors. But these are very few and by their nature, usually very minor.

People studying the Bible, not from the point of view of looking for errors, but to learn from it, are unlikely to be much affected by copying and translation errors. Whether the members of Jacob's family who settled in Egypt originally numbered 70 or 75 (one frequently cited contradiction, see issue 7.3) has little impact on their understanding of the text. It's hard to see any moral or theological importance at all, and the historical significance of such a distinction is trivial.

Regardless of how serious these errors are, the fact that the Christian's actual position is difficult to refute does not give the critic the right to put another position in his mouth. You can't decide what positions your opponent is allowed to take. You especially cannot tell him that he is not allowed to take a certain position because it's too difficult for you to argue against and is therefore unfair. It is not "cheating" to decline to take positions that you know are weak.

4.7. Literalism

Christians claim that we must take the Bible literally. This is clearly absurd. The Bible is full of statements that cannot possibly be meant literally, like, "The mountains and the hills shall break forth into

**singing before you, and all the trees of the field shall clap their hands."
[Isaiah 55:12]**

This specific example of the criticism comes from one of my college professors. Actually he quoted the Bible as saying, "The mountains clapped their hands", but the above verse is the closest I can find to what he claimed the Bible said and is probably what he had in mind. He told the class that when he showed this verse to a Biblical literalist and said, "You don't really believe that mountains have hands, do you?", that the ignorant Christian replied, "Well, in those days they did."

I can't speak for all Christians in the world. It's possible that he really found one this foolish.

When I say that I take the Bible literally, I don't mean that statement literally! What I mean is that I read the Bible as I would read any other book.

There are statements that are clearly intended to be read literally. When the Bible says, "On the same day Jesus went out of the house and sat by the sea," [Matthew 13:1] I take this as an obviously literal statement. There was an actual, physical house that Jesus had been inside. He really walked out the door to a real-life sea, etc.

There are statements that are clearly intended to be read figuratively. When the Bible says, "The LORD is my rock and my fortress and my deliverer; My God, my strength, in whom I will trust; my shield and the horn of my salvation, my stronghold," [Psalm 18:2] I do not for a moment suppose that God is literally a rock or a shield or a military fort. Obviously this language is symbolic and poetic. God is like a shield or a fort in that he protects us, etc.

Granted, there are places in the Bible where it is not clear whether the language is intended to be literal or symbolic. The Bible sometimes describes things outside normal human experience, like angels and demons and Heaven and Hell. When it talks about these things, there is sometimes legitimate question how we are supposed to read the text. Much of the book of Revelation falls into this debatable category.

The Bible is not unique in this. We have this problem when reading other books about things outside our experience. For example, books about computers often talk about the computer in human-sounding terms, like discussing its "memory" or referring to it as "thinking". People who are not familiar with computers can be unsure when or to what extent such statements are to be understood literally and to what extent they are simply analogies.

The reason why some Christians find it necessary to say that we take the Bible "literally" is because there are sections that by any normal reading are intended to be taken literally, but which some people insist on taking figuratively. Stories of miracles like Jesus turning water into wine or walking on water are written in the same straightforward, factual manner as mundane statements like Jesus walking outside and sitting by the water. There is no reason to believe that these stories are intended to be allegories. No reason except that the compromising Christian finds these stories too difficult to believe, and so in an effort to "save" the Bible he re-interprets them as allegories.

If you find these stories difficult to believe, fine, tell us why you find them difficult to believe and we can discuss the evidence for and against. Maybe the writer is a fool who completely misunderstood what was happening around him. Maybe the writer is a liar trying to deceive us into believing a hoax. Or maybe he is telling the truth and your incredulity is your own problem.

5. History

5.1. Sodom and Gomorrah Never Existed

The story of Sodom and Gomorrah is a fable with no basis in fact. History does not record any such cities ever existing.

Business records

In the late 1960s, archaeologists exploring in north-western Syria dug up a city which turned out to be the ancient city of Ebla. While not well known today, in its time – around 2300 BC – Ebla was the center of a powerful and important empire. In 1975 the archaeologists discovered an archive, containing about 15,000 clay tablets with ancient writing.

While the tablets were written in an unknown language, the archaeologists had a huge stroke of luck: among the tablets found were over 100 dictionaries translating between the Eblahite language, which they called "Paleo-Canaanite", and Sumerian. As the Sumerian language was already known, this greatly speeded the work of deciphering the language.

But alas, for anyone hoping that this library would yield up fascinating new historical tales, the bulk of the tablets turned out to be mundane business records. Many consist of lists of goods to be delivered to various places: 200 blankets to this city, 50 goats to that town, etc. Others are basically salesmen's expense accounts: How much was allowed for food and lodging on a caravan trip. Perhaps archaeologists of the future will have a similar experience if they unearth an "ancient American" city and find a room full of records, excitedly expecting it to contain all sorts of interesting books about American life, and it turns out to be a pile of tax audits.

Amidst all of these boring business records they found several references to business dealings with people in Sodom and Gomorrah. One tablet even listed a trade route that included over a hundred cities to be visited, including Sodom, Gomorrah, Admah, Zeboiim, and Zoar, not only the same five cities listed as the "Cities of the Plain" in Genesis 14, but in the same order. There is also a reference to a "King Birsha" of Admah. According to Genesis 14, there was a "King Birsha" of Gomorrah. The association with different cities makes it unlikely that they are the same person. But it is certainly interesting to see the same name show up. They may have been related, or it may have been a common name in that time and place. [Wilson, Clifford. *Ebla Tablets: Secrets of a Forgotten City.* San Diego: 1979. pp 36-37, 127-131]

Debate

On the other hand, in the years following, the identification of these cities in the Ebla tablets has been challenged, and one of the archaeologists who originally supported it has retracted. Remember that we are talking about translating names between multiple languages. Sometimes it can be difficult to tell if a name is really the same or just similar sounding. On the third hand, there is more to the identification than just the sound of the names. There is the geographical location and other clues. Furthermore, this retraction came after heavy pressure by the Syrian government. The Syrians have openly stated that discussion of Ebla should center around the glories of ancient Syrian civilization, and not any connection to Israel. They have accused archaeologists who talk about connections to the Bible of being involved in a "Zionist plot". The Syrian Department of Antiquities pressured one of the archaeologists into signing an "Official Declaration" renouncing any connection between Ebla and the Bible. The Syrian ambassador to the US told *Biblical Archaeology Review* (a semi-technical magazine about Middle-Eastern archaeology), "We are able to close the whole thing down, but we don't want this." That's a not-very-thinly-veiled threat that any archaeologist who talks about connections to the Bible will be denied access to the site. ["Ebla Update: The Known, the Unknown, and the Debatable". *Biblical Archaeology Review.* May/June 1980. pp. 48-49]

Conclusion

While there have been criticisms of the findings at Ebla, these are so obviously motivated by political chauvinism and anti-Jewish bias that they should be taken with a grain of salt.

I conclude that the original reports about Ebla are correct. Merchants from Ebla routinely traded with Sodom and Gomorrah. If this was a hoax, it was a very elaborate hoax: They created thousands upon thousands of authentic-looking business records, just so they could conceal obscure references to these cities in them. It was also a hoax with amazing foresight. There is no evidence that people in 2300 BC debated the existence of Sodom and Gomorrah. They must have anticipated that this would be a controversial issue 4000 years in the future, and carefully planned for it. The critics want us to believe that the prophets in the Bible are fiction, but that Ebla had some truly amazing prophets.

This doesn't prove that Sodom and Gomorrah were destroyed by God. But it does prove that they really did exist.

5.2. Nod

The Bible says that after Cain killed Able, he lived in the land of "Nod". But the word Nod is Hebrew for "wandering". This wasn't an actual place. The author of Genesis confused a verb for a noun.

The fact that the word "Nod" has meaning hardly proves that it was not a real place. Lots of places have picturesque or descriptive names. Here in the U.S. we have Coffee City, Texas and Two Egg, Florida; Boring, Oregon and Happy Land, Oklahoma.

If the area became well known as the place where Cain wandered after killing his brother Abel, maybe people came to call it Nod after this event. Or maybe Cain named it himself. Apparently he didn't wander forever, nor did he live there alone, as we are told he eventually built a city that he named Enoch.

5.3. Ur ... Where?

Genesis 11 refers to the city of Ur as "Ur of the Chaldeans". But the ancient city of Ur was not in Chaldea: it was in Sumer. Chaldea was

in what today is the southern tip of Iraq and Kuwait. Sumer was in central Iraq.

Christians generally offer two replies.

Some suggest that the phrase "of the Chaldeans" may not refer to geographical location but to social and/or political dominance. Sumer and Chaldea were neighbors, and Sumer was in decline at this time, so perhaps Chaldeans were taking over Ur.

Possible, but there's another, simpler explanation I find more convincing: There was more than one city at the time named "Ur", and the writer wanted to make clear which he was referring to. Modern scholars have difficulty identifying just what city Genesis is referring to, partly because there were a number of cities at the time with similar names. Archaeologists have found references to cities named Ouria, Orek, Urnki, Urfa, Urima, Uru, and others, any of which could be translated to "Ur" or something similar in Hebrew.

The Bible does not generally attach the name of a nation to the name of a city like this. For example, the same verse that mentions "Ur of the Chaldeans" ends, "… and they came to Haran and dwelt there." [Genesis 11:31] It doesn't say "Haran of Assyria", but simply "Haran". Et cetera, for almost all other references to cities.

So why would the writer tack on the "of" for this city but no others? The obvious reason would be that there was more than one city named Ur, so the reference would be ambiguous or misleading without specifying just which Ur he was talking about.

Suppose you read that someone lived in "Rome, New York". Would you say that this is clearly a mistake, because Rome is in Italy? No, even if you were unaware of the existence of a city named Rome in New York State, you would likely realize that the writer was trying to make clear that he was not talking about the well-known city in Italy, but about a less-well-known city in New York.

5.4.   Hittite Empire Never Existed

The Bible contains over 50 references to a nation it calls the "Hittites". No such nation is mentioned in the histories of Greece, Egypt, or any other ancient nation. There never was any such nation. The Bible account is fiction.

Hittites Rediscovered

This was a popular criticism of the Bible in the 19th century. You don't hear it so much anymore. This is probably because in 1884 archaeologist William Wright discovered a monument near the modern Turkish city of Bogazkoy identifying the site as Hattusas, the capital of the Hittite Empire. In 1905 Hugo Winckler excavated sections of the city, including the royal archives. These discoveries helped explain Egyptian documents found in 1887 in El-Amarna containing letters between the pharaohs Amenhotep III and his son Akhenaton and a previously-unknown kingdom that the Egyptians called "Kheta". Historians now generally believe that Kheta is the Egyptian word for Hittites.

Further excavations have revealed that the Hittites were probably the first people to smelt iron, thus beginning the Iron Age. It is now known that they had extensive trade relations with Greece, Assyria, and Egypt, and thus helped to transmit knowledge between these three civilizations.

The Hittite Empire collapsed sometime after 1280 BC. Exactly what happened to them is not known. After this they rapidly faded from history, all references to them outside the Bible were lost, and they were practically forgotten until their rediscovery by Wright and Winckler. Thus enabling the critics to deny their existence.

Second Try

That's where I intended to leave this section. But when doing research for this book, I discovered that the critics have a new argument: The rediscovered Hittites are not the same people as the Hittites of the Bible. Their reasoning is that they can't be the same because the Bible describes the Hittites as a small nation in Palestine, while the rediscovered Hittites were a major empire in Turkey. The similarity in names is just a coincidence.

This criticism simply misreads the Bible. It is true that the references to the Hittites in Genesis, Exodus, and Judges talk about them being in Palestine. Throughout Exodus and Judges we find lists of the nations that Israel is fighting in Palestine that often include the Hittites. For example, in Exodus God says that he will bring the Israelis "to a good and large land, to a land flowing with milk and honey, to the place of the Canaanites and the Hittites and the Amorites and the Perizzites and the Hivites and the Jebusites." [Exodus 3:8]

But nowhere does it say that the only place one could find Hittites is in Palestine. It just says that they were there. There is no solid evidence from non-Biblical sources that the Hittites controlled territory in Palestine. But ancient histories consistently agree that the Hittites were in contact with Greece, Assyria, and Egypt. Look at a map and you will quickly see that to do this they had to travel through Palestine. They were a warlike nation. It is likely that they would have tried to conquer lands that they saw as important trade routes. For that matter, the Bible doesn't say they controlled land there, just that they were there. It's possible that they had an economic and military "presence", much as the United States has an economic and military presence in many places around the world without claiming any territory. Perhaps future historians will declare that stories of the United States fighting wars in Kuwait and Iraq are absurd because the United States was in North America, not the Middle East.

The Bible continues to refer to the Hittites after Israel had conquered Palestine. We are told that under Solomon Israeli merchants bought horses and chariots from Egypt and "through their agents, they exported them to all the kings of the Hittites and the kings of Syria." [1 Kings 10:29] If the Hittites were still around after Israel conquered all of Canaan, then they couldn't have been a small nation in Canaan. If they still had their own kings, this can't be referring to them as an ethnic group as opposed to a nation.

Similarly, during the time of the prophet Elisha, the Syrians attacked Israel, but withdrew because they believed (incorrectly, it turns out, but they believed), "The king of Israel has hired against us the kings of the Hittites and the kings of the Egyptians to attack us!" [2 Kings 7:6] The fact that they say the Hittites and the Egyptians in one breath, as it were, could mean that the two were of comparable military strength.

I don't know how you could literally prove that the two "Hittites" are the same people. The Bible does not describe who the Hittites it is talking about are: it assumes the name is sufficient to identify them. But the references are consistent with it being the rediscovered Hittites.

Conclusion

The recent revival of this criticism is clearly much weaker than the original. "We have proof that there is no such thing, so the Bible is in error" sounds like a convincing argument. "This may or may not be the same thing, and you can't conclusively prove that it is" is clearly much weaker. Even the most virulent critics today don't claim that their new doubts prove that the Bible is wrong. Rather, their argument is that the Christians who hold up the story of the Hittites as a humiliation of the critics are being smug and premature. They have shifted from boldly proclaiming victory to covering their retreat. Now they can only say that the Christians may have overreached in declaring complete victory.

Despite the recent revival, this is largely a dead issue. The critics have lost this one and only a few still cling to it. I include it here for one reason: It demonstrates the type of flawed argument that Bible critics will use, and thus is a useful model for examining current criticisms.

The substance of the criticism was that a claim of historical fact in the Bible could not be corroborated from other sources. If we were talking about any other ancient historical document, no one would have thought much about this. There are many events in ancient history known to us from only one source. There are many events in ancient history that are not known to us at all because no written record was ever made of them, or because all written records have been lost. When there is only one source, historians are cautious about believing all the details. That source may be biased, wishing to portray his nation or his faction in the best light, or to make some political or moral point. Or the source may simply be misinformed. And yes, historians consider the possibility that the account we have may be complete fabrication. But no serious historian declares that a source is false simply because it cannot be corroborated. That would be highly premature and presumptuous. Only when it comes to the Bible do people seriously state that because we cannot independently prove it true, that therefore we must conclude that it is false.

5.5. Moses Was Pre-Literate

Moses could not have written the "Law of Moses" because writing had not been invented yet in his time.

Christian scholars generally place Moses and the Exodus about 1440 BC. Secular scholars tend to put the Exodus later, at more like 1290 BC. (See issue 5.7.) Even if we take the earlier date, there are many examples of writing from that time and earlier.

In the 1970's archaeologists excavated the city of Ebla in what is today northern Syria. They found an archive with about 15,000 clay tablets inscribed with ancient writing. They were dated to circa 2300 BC. Most of the texts were pretty boring – mostly mundane business records. So writing was not only in existence in the Middle East 1000 years before Moses, but that it was common enough that people were using it not just to record great epics or important royal decrees, but also the trivial details of day-to-day life. [Wilson, Clifford. *Ebla Tablets: Secrets of a Forgotten City*. San Diego: 1979. pp. 12, 16]

The Egyptians had a variety of writing systems, but they had some sort of alphabet by around 1700 BC. The Sumerians had an alphabet by 1300 BC.

Writing existed for hundreds of years before Moses.

5.6.   Moses Plagiarized Hamurrabi

The "Law of Moses" – the Ten Commandments and the other laws in Exodus, Leviticus, and Deuteronomy – are all obviously copied from the Code of Hamurrabi. Hammurabi was a king of Babylon who compiled a code of laws about 1790 BC, at least 300 years before Moses. There are so many similarities between the Code of Hamurrabi and the Law of Moses that they can't be coincidence. In some cases they even have almost identical wording, like "an eye for an eye". Moses, or whoever really wrote the so-called "Books of Moses", plagiarized Hammurabi.

Written Law

No one denies that Hammurabi wrote down a code of laws centuries before Moses. If the question is whether Moses invented the idea of having written laws, clearly the answer is that he did not. I don't know of any Christian or Jewish scholar who claims he did.

But it is quite a stretch to say that the Law of Moses is copied from the Code of Hammurabi. Yes, both are collections of laws. As such, they have some similarities. Both have penalties for murder, stealing, and kidnapping. But then, almost any collection of criminal laws would be expected to include laws against murder, stealing and kidnapping.

Scope

The Code of Hammurabi is mostly concerned with assault, divorce, inheritance, responsibilities of renters and tenants, and a long list of government-set prices for various products. The Law of Moses also discusses assault and divorce. It also deals with theft and other property crimes, public health, safety regulations, and many religious matters such as kosher foods and religious rituals. If Moses copied from Hammurabi, he also added a lot of original material. Moses does not include any government-mandated price-fixing, so apparently he decided not to plagiarize that part.

Ordeal versus Evidence

There are significant differences between Moses and Hammurabi. For example, throughout Hammurabi's laws you find rules like this:

> If anyone bring an accusation against a man, and the accused go to the river and leap into the river, if he sink in the river his accuser shall take possession of his house. But if the river prove that the accused is not guilty, and he escape unhurt, then he who had brought the accusation shall be put to death, while he who leaped into the river shall take possession of the house that had belonged to his accuser.
>
> Hammurabi. *Code of Hammurabi.* #2

Compare this to a typical rule from the Law of Moses:

> You shall appoint judges and officers in all your gates, which the LORD your God gives you, according to your tribes, and they shall judge the people with just judgment. You shall not pervert justice; you shall not show partiality, nor take a bribe ...
>
> Deuteronomy 16:18-19

That is, if someone was accused of a crime, the way Hammurabi said to determine guilt or innocence was to throw the accused person into a river. If he drowned, he must be guilty. If he was able to swim to safety, he must be innocent. The way Moses said to determine guilt or innocence was to have judges examine the evidence and make an unbiased decision.

Eye for an Eye

The biggest similarity that critics like to point out is that both Hammurabi and Moses have the idea of "an eye for an eye".
Moses says:

If a man causes disfigurement of his neighbor, as he has
done, so shall it be done to him — fracture for fracture, eye
for eye, tooth for tooth.

Leviticus 24:19-20

That is, if you were convicted of attacking another person and
gouging out his eye without provocation, as punishment the court
would gouge out your eye.

(Many modern people say they find such a law barbaric. We
could certainly debate this. Personally I find modern American law
much more barbaric. I saw a news story once about some thug who
had raped a teenage girl, beaten her senseless, cut off both her arms,
and left her to bleed to death. Miraculously she survived. He was
caught and sent to prison. After five years he was released and
returned to the town where he had committed his crimes. The point of
the news story was that he was unwelcome there and people tried to
run him out of town, and how unjust this was to this poor man who
had, after all, served his time. Personally, I think that he should have
been kept in prison until the girl's arms grew back. But my goal here is
not to defend the Bible's ethical standards but its factual accuracy, so
this is really beside the point.)

Hammurabi does indeed have a similar law, but it has
important differences:

If a man put out the eye of another man, his eye shall be
put out. ... If he put out the eye of a freed man, or break
the bone of a freed man, he shall pay one gold mina. If he
put out the eye of a man's slave, or break the bone of a
man's slave, he shall pay one-half of its value.

Hammurabi, #196, 198, 199

Under Hammurabi's law, assaulting and injuring a slave is a
minor crime calling for a fine. Assaulting and injuring a freed man, i.e.
a former slave, is a bigger fine. But assaulting someone of higher
social status is a serious crime. Under Moses law, there is no
distinction based on social status.

Moses does add one special case about injuring slaves:

If a man strikes the eye of his male or female servant, and
destroys it, he shall let him go free for the sake of his eye.

- 152 -

And if he knocks out the tooth of his male or female servant, he shall let him go free for the sake of his tooth.

Exodus 21: 26-27

You may note from the references that this is in a separate place in the law, so it appears that the slave is freed in addition to the master being punished. But this is not entirely clear.

Justice and Social Status

Many of the laws in the Code of Hammurabi have different punishments depending on whether the victim is slave or free, common or noble. The only comparable distinctions in Moses are a few cases involving a crime against a person's own slave. For example, in general if you injure someone, you have to compensate him for the time he must take off from work to recover. But this law does not apply if a master injures his own slave. Presumably because the lost work would have gone to the benefit of the master, so he would be compensating himself.

Rather, the Law of Moses calls for absolute impartiality:

You shall do no injustice in judgment. You shall not be partial to the poor, nor honor the person of the mighty. In righteousness you shall judge your neighbor.

Leviticus 19:15

Judges are forbidden to either show favoritism to the poor out of sympathy, or to the rich out of respect. Justice is supposed to be completely impartial.

Family Law

Hammurabi had an interesting take on family law.

If the prisoner die in prison from blows or maltreatment... If he was a free-born man, the son of the [jailor] shall be put to death.

Hammurabi. *Code of Hammurabi.* #116

If a man strike a free-born woman so ... the woman die, his daughter shall be put to death.

Hammurabi. #209-210

There are a number of laws in the Code of Hammurabi that punish the son or daughter of the person who committed the crime instead of the criminal himself.

Moses says the opposite:

> Fathers shall not be put to death for their children, nor shall children be put to death for their fathers; a person shall be put to death for his own sin.
>
> Deuteronomy 24:16

Conclusion

There are a few similarities between the Law of Moses and the Code of Hammurabi, like both saying that murder and assault are illegal. But these are things you would be likely to find in any legal code.

There are huge differences between the two. The Law of Moses calls for trials in which judges examine the evidence. The Code of Hammurabi calls for trials in which the accused is thrown in the river and his guilt is supposed to be magically determined by whether he sinks or swims. The Code of Hammurabi makes numerous distinctions between the rights of nobles, commoners, freed men, and slaves. The Law of Moses says justice must be equal for all. The Code of Hammurabi punishes children for the crimes of their parents. The Law of Moses says that each person must pay for his own crimes.

The critics' claim that the Law of Moses is plagiarized from the Code of Hammurabi really comes down to one similarity that might be considered surprising: the idea of "an eye for an eye". Note that they do not use the same words: Hammurabi does not use the "eye for an eye" formulation. They have similar ideas, not words. Is this idea so distinctive that we cannot imagine both God and Hammurabi thinking of it independently? If Hammurabi brought a copyright violation suit in a U.S. court, it's hard to imagine how he could win.

Side Note: Any Way You Can

Do you notice that this criticism is exactly the opposite of 5.5? With one breath the critic will say that Moses could not have written the Ten Commandments because writing hadn't been invented yet. When this is shot down, he promptly replies that Moses could not have written the Ten Commandments because written codes of law were in existence for centuries before Moses. He faults Christianity for being too fat, and when that is refuted, he replies, oh yeah, it's really too thin. Any theory is good as long as it is anti-Christian.

5.7.   Exodus Never Happened

If the plagues described in the book of Exodus – the Nile turning to blood, death of livestock, terrible hailstorms, etc. -- had really happened, Egypt would have been devastated. There would have been some mention of it in Egyptian history, but there is nothing. Egyptian history has no record of the supposed Exodus. Therefore the Exodus and the plagues could never have happened.

You might think that matching up the histories of two civilizations would be straightforward. For example, who was pharaoh of Egypt when Moses was leading Israel? Modern historians generally put Moses and the Exodus at about 1250 BC. All we have to do is look up who was pharaoh in 1250 BC, which turns out to be Ramesses II. Problem solved.

In real life, it's not that simple. Neither ancient Israel nor ancient Egypt used our modern Gregorian calendar (365 ¼ days per year, AD/BC, etc.) Historians routinely struggle with how to connect dates from one calendar to those from another. The dates of events in ancient history are often uncertain. This uncertainty is often decades and sometimes centuries.

When I was researching this chapter, I found theories on the pharaoh of the Exodus that ranged from Pepi II, conventionally put at about 2200 BC, to Ramesses II, at 1250 BC. Historians trying to connect Moses to Pepi will say that Pepi was really much later than that and Moses much earlier than generally thought. Historians connecting Moses to Ramesses II usually accept the conventional date for Ramesses but say Moses lived later than typically accepted.

Christian scholars generally put the Exodus at about 1450 BC. If so, then the pharaoh of the Exodus was Thutmose II or Thutmose III.

Most theories about the identification of the pharaoh of the Exodus center on better-known pharaohs. This tends to mean the more successful pharaohs. Some make the interesting argument that the pharaoh of the Exodus would more likely have been an *unsuccessful* pharaoh. By this reasoning, Thutmose II is a good candidate: he ruled at the right time, and his reign is undistinguished.

Thus, the sad reality is that we can't say for certain just where the Exodus fits in Egyptian history. This makes identifying references tricky.

Biblical Date Evidence

The main Biblical reason for assigning a 1250 BC date is Exodus 1:11, "And they built for Pharaoh supply cities, Pithom and Raamses." The city of Raamses, or Ramesses, was named after Ramesses II, who by the conventional timeline reigned in the 13th century BC. The Exodus happened after these cities were built, so it must have happened at the time of Ramesses II or later.

The main Biblical reason for a 1450 BC date is 1 Kings 6:1, which says that the fourth year of King Solomon's reign was 480 years after the Exodus. Matching this with other historical events that can be connected to Solomon puts us in the 15th century BC.

Advocates of the 1450 date rebut the conclusions from Exodus 1:11 by theorizing that a later editor updated the name of the city to make it recognizable to later readers. When the Jews built the city, it had some other name. Later Ramesses changed the name of the city to name it after himself. An editor then updated Exodus with the new name so that readers would know what city it was talking about. Contemporary writers often use modern place names for ancient places to avoid confusion, like saying "in the country today called Turkey".

Propaganda

Critics make much of the fact that no contemporary Egyptian historical records have been found that describe the country being destroyed in plagues sent by a foreign God, and then a mass of slaves escaping and destroying an army sent to pursue them.

A review of official Egyptian historical records shows that the greater mystery would be if Egyptian history *did* record such an event. Ancient Egypt was a dictatorship. Dictators then, like dictators today, have a tendency to censor the news.

According to official Iraqi news sources, in Saddam Hussein's run for re-election in 2002 he won with 100% of the vote. We are expected to believe that not one person in the entire country voted against him. Even the people he tortured, or the families of the people he killed, no doubt understood that he had to do these things for the good of the country, and respected him for it.

In 1953 the head of the Soviet secret police, Lavrentiy Beria, fell out of favor with Krushchev and was arrested and executed. The government sent a letter to all the owners of the official Soviet Encyclopedia instructing them to rip out the article on Beria, and replace it with an article on the Bering Sea conveniently enclosed with the letter. [Burnette, O. Lawrence, Jr. and Haygood, William Converse. *A Soviet View of the American Past*. Chicago: Scott Foresman, 1964. p. 7]

It is difficult to find any mention in all of official Egyptian history of Egypt ever losing a battle. We have an Egyptian account of the Battle of Kadesh, fought against the Hittites, that describes it as a glorious victory for the Egyptians. It goes on at great length about how Pharaoh personally led the charge. Indeed, the account repeatedly tells how "his majesty alone by himself" defeated the enemy. ["Official Egyptian Record of the Battle of Kadesh". http://www.reshafim.org.il /ad/egypt/kadeshaccounts.htm. ca. 1270 BC. Retrieved November 26, 2010.] Apparently the rest of the army just watched as Pharaoh single-handedly took on 2500 Hittite chariots. However, the end result of the battle was that Egypt signed a treaty giving up all claims to Kadesh and the surrounding territory. [Fox, Troy. "Ramesses II: Anatomy of a Pharaoh: The Military Leader". http://www.touregypt.net /featurestories/ramessesiimilitary.htm. Retrieved August 22, 2010.] Curious, isn't it, that after winning a great victory in battle, they would promptly surrender?

If a large group of slaves really did escape from Egypt, and destroyed an Egyptian chariot corps on their way out, it would be surprising indeed if official Egyptian history recorded it. That is exactly the sort of story that the official government news sources would either censor completely or spin in some way to make it sound like a triumph of the Egyptian government.

Nevertheless, there are several possible links from Egyptian history to the Exodus.

First Mention

A monument from the time of Pharaoh Merenptah contains a brief reference to Israel. It is generally dated to circa 1210 BC. It is the oldest reference yet found from a non-Jewish source that uses the name "Israel".

Disappointingly, it doesn't say much. The Pharaoh boasts about his victories over several enemies during a campaign in Canaan: "Plundered is Canaan with every evil; Carried off is Ashkelon; seized upon is Gezer; Yanoam is made as that which does not exist; Israel is laid waste, his seed is not." That's it. There is no further reference to Israel.

Nevertheless, we can learn two interesting things from this inscription.

First, it tells us that the Exodus must have happened before the time of Pharaoh Merenptah. After all, if the pharaoh fought them in Canaan, then they must not have been in Egypt anymore. This would seem to refute any theory that puts the Exodus after the time of Merenptah.

Second, there is a technical linguistic point: The word used for Israel has the form used in Egyptian for an ethnic group rather than a nation. This is curious, as the other places listed are identified as nations. It would be like a modern general saying, "I defeated Germany, Italy, and the Frenchmen." This would be consistent with Israel being in the period of the Judges. They had no central government and no king, and so other nations may have seen them as a curious anomaly: Not exactly a nation, but ... what?

Habiru

Surviving records of many nations in the ancient Middle East talk about a group call the "Hapiru" or "Habiru". They were not a nation, at least not in the sense of having national territory, but rather a collection of migrants. They wandered from Mesopotamia to Syria to Egypt. Other nations routinely talked about hiring them for manual labor and as mercenary soldiers.

Egyptian records talk about the "Apiru", which appears to be the same people. An Egyptian monument dated to the reign of Thutmose III, ca. 1470 BC, depicts people doing manual labor with captions saying that they are Apiru. A papyrus of routine administrative matters from about 1250 BC includes the statement, "Issue grain to the men of the army and to the Apiru who draw stone for the great pylon of Rameses II." ["The Mysterious Habiru and the Hebrews". http://www.imninalu.net /Habiru.htm. Retrieved Oct 16, 2010.]

The "Amarna Letters" are a collection of letters between the Egyptian government and various officials and allies, which were found in the city of Amarna. (Hence the name ...) One of these is from Abdu-Heba, the Canaanite king of Jerusalem, written somewhere between 1390 and 1340 BC, requesting military help from Egypt:

> May [pharaoh] send troops of archers against the people who commit evil deeds against the king, my Lord. If this year there are troops of archers, there will be countries and governors for the king, my Lord; if there are no troops of archers, there will be no countries nor governors for the king. See, the country of U-ru-sa-lim [Jerusalem], has not been given to me by my father nor by my mother; the strong arm of the king has given it to me. See, this is the work of Milkili [the ruler of Gezer] and the deed of the sons of Labayu [the ruler of Shechem], who have given the country to the Has-pi-ri [Hapiru]. See, oh king, my Lord, the right (is) with me.

Abdu-Heba. Amarna Letter EA 287. Available online at http://www.reshafim.org.il /ad/egypt/a-abdu-heba3.htm

There is an obvious similarity between the words "Habiru" and "Hebrew", especially considering that the "u" on the end is a plural suffix, like "s" in English. The description of the Habiru as people without a country matches what the Bible says about the Hebrews before the conquest of Canaan. In general, descriptions of the Habiru are consistent with what the Bible says about the Hebrews.

We must add the important qualifier that the Habiru were a bigger group than just Israel. Some have pointed to this as an argument against identifying the Habiru with the Hebrews. The Bible also indicates that "Hebrew" was a bigger group than just the Israelis: Israelis are the descendants of Jacob, while Hebrews are the descendants of his ancestor several generations back, Eber. All Israelis are Hebrews, but not all Hebrews are Israelis. There is the fact that ancient sources do not describe the Habiru as an ethnic group but more as a "lifestyle". This is a contradiction, but a trivial one. Unrelated people may have joined the Hebrews, just as immigrants move in to any country. Or outsiders may have lumped several groups together, like modern Americans often carelessly refer to Iranians and Afghans as "Arabs", even though they are not of Arab descent, do not speak Arabic, and do not call themselves Arabs.

If the traditional date of the Exodus of circa 1450 BC is correct, the Egyptian references to the Apiru fit well. According to the

Bible, before the Exodus the Jews were slaves in Egypt. The monument showing Apiru doing manual labor a few decades before the Exodus fits quite nicely with this. After the Exodus, beginning about 1400 BC, the Jews conquered Canaan. A desperate plea from a Canaanite ruler for military help to prevent the Apiru from taking over all of Canaan also fits this.

It is interesting that Abdu-Heba says that the sons of the ruler of Shechem are the leaders of these Habiru. According to Joshua 24, early in the conquest of Canaan the Jews made their military headquarters at Shechem.

Egyptian writings refer to Apiru in Egypt after the likely date of the Exodus. But this is not difficult to explain: Some Jews may have stayed behind, and Apiru who were not Jews may still have lived there.

Some scholars reject the idea that the Habiru and the Hebrews are the same people. If they are not the same people, there are a lot of coincidences.

Ipuwer

The Egyptian writer Ipuwer described a terrible calamity that had fallen on Egypt. He wrote:

> Pestilence is throughout the land, blood is everywhere, death is not lacking ... Indeed, the river is blood, yet men drink of it. Men shrink from human beings and thirst after water.

Ipuwer. *The Admonitions of Ipuwer*. Part II.

Ipuwer blames all these problems on "barbarians" and "foreigners":

> Barbarians from abroad have come to Egypt. Indeed, men arrive [indecipherable] and indeed, there are no Egyptians anywhere.

Ipuwer. *The Admonitions of Ipuwer*. Part III.

> The troops whom we marshaled for ourselves have turned into foreigners and have taken to ravaging.

Ipuwer, Part XV.

Nothing Ipuwer wrote identifies the Israelis as the despicable foreigners who have destroyed the country. He might be talking about Libyans or Syrians or anyone else. But blaming the problems on foreigners "whom we marshaled for ourselves" is consistent with the idea of it being Jews, as the Jews were invited into the country during the time of Joseph.

The reference to "pestilence" and other similar statements about death and destruction are also consistent with the account in Exodus. However, we must admit that these things are not unique to the Exodus. This could be a description of many disasters.

The reference to the river becoming blood is a very clear parallel to the account in Exodus. Note Ipuwer doesn't say that the river was filled with blood, which might mean that many people died and their blood flowed into the river, but that "the river *is* blood", indicating that something happened to the water.

Some critics dismiss the similarity as a metaphor, that Ipuwer didn't mean that the river literally turned to blood, but simply used this as a poetic way of saying that the situation in the nation was very bad. The resemblance to Exodus is just coincidence. As one put it:

> If I were to say that 'Society is going to the dogs' would [you] be justified in supposing that I was speaking of a band of wild dogs who had entered my city and were devouring its inhabitants?
>
> Asimov, Isaac. *The Stars in their Courses*. New York: 1971. p. 50

A cute comeback, but if we read Ipuwer carefully, there is no indication that he is writing poetic metaphor. Many of his statements of the tragedies that have befallen the country are quite prosaic, like "public offices are opened and their inventories are taken away", and that the cities of Elephantine and Thinis are "not paying taxes due to civil strife". Not exactly the stuff of epic poetry. Ipuwer certainly relies heavily on anecdotal descriptions of problems and often trite symptoms, like "there is none whose clothes are white in these times" and "female slaves are free with their tongues", but there is no reason to believe that he does not mean these statements literally, as examples of the tragedy. There are a few similes: "No offices are in their right place, like a herd running at random without a herdsman." If the statement about the river turning to blood is a metaphor, it is, as far as I can see, the only metaphor in the entire book.

If I were to say, "On 9/11 the World Trade Center buildings collapsed", would you be justified in supposing that I was speaking metaphorically of an economic crisis, and no buildings actually collapsed? In either case, you must look at the context. The main reason to suppose that Ipuwer is speaking in metaphor is a prior, dogmatic belief that the account in Exodus is a myth.

Another objection made to associating Ipuwer with Exodus is related to dating. According to the same critic cited above, Ipuwer wrote in 2200 BC and the Exodus (if it happened at all, which he doesn't believe) was in 1200 BC [Asimov, pp. 49-50]. This may sound like a devastating critique, but it contains two critical flaws.

First, the Exodus could not have been as late as 1200 BC. The Merenptah inscription proves that Israel was already in Canaan by that date, and had been there long enough to establish a presence strong enough for a Pharaoh to boast about defeating them and to name them in the same breath with several established nations.

Second, this dating of Ipuwer is only conjecture. The oldest surviving copy of Ipuwer is from the 19th Dynasty, about 1290 to 1190 BC. This is a copy of an older book, but there is no concrete evidence when the book was originally written, and whether the author was writing about his own time or events that were past for him as well as us. While Ipuwer goes into great detail about the calamities that Egypt suffers, nothing he says enables us to attach a specific date to his book. He does not name the pharaoh in power at the time, link it to any dateable astronomical events like an eclipse or planetary conjunction, etc. Many Egyptologists theorize that the original book was written about 1800 BC plus or minus centuries based on the writing style, and then further theorize that he must be talking about events in the First Intermediate Period, about 2100 BC, because that was a time of great chaos and upheaval such as Ipuwer describes. But that bare statement is pretty much all the evidence for such a date. The reasoning is, "Ipuwer describes a time of great calamity, the First Intermediate Period was a time of great calamity, therefore Ipuwer must have been describing the First Intermediate Period." The plagues of the Exodus were also a great calamity, so that could be the time that Ipuwer is describing. The critic dismisses Ipuwer's testimony as evidence that the Exodus really happened because he associates Ipuwer with a different era. He associates Ipuwer with a different era based on the assumption that the Exodus never happened. It's circular logic.

Some critics assert that the writer of Exodus must have read Ipuwer and copied his descriptions of the disasters. After all, they say, the writer obviously lived in Egypt and so Ipuwer would have been part of the popular culture. Of course if the Exodus account is a myth invented by Jews living in Israel centuries after the events were supposed to have happened, then the writer never lived in Egypt. The critic is getting his own story confused. And why would a Jewish writer creating myths for a Jewish audience make allusions to an Egyptian story? If his readers didn't know the story, it would be irrelevant. If they did know the story, then that would make his account less credible, not more. If I read a book claiming that there was a conspiracy behind the assassination of President Kennedy, and I realized that many elements of the story appeared to be copied from Shakespeare's play about the assassination of Julius Caesar, would that make me more or less likely to believe the story was true?

The fact that anyone would make such a suggestion is a tacit admission of the similarities between Exodus and Ipuwer.

A more serious argument against the theory that Ipuwer is talking about the Exodus is this: Of the ten plagues that the Bible says God brought on Egypt, we find clear parallels in Ipuwer for only three, and two of those are not very interesting. As I've noted, there is plague number one, turning the rivers to blood. Ipuwer discusses a plague on the livestock which matches plague number five, but that's pretty generic, as there have been many plagues on livestock in history. He mentions children being killed, including "children of princes", which could match plague number ten, the death of the firstborn. But then any calamity causing many deaths would surely include the death of children. Though children of princes would usually be relatively safe. I see nothing that obviously connects to the other seven plagues. There are other similarities, like slaves robbing their masters and foreigners ruining the country. But again, these are things that have happened many times in history, and there is not enough detail to say that the resemblance between Ipuwer and Exodus is particularly remarkable on these other points. 90% of the argument for connecting Ipuwer to Exodus is his description of the river turning to blood.

All told, the fact that critics work so hard to explain away the similarity between Ipuwer and Exodus is evidence that the similarity is significant.

We do not know just when Ipuwer lived, or for that matter whether he was describing his own time or a time in his past. Egyptian scholars have given a wide range of dates to Ipuwer. As I said, dating of events in ancient history is often difficult. Even fitting one Egyptian document with other Egyptian documents can be tricky. Is Ipuwer describing the Exodus, or some other time of crisis in Egypt?

The Hyskos

Egyptian history contains many references to the "Hyskos", a mysterious group of invaders who came from Palestine and who dominated the country for about 100 years before the Egyptians rose up and threw them out.

Some historians theorize that the Jews may have been a subgroup within the Hyskos. No one says that the Jews *were* the Hyskos. For one thing, the Hyskos conquered a number of Egyptian cities, something no one supposes the Jews ever did. However, both Jews and Hyskos were Semitic people from Palestine. One Hyskos leader mentioned in Egyptian histories is named "Jacob-Hur" or "Jacob-El". This may be the Jacob of the Bible. The evidence is slim, but even if it's just a common name, the fact that Hyskos and Jews used the same names is evidence of a relationship. If they were in the country at the same time, it is likely they would have been associated with each other, especially in the Egyptian mind. Much as modern Americans lump immigrants from Mexico in with immigrants from Guatemala and Costa Rica as "Hispanics", the Egyptians might have lumped all Palestinian Semites together as "Hyskos".

Thus, some historians equate the Exodus with the expulsion of the Hyskos. Perhaps Jews and Hyskos left Egypt together. Maybe as the political power of the Semites declined, the Jews and Hyskos decided that it was time to leave Egypt, but the Egyptians tried to force them to stay. Given the Egyptian government's tendency to propaganda, it would not be surprising if Egyptian historians reported a failed attempt to prevent an ethnic group from escaping as a great victory in which they were successfully thrown out.

On the other hand, the Hyskos departed about 1535 BC. This is too early to coincide with the Exodus by most chronologies. Also, could the Jews have been associated with both the Habiru and the Hyskos? Possible, though unlikely.

A more likely theory is a more tenuous relationship: When the Hyskos were in power, they favored the Jews because of their common ethnic and geographic heritage. When the Egyptians overthrew the

Hyskos, they resented the Jews, and this was a factor in their subsequent bad treatment.

Akhenaten

One pharaoh, Amenhotep IV, attempted to replace Egyptian polytheistic religion with the worship of one god. He called this god Aten and changed his own name to Akhenaten, meaning "spirit of Aten". He claimed that Aten was a god of love, in contrast to the warlike gods of traditional Egyptian religion. Akhenaten reigned for 17 years, dying about 1334 BC. By a late chronology, Exodus ca. 1250 BC, this puts him between the time of Joseph and the time of Moses. Is it possible that Amenhotep got his ideas about one God from the Jews? Maybe one of Joseph's descendants converted a later pharaoh to belief in Yahweh. By the more likely early chronology, Exodus ca. 1450 BC, Akhenaten is well after the Jews were gone. Perhaps his faith in traditional Egyptian religion was shaken at the thought that the Egyptian gods were beaten by the God of the Hebrew slaves.

It could be that an Egyptian thought of the idea of monotheism with no help from any Jews. There's some interesting material here, but there's a lot more speculation than fact.

In any case, when he died, the old religion came back and his efforts were quickly buried. His son even changed his name from Tutankhaten, "Image of Aten", to Tutankhamun, "Image of Amun", one of the traditional Egyptian gods. (This Tutankhamun being perhaps the best known of all Egyptian pharaohs: King Tut.) Apparently he did not distance himself enough from his father, as later pharaohs had the names of both Akhenaten and Tutankhamun – plus Smenkhkare who ruled in between them, possibly Tutankhamun's older brother – purged from all inscriptions and historical records. It was not until the late 19th century that students of Egyptian history re-discovered their existence when archaeologists unearthed the city of Amarna, which Akhenaten had built as a center for the worship of one god.

If the later pharaohs could successfully wipe the names of three pharaohs out of their history books because they found their existence embarrassing, they could also wipe out references to a slave revolt.

This was not the only time a pharaoh tried to erase a previous ruler. Thutmose III – possibly the pharaoh of the Exodus – tried to destroy all mentions of his stepmother, Hatshepsut, who had ruled as his regent when he was a boy, and whose domination he apparently resented. He destroyed many documents and monuments, but he did not succeed in destroying the memory of her completely.

How Bad?

Critics say that the Exodus is impossible because an event like the Ten Plagues would have destroyed Egypt, and yet Egypt continued to survive after any date that has been associated with the Exodus.

This is an exaggeration. Yes, the plagues would have been bad for the economy, to say the least. But they would not have destroyed the country. The United States suffered two "plagues" in the 1930s: the stock market crash and the Dust Bowl. Yet by the 40s it was back on its feet, and in the 50s and 60s even had an economic boom.

Similarly, while events like Exodus describes would have devastated Egypt, under competent leadership the country could have recovered within a decade or two. That's a long time for the people living through it, but the blink of an eye to historians looking back from 3000-plus years.

Moses

I don't know that this proves anything, but it's an interesting side note: We all know the name of Moses. In Egyptian, the name "Ramesses" is pronounced more like "Ra-mo-ses". "Thutmose" is "Thut-mo-ses". "Ahmosis" is "Ah-mo-ses". "Moses" is Egyptian for "son" or "drawn from". Thus Ramesses is "son of Ra" or "drawn from Ra", Thutmose is "son of Thut", etc. A number of pharaohs had the word "moses" in their names.

Conclusion

It is not accurate to say that the Exodus could not have happened because there is no reference to it in Egyptian history.

For one thing, there may well be a reference to it in Egyptian history: Ipuwer.

Official Egyptian history was heavily censored and spun by the government. We know, for example, that they wrote an account of an important battle that made a defeat or stand-off sound like a great victory, and they erased all reference to three pharaohs they considered an embarrassment. A group of slaves winning a showdown with the pharaoh, escaping from the country, and destroying an army sent to pursue them is exactly the sort of thing the government would censor.

Other Egyptian references are consistent with the Exodus and difficult to explain without it.

Egyptian history records Hebrews as manual laborers on government projects before the traditional date of the Exodus, and Jews conquering Canaan shortly after. There is also a reference to fighting Israel during the time of the judges.

If there never was an Exodus, then what happened to the Apiru in Egypt? Did they just disappear? Where did the Israelis who conquered Canaan come from? Did they appear out of nowhere? Both mysteries evaporate if we theorize that the two are the same people, and so they must have left Egypt and invaded Canaan somewhere around 1400 BC.

Two more tentative connections are the Hyskos and the monotheism of Akhenaten. These are interesting, but inconclusive.

5.8.   Jewish Slaves Didn't Build Pyramids

The Bible says that the pyramids were built by Jewish slaves. This is impossible. Recent archaeological finds show that the pyramids were built by well-paid freemen. Egypt never practiced slavery. Major public works projects were built by corvee, that is, conscript labor, not by slaves.

Note: This could rightly be considered part of issue 5.7, but I discuss it separately because the arguments are different.

Giza graves

Critics have made much of some archaeological discoveries of the 1990s and 2000s that purport to prove that the pyramids were not built by slaves, but by free and well-paid workers. Archaeologists dug up graves in Giza in Egypt, the site of the great pyramids. These are likely graves of people who built the pyramids.

The archaeologists say that the life of these people was hard. Many of the skeletons show arthritis and damaged vertebrae, indicating lives of difficult manual labor. And they appear to have died quite young. According to Adel Okasha, supervisor of the excavation, "Their bones tell us the story of how hard they worked."

But they could not have been slaves because they were buried near the pyramids, and jars were found in the graves which probably at one time contained food or other supplies, in accordance with Egyptian religious burial practices. "No way would they have been buried so honorably if they were slaves," said Egyptian archaeologist Zahi Hawass. [Kratovac, Katarina. "New Discovery Shows Slaves Didn't Build Pyramids, Egypt Says". *Huffington Post*. Jan 11, 2010.]

Proving What?

It is not clear, from the reports I have read anyway, how any of this proves that the pyramid builders were not slaves. Maybe the fact that they were buried near the pyramids they were building is a sign of reverence for the dead, that they were worthy to be buried near these great monuments. Or maybe it means that the Egyptians couldn't be bothered to send the bodies back to their homes and just dumped them in the nearest convenient place. The fact that they put a jar of food in the grave is comparable to the American practice of putting flowers on a grave. It shows some level of respect for the dead and that's a nice thing. But it doesn't prove that these people weren't slaves, just that they were treated with some minimal level of dignity. The Egyptian archaeologists themselves note how hard these people's lives were. These people were certainly not the pampered children of nobility.

In any case, the whole discussion is almost certainly irrelevant. I don't know of any serious Christian or Jewish scholar who claims that the pyramids were built by Jewish slaves. The Bible never says that the Jews built the pyramids. Exodus 1:11 says, "Therefore [the Egyptians] set taskmasters over them to afflict them with their burdens. And they built for Pharaoh supply cities, Pithom and Raamses." According to the Bible, the Jews were forced to build "supply cities", not pyramids. The idea that Jewish slaves worked on the pyramids probably comes from simple leaping to conclusions: the Egyptians forced Jewish slaves to work on construction projects, the biggest construction projects in Egypt were the pyramids, therefore Jewish slaves worked on the pyramids.

The famous pyramids of Giza referenced in the news reports were built around 2630 to 2610 BC. Most conservative Bible scholars put Joseph and the arrival of the Jews in Egypt at around 1880 BC. So the pyramids of Giza were built centuries before the Jews arrived. The last pyramid I can find a date for is that of Amenemhat III in 1814 BC. While there were Jews in Egypt by then, it is before they were slaves and centuries before the Exodus.

Slavery in Egypt

The claim that there was no slavery in Egypt is simply false.

One of the terms of the Treaty of Kadesh, a treaty between Egypt and the Hittites, was that the Hittites agreed to return any slaves who escaped from Egypt and sought refuge in Hittite country. "Or if there flee a man, or two men who are unknown, and they shall come to the land of Kheta, to become foreign subjects, then they shall not be settled in the land of Kheta, but they shall be brought to Ramses-Meriamon, the great ruler of Egypt." [*Treaty of Kadesh* ca 1274 BC. Provision 10]. If someone who attempts to quit his job can be arrested, dragged back, and forced to go back to work, that's pretty much half the definition of slavery.

Pharaoh Amenhotep III sent a letter to Milkilu, prince of Gezer in Canaan, which was basically a purchase order for slave girls. He requires, "In total: forty concubines - the price of every concubine is forty [coins] of silver. Therefore, send very beautiful concubines without blemish." [Amenhotep III. "From Amenhotep to Milkilu". *Amarna Letters*. ca. 1350 BC] When human beings are bought and sold for money, that's pretty much the other half of the definition of slavery.

Inscriptions on monuments boast of how many slaves were brought back after an enemy was conquered. There are numerous surviving Egyptian documents that specify the price that was paid for a slave. We have wills in which people talk about which friend or relative they will leave their slaves to.

This doesn't prove that Jews were slaves, but it is absurd to say that there was no slavery in Egypt.

Slavery versus Forced Labor

A number of critics say that the Jews were not slaves but were simply subject to a "corvee". The corvee was a common practice in ancient times. Instead of requiring people to pay taxes in cash, governments required manual labor on state projects. Usually these were construction projects, like forts or roads or irrigation channels. Typically the obligation was seasonal: you would work a few months for the government, then you would be free to go home and work on your own farm. I presume the reasoning was that most of the common people were farmers, and farming is a seasonal business – very busy at spring planting time and then again at fall harvest, but less work during summer and winter. So they had free time that they might as well spend working for the government. If this sounds outrageous to you, it's less onerous than being drafted into the army. At least on a construction project there aren't people trying to kill you. The practice isn't entirely dead. A few years ago my city required everyone on my street to repair the sidewalks: We could either do the work personally or we could hire someone to do it. I paid a contractor, but I'm sure some did the work themselves. The principle is the same as the corvee. Of course a day or two of work is much less of a burden than months.

Most history books that describe the corvee refer to it as "forced labor". To the person subject to it, it surely seems little different from slavery. If the government sent police to your home and forced you to go with them to some far-away place and do hard manual labor at a construction project, I think you might refer to this as "slavery", even if it does not meet some arbitrary definition.

None of the sources I have for this criticism give any historical evidence that the Jews were forced labor and not technically slaves. They just say that it is so. But even if this is true, so what? They might well have described it as slavery, and the distinction is just a quibble.

Afterword: Jews, Hebrews, Israelites

When I was researching this section, I came across a number of articles by critics that start out saying that they can prove that "Jews were never slaves in Egypt", and it turned out that their proof was that the term "Jew" did not come into use until centuries later. Some went on to talk about the difference between the words "Jews", "Hebrews", and "Israelites". They say that you cannot talk about "Israelites" until Israel became an independent nation, and you can't talk about "Jews" until at least the time when Judah became a separate country, as the word "Jew" comes from "Judah".

This is at best debatable, and mostly a red herring. The name Israel is the nickname that God gave to Jacob, and which came to be applied to all his descendants. It might rationally be applied to descendants of Jacob regardless of whether they were a country with definable borders or not. A group of people can have a name even if they are not a nation. There is no nation of "Accountia", but that doesn't mean that the term "accountants" is therefore meaningless. Yes, the word "Jew" did not come into use until centuries later. But so what? Today the English word is understood to refer to anyone descended from Jacob. This objection is rather like saying that the United States was never really at war with Germany ... because the Germans don't call their country "Germany" but "Deutschland". If you want to argue that our terminology is flawed, okay, make that case.

But don't play this silly game of pretending that a debate about what a group of people should be properly called proves something about where they lived.

Conclusion

It is true that the pyramids were almost certainly not built by Jewish slaves. The pyramids were built long before they arrived in Egypt. But this is not an argument against the Bible, because the Bible does not say that Jewish slaves built the pyramids. It says that they built "supply cities".

The claim that the Jews could not have been slaves in Egypt because Egypt did not practice slavery is completely false. There are many surviving Egyptian documents that discuss slavery.

5.9. Supplying the Exodus

The Bible says that Moses and the Israelites wandered in the desert for 40 years. It also says that they numbered over 2 million. How could Moses possibly have kept all these people fed? It would have taken thousands of trainloads every day just to supply the food for such a population, never mind clothes and other supplies. It is a logistical impossibility.

Actually "thousands of trainloads" is rather high. According to the U.S. Department of Agriculture, the average American eats 4.7 pounds of food per day. Americans eat more than most people throughout history, but let's suppose the Israelis ate a similar amount. Multiply by 2 million people makes 9.4 million pounds of food per day. Say 10 million. A railroad car can carry about 200,000 pounds. So it would have taken 50 railroad cars per day, i.e. one small train, not thousands of trainloads.

Still, that's a lot. And of course Moses didn't have access to any trains.

The author of Exodus knew full well that supplying such a population in the desert would be an incredible challenge.

Then the whole congregation of the children of Israel complained against Moses and Aaron in the wilderness. And the children of Israel said to them, "Oh, that we had died by the hand of the LORD in the land of Egypt, when we sat by the pots of meat and when we ate bread to the full! For you have brought us out into this wilderness to kill this whole assembly with hunger."

Exodus 16:2-3

But then God miraculously supplied food to the people.

And the LORD spoke to Moses, saying, "I have heard the complaints of the children of Israel. Speak to them, saying, 'At twilight you shall eat meat, and in the morning you shall be filled with bread. And you shall know that I am the LORD your God.'" So it was that quails came up at evening and covered the camp, and in the morning the dew lay all around the camp. And when the layer of dew lifted, there, on the surface of the wilderness, was a small round substance, as fine as frost on the ground. ... And the house of Israel called its name Manna. And it was like white coriander seed, and the taste of it was like wafers made with honey.

Exodus 16:11-14, 31

The critic denies the possibility of a miracle. The instances I have seen of this criticism do not even mention the manna. Then having ignored the solution clearly spelled out in the text, they declare the problem unsolvable. They just assume that half the story is false, and then use this "fact" to prove that the other half must be false also.

Even without a miracle, the problem is not unsolvable. The Bible says that the Israelis brought along flocks and herds of animals. The Sinai is a barren place, but there are springs and vegetation and oases. There have been plenty of nomadic people in history who have managed to survive wandering about a wilderness with their herds.

5.10. Jericho

The Bible says that Joshua and the Israelites attacked and conquered the city of Jericho. This is impossible. Most historians place the Israelite invasion of Canaan at about 1400 BC. Some give dates as late as 1200 BC. When archaeologist Kathleen Kenyon excavated the site in the 1950s,, she proved that Jericho was destroyed about 1550 BC. Whether you take the 1400 date or the 1200 date, the city had been

abandoned long before Joshua arrived, so Joshua could not have been involved in the destruction of the city.

Dating Old Places

To understand this criticism, you have to know something about how archaeologists determine the date of an historical site.

Laymen often assume that archaeologists use some highly technical method, like Carbon-14. In fact such technical means are only a secondary method for dating historical sites.

Perhaps the most common category of dating methods is what is called "seriation". In this technique, archaeologists look for artifacts that show recognizable changes in design or style over time. If archaeologists of the future sought to use this technique on our era, they might look at styles in automobiles. They could trace styles in automobiles from the Model T to the Mustang to the Prius. Some of the changes would be technological, others would simply be fashion, but either way they would be recognizable. Once they had determined that the original Mustang was produced in 1964 and the styling changed noticeably by the mid 70's, then any time they excavated a site and found early-style Mustangs, they would know that the site could not be pre-1964 and is probably from the 60s or 70s. Of course an old car could be kept long after it was built, but a likely end date could be found by looking at the latest style of car found there.

When studying ancient sites, archaeologists routinely look at pottery. There have been many distinctive styles of pottery over the centuries. Archaeologists have constructed detailed charts of the pottery of various times and places. When a site is excavated, they can examine the pottery found and match it against the charts to date the site.

Dating Jericho

So now let's discuss Jericho specifically.

Archaeologist John Garstang excavated Jericho in the 1930s. He concluded that the city was destroyed about 1400 BC. He found the remains of city walls that had collapsed, apparently by an earthquake, and evidence that the city had been devastated by fire. He concluded that the physical evidence matched the Biblical account of the fall of Jericho as well as placing it at about the right time.

Garstang's report caused some controversy, so in the 1950s Kathleen Kenyon conducted a fresh investigation. She agreed with

Garstang that the city had been surrounded by a wall that had collapsed, and that it had been burned down. But she came to a very different conclusion about dates: she determined that the city was destroyed and abandoned about 1550 BC, so when Joshua and the Israelis arrived in 1400 there would have been almost no one there for them to fight.

Kenyon published some non-technical accounts of her findings explaining her conclusions, but she did not publish the raw data, i.e. the evidence that led to those conclusions. It was not until after her death in 1978 that the raw data was finally published, so that other archaeologists could review and critique her analysis.

Critics of Christianity seized on Kenyon's conclusions to declare that the Bible had been proven wrong. I recall seeing a television documentary in early summer of 1990 in which the narrator looked into the camera and asked, "In what sense is the Bible true?" Is it literally true, he asked, or just true in some spiritual sense? The Bible cannot be literally true, he concluded, because Kathleen Kenyon had "proven, beyond a shadow of a doubt" that the Biblical account of the fall of Jericho could not be true.

Revisiting the Jericho Date

But just a couple of months before that program aired, *Biblical Archaeology Review* published an article by Dr. Bryant Wood that found serious flaws in Kenyon's thesis. [Wood, Bryant. "Did the Israelites Conquer Jericho? A New Look at the Archaeological Evidence". *Biblical Archaeology Review*, Vol. XVI, No. 2, March/April 1990, pp. 44-58.]

Kenyon dated the city based on pottery seriation. She observed that in 1400 BC, pottery imported from Cyprus was popular in Canaan. But the only examples of this Cypriote pottery that she found in Jericho were in a few outlying houses, and not within the central city. Thus she concluded that the city must have been destroyed before Cypriote pottery became popular. She interpreted the Cypriote pottery found on the outskirts to mean that there were a few scattered people living among the ruins.

But Dr. Wood pointed out that Kenyon's reasoning was based not on something that was found, but on what was not found. Furthermore, all of Kenyon's conclusions were based on excavations in an area 26 feet square. As she herself described it, the part of the city that she studied was apparently a poor section. It also appears that at this time Jericho was not on the major trade routes.

> The picture given... is that of simple villagers. There is no suggestion at all of luxury.... It was quite probable that Jericho at this time was something of a backwater, away from the contacts with richer areas provided by the coastal route.
>
> Kathleen Kenyon. Digging up Jericho, p 271. As quoted in Wood.

So in a small segment of the poor section of town, in a city that was "something of a backwater", she did not find expensive imported pottery. This does not seem to be a particularly startling discovery.

When Garstang did his excavation, the significance of Cypriote pottery was not yet known, so he was not looking for it. But Garstang wrote descriptions and drew sketches of all the pottery he found. Among his sketches are a number of pieces that appear to be Cypriote. He found these pieces at the bottom of a slope, where they apparently fell when a large building at the top was destroyed. Garstang theorized that this building was a palace. Thus it appears that there was Cypriote pottery in Jericho, not in the poor section where Kenyon excavated, but in the rich section.

A number of other lines of evidence also indicate an age of 1400 BC:

The domestic pottery found at the site was consistent with pottery found at other 1400 BC sites.

A Carbon-14 sample was dated to 1410 BC by the lab at the British Museum.

Egyptian scarabs were found buried with people in the cemetery. These are little trinkets shaped like beetles and often with inscriptions, often the name of the reigning pharaoh. The pharaohs named stretched from 1800 BC to 1380 BC.

There was considerable demolition and rebuilding. One section of the city was rebuilt 20 times. By Kenyon's chronology, all this rebuilding had to happen in just 100 years.

Defending Kenyon

In the 20 years since Wood published his article in *Biblical Archaeology Review*, a number of critics have attacked his conclusions. They consistently make the same two arguments:

1. The traditional date for the Israeli invasion of Canaan, 1400 BC, is incorrect. The invasion really occurred much later, about 1200 BC. Therefore, whether Jericho was destroyed in 1550 BC or 1400 BC, it was still gone before Joshua arrived.

Reply: Scholars have been debating this for decades and it is itself a controversial question. But as a debating point, this is very weak: You can't assume you're right on one hotly-debated question and then use that "fact" as an argument on another hotly-debated question. (Like: "As everyone knows that President Kennedy was really assassinated by the CIA, then 9/11 must also have been a conspiracy, probably by the same people at the CIA.") One might just as well argue that a 1400 BC date for the destruction of Jericho is evidence that the conquest of Canaan occurred at that time.

2. The British Museum has retracted its date for the Carbon-14 sample. They discovered that the original result was caused by a calibration error. After correcting for this error, they now date the sample to 1550 BC, in perfect agreement with Kathleen Kenyon's conclusions.

Reply: This is a complicated question all by itself.

Carbon-14 dating is routinely explained as a straightforward, irrefutable technical method. Carbon-14 undergoes radioactive decay into Carbon-12 at a known rate. Plants and animals are constantly taking in carbon from the environment while they are alive, but once they die, of course they stop breathing and eating. Thus, at the moment of death the ratio of Carbon-14 to Carbon-12 should be the same as that in the general environment. But once the creature dies, the Carbon-14 begins decaying into Carbon-12. By measuring the relative amounts of Carbon-14 to Carbon-12, we can tell how long ago it died.

But such "pure" Carbon-14 dates have long been rejected by archaeologists because they do not match the dates gained by any other method. If we believe the raw dates we get from Carbon-14 analysis, we must conclude that the calendars of every civilization in the ancient world are wrong. If Carbon-14 dates disagreed with dates from Roman historians but agreed with Egyptian historians and Greek historians and Syrian historians, it would be plausible to suggest that the Roman histories are wrong or that we are mis-reading their calendars. But when Carbon-14 disagrees with all of them, the unavoidable conclusion is that the Carbon-14 dates are wrong.

So historians "calibrate" the Carbon-14 dates, that is, correct them by various techniques, until they agree with widely-accepted historical dates.

So let's get back to the British Museum and the Carbon-14 samples from Jericho. Initially the British Museum dated the sample and came up with a date that agreed with the Bible. But of course this was impossible, as Kathleen Kenyon had proven that the Bible was wrong and the site was really much older. They took a lot of criticism from archeologists and historians who said that this dating was obviously wrong and they were embarrassing themselves by publicizing such a date. So the British Museum re-examined their data and discovered that their calibration was flawed. After correcting for these errors, they came up with a date that agreed with Kathleen Kenyon.

Many archaeologists continue to challenge current calibration techniques because it gives Carbon-14 dates that contradict other historical documents. No serious archaeologist accepts a Carbon-14 date as definitive. Rather, it is one of many pieces of evidence to be used in dating a site.

While the critics continue to harp on the Carbon-14 date as confirming Kenyon and refuting Wood, I have yet to see anyone offer a serious rebuttal to Wood's other arguments. In Wood's analysis, the Carbon-14 date was only one of several pieces of evidence that came together to confirm a 1400 BC date. If we accept that the "true" Carbon-14 date is 1550 BC, we are left with one piece of evidence arguing for the old date and at least three or four arguing for a 1400 BC date.

Jericho and the Bible

There are some interesting features of the site that are consistent with the Biblical story of the fall of Jericho.

The most obvious is that there is a wall around the city that collapsed. Both Garstang and Kenyon said it looked like the wall fell during an earthquake. Bricks that were on the top of the inner wall were found outside the outer wall lying in heaps. The Bible says that God made the wall fall down when the Israelis arrived. What would we expect to find if God knocked down the wall miraculously? For that matter, maybe God did it with an earthquake.

The city was destroyed by fire. The Bible says that the Israelis burned the city down.

The archaeologists found large quantities of grain in storage areas throughout the city. This was very rare find. Usually when a walled city was conquered, it was after a long siege, in which all the food in the city would have been eaten until the people were reduced to starvation. But at Jericho, the food was all still there. This is consistent with the Biblical account which says that the city fell very quickly.

It is also interesting that the conquerors did not take the grain. Grain was valuable. Why wasn't it looted? The Bible says that God told Israel not to take anything of value from the city.

Conclusion

Kenyon's declaration that Jericho was abandoned before Joshua and the Israelis arrived was premature, based only on negative evidence. The actual evidence is consistent with the Bible story. Jericho was destroyed at the time that Joshua and the Israelis arrived. The walls collapsed like the Bible describes -- though archaeology cannot tell us whether this was by natural causes or a miracle. The city was destroyed by fire like the Bible describes.

The archaeological evidence supports the Bible story.

5.11. Esther, Beauty Queen

According to the Biblical book of Esther, King Xerxes chose his wife and queen by holding a beauty contest in which he sent talent scouts throughout the country to recruit contestants, and then personally choosing a winner from the finalists. This story is absurd and impossible. No king would choose a queen by such an irrational method.

I have to wonder whether the people who make this criticism have ever met a real-live human male. While I have not conducted a scientific poll on the subject, I suspect that if you asked men whether they would like to marry a beauty contest winner – especially if they could personally choose the winner – 90% would say "Of course!" and half the remainder would be lying.

Nowhere does the Bible say that this is how all kings choose their queens or even that this was a common practice. Nor does it say that this was a good idea. It just says that in this one particular case, this one king did it. Even if this was some truly far-out, bizarre behavior, if you had never met anyone in your life who would want to do such a thing, it would still be quite a stretch to say that not one person, anywhere, at any time in history, would ever have done it.

A friend of mine who lived in Kuwait for many years tells me that in the 1980s the prince of that country had a similar practice. As a Moslem he was allowed to have four wives, so he had three permanent wives and one rotating position. According to my friend, the prince filled the latter by sending talent scouts out to hold beauty contests. He would then select a winner from among the finalists, and marry her for a year or so. Then he would divorce her, give her a house and a bunch of money as a divorce settlement, and hold a new contest. I haven't been able to confirm this story, but you can find similar things about the Kuwaiti prince in People magazine and the like. Even if the story is unconfirmable, would you really say that it is so outrageous that it is impossible?

5.12. God's Girlfriend

The Bible says that there is only one God. But recent archaeological discoveries show that the Jews of Old Testament times also worshipped a goddess. Apparently Jehovah had a girlfriend.

"And it will come as an unpleasant shock to many that the God of Israel, Jehovah, had a female consort." [Herzog, Ze'ev. "Deconstructing the walls of Jericho". http://www.truthbeknown.com /biblemyth.htm, 1999. Retrieved September 2010.]

The Old Testament clearly states that the ancient Jews worshipped a goddess. Her name was Asherah or Astarte. She was a god of the Canaanites that the Israelis borrowed. The Old Testament repeatedly criticizes the Jews for straying from the worship of Jehovah to worship her.

> So the children of Israel did evil in the sight of the Lord. They forgot the Lord their God, and served the Baals and Asherahs.
>
> Judges 3:7

The Israelis tried to mix worship of Asherah with worship of Jehovah.

> [King Manasseh] did much evil in the sight of the Lord, to provoke Him to anger. He even set a carved image of Asherah that he had made, in the house of which the Lord had said to David and to Solomon his son, "In this house

and in Jerusalem, which I have chosen out of all the tribes of Israel, I will put My name forever."

2 Kings 21:6-7

The Bible makes it clear that the Jews worshipped a goddess, and that they even put statues of her in the temple of Jehovah. The archaeological finds of such worship do not prove the Bible wrong. They prove it true.

5.13. Jesus Never Lived

There never was any such person as Jesus. He is a fictional character invented by the writers of the Gospels. There is no evidence for the existence of Jesus outside of the Gospels, and those are obviously biased sources.

The Gospels

First of all, it is quite capricious to simply dismiss the Gospels as evidence for the life of Jesus. Here we have four biographies written by four different people about the same person. There are plenty of people in ancient history who are known to us today from only one source. For Jesus we have not one but four. These by themselves make Jesus' life better documented then all but a tiny number of ancient people: a few kings and emperors and a handful of other notable people.

Most of what was written in ancient times does not survive today. We know from references in other surviving books that the Roman writer Suetonius wrote at least 17 books, but only one survives in its entirety today, *The Twelve Caesars*, and we have fragments of three others. There could have been any number of references to Jesus from non-Christian sources that have been lost over the centuries.

The fact that the Gospels are all included in the Bible does not turn them into a single source. The Bible is an anthology of books written by many people. Four biographies of Jesus are included because he is a subject of particular interest to Christians. (It's like the old joke that Shakespeare wasn't such a prolific writer. After all, in his whole life he only wrote one book: "The Complete Works of Shakespeare".)

It is true that the four Gospel writers all viewed Jesus positively. But again, most people in ancient history are known to us from only one or two sources, and favorable or unfavorable, that's all we have. Many writers of biographies have an opinion about the person they're writing about. Some allow that opinion to make them biased. But we don't completely ignore a biography and declare the subject person to be complete fiction just because the author has an opinion. Winston Churchill wrote a history of the Second World War which talks a lot about things done by Winston Churchill. Historians don't ignore this book because Churchill has an obvious bias to present himself positively. Rather, they see it as an incredibly valuable resource, a history written by someone who knows it all first hand.

Apathy

Second, it is not surprising that contemporary Greek and Roman writers generally ignore Jesus. We wouldn't expect them to take notice unless and until Jesus' followers became a politically-significant force. How often are religious leaders from other countries mentioned in your nation's media? Americans had little interest in the preaching of Ayatollah Khomeini in Iran – until he and his followers overthrow a government that had been friendly to America. Then America's interest in Moslem religious leaders again lapsed – until they led to terrorist attacks. Quick: Name a religious leader from Pakistan.

That said, there are a number of surviving ancient non-Christian sources that mention Jesus.

Suetonius: Mildly Hostile View

The Roman writer Suetonius that I mentioned above made a brief reference to Jesus:

> [Emperor Claudius] banished from Rome all the Jews, who were continually making disturbances at the instigation of one Chrestus.
>
> > C. Suetonius Tranquillus. "Claudius, XXV". *The Twelve Caesars*. ca. AD 110.

During the reign of Claudius there was conflict among the Jews in Rome between those who accepted Christ and those who didn't. In AD 49 these religious debates disturbed the government enough that they kicked all the Jews out of Rome so they wouldn't have to put up with it.

(The Bible also mentions this incident. Acts 18:2 tells us that the apostle Paul met Priscilla and Aquilla in Corinth in Greece, and they were there "because Claudius had commanded all the Jews to depart from Rome".)

It's not a lot. Suetonius words might be taken to mean that he thought that Christ was alive and in Rome in Claudius's time. Still, a Roman historian writing in AD 110 tells us that in AD 49 the Roman government was aware of this Christ person.

Tacitus: Hostile View with Reservations

A terrible fire swept through Rome circa AD 64. It was widely suspected that the emperor Nero had the fire deliberately set so that he could have the city rebuilt in a style more to his liking. Nero had talked about "building a new Rome" before the fire, but the Senate was unwilling to appropriate the money for such a project. Nero was well known for indulging his whims.

According to the Roman historian Tacitus:

> But all human efforts, all the lavish gifts of the emperor, and the propitiations of the gods, did not banish the sinister belief that the conflagration was the result of an order. Consequently, to get rid of the report, Nero fastened the guilt and inflicted the most exquisite tortures on a class hated for their abominations, called Christians by the populace. Christus, from whom the name had its origin, suffered the extreme penalty during the reign of Tiberius at the hands of one of our procurators, Pontius Pilatus, and a most mischievous superstition, thus checked for the moment, again broke out not only in Judaea, the first source of the evil, but even in Rome, where all things hideous and shameful from every part of the world find their center and become popular. Accordingly, an arrest was first made of all who pleaded guilty; then, upon their information, an immense multitude was convicted, not so much of the crime of firing the city, as of hatred against mankind. Mockery of every sort was added to their deaths. Covered with the skins of beasts, they were torn by dogs and perished, or were nailed to crosses, or were doomed to the flames and burnt, to serve as a nightly illumination, when daylight had expired.

Tactitus. *Annals*. Book XV. ca. AD 120.

The wording makes it pretty clear that Tacitus was not a Christian or in any way sympathetic to Christians. But from this short passage we can see that he accepted as fact that Jesus lived, that he was from Judea, that he was a religious leader, and that he was executed under Pontius Pilate. Tacitus wrote this about AD 120, and he is describing events that occurred in AD 64.

Pliny the Younger: Clinically Hostile View

Pliny the Younger published a book of letters he had sent and received over his lifetime. About AD 111, Pliny was appointed governor of Bithynia, in what is now Turkey. He was apparently a very indecisive governor, because the letters include numerous questions sent back to Emperor Trajan for instructions on everything from whether to create a fire department to how to dispose of the estates of people who died without writing a will.

One of the problems that he refers to Trajan is how to deal with Christians. Here are some key excerpts from his letter:

> To THE EMPEROR TRAJAN
> It is my invariable rule, Sir, to refer to you in all matters where I feel doubtful; for who is more capable of removing my scruples, or informing my ignorance? Having never been present at any trials concerning those who profess Christianity, I am unacquainted not only with the nature of their crimes, or the measure of their punishment, but how far it is proper to enter into an examination concerning them. Whether, therefore, any difference is usually made with respect to ages, or no distinction is to be observed between the young and the adult; whether repentance entitles them to a pardon; or if a man has been once a Christian, it avails nothing to desist from his error; whether the very profession of Christianity, unattended with any criminal act, or only the crimes themselves inherent in the profession are punishable; on all these points I am in great doubt. ...
> They affirmed the whole of their guilt, or their error, was, that they met on a stated day before it was light, and addressed a form of prayer to Christ, as to a divinity, binding themselves by a solemn oath, not for the purposes of any wicked design, but never to commit any fraud, theft, or adultery, never to falsify their word, nor deny a trust when they should be called upon to deliver it up; after which it was their custom to separate, and then reassemble, to eat in common a harmless meal. From this

custom, however, they desisted after the publication of my edict, by which, according to your commands, I forbade the meeting of any assemblies. After receiving this account, I judged it so much the more necessary to endeavor to extort the real truth, by putting two female slaves to the torture, who were said to officiate in their religious rites: but all I could discover was evidence of an absurd and extravagant superstition. I deemed it expedient, therefore, to adjourn all further proceedings, in order to consult you. ...

> Pliny the Younger. "Letter XCVII". *Epistles*. ca AD 100.

Pliny wrote this letter about 70 years after Jesus' death. It tells us nothing directly about Jesus himself. Pliny does not recount any incidents from the life of Jesus. So this does not give us any direct corroboration for much of anything in the Gospels.

But it does prove that Christians existed by this time, and that they believed that Jesus was the Son of God, as opposed to simply believing that he was a good teacher or some such.

The emperor gave this concise reply:

TRAJAN TO PLINY
You have adopted the right course, my dearest Secundis, in investigating the charges against the Christians who were brought before you. It is not possible to lay down any general rule for all such cases. Do not go out of your way to look for them. If indeed they should be brought before you, and the crime is proved, they must be punished; with the restriction, however, that where the party denies he is a Christian, and shall make it evident that he is not, by invoking our gods, let him (notwithstanding any former suspicion) be pardoned upon his repentance. Anonymous information ought not to he received in any sort of prosecution. It is introducing a very dangerous precedent, and is quite foreign to the spirit of our age.

> Pliny the Younger. "Letter XCVIII". *Epistles*. ca. AD 100

This adds little to our knowledge of Jesus but it is interesting. The emperor's sense of justice demands that no one be convicted without proper evidence, that anonymous accusations should be ignored, that there be no witch hunts, and that people arrested should be given the opportunity to escape punishment by demonstrating that they have rehabilitated themselves. But his justice is not offended at all by the idea of arresting, torturing, and killing people for the "crime" of following an unpopular religion. It is okay to kill someone for being a Christian, as long as he is first given a fair trial!

Mara bar Serapion: Sympathetic View

A man named Mara bar Serapion wrote a letter from prison to encourage his son, Serapion. The exact historical circumstances of this letter are uncertain. It has been dated at anywhere from AD 72 to 200 years later. Thus, it *may* be the oldest surviving non-Christian, non-Jewish reference to Jesus.

In any case, it is clear from what Mara writes in the letter that he saw himself as a victim of persecution. And so he assured his son:

> What advantage did the Athenians gain from putting Socrates to death? Famine and plague came upon them as a judgment for their crime. What advantage did the men of Samos gain from burning Pythagoras? In a moment their land was covered with sand. What advantage did the Jews gain from executing their wise King? It was just after that their Kingdom was abolished. God justly avenged these three wise men: the Athenians died of hunger; the Samians were overwhelmed by the sea; the Jews, ruined and driven from their land, live in complete dispersion. But Socrates did not die for good; he lived on in the teaching of Plato. Pythagoras did not die for good; he lived on in the statue of Hera. Nor did the wise King die for good; He lived on in the teaching which he had given

> Mara bar Serapion. As quoted in F. F. Bruce. *Jesus & Christian Origins Outside the New Testament.* London: 1974. p. 31

Some critics point out that the letter nowhere uses the name Jesus, and so the "wise King" mentioned may be someone else entirely, perhaps a literal Jewish king who lived and died before the Babylonian captivity. But this is very unlikely from the context of the letter. Mara is clearly talking about philosophers, not political leaders, and about people who were killed for their beliefs, not killed in war or by political assassination. It is difficult to think of anyone besides Jesus who would make sense in context.

Mara is clearly neither a Christian nor anti-Christian. He respects Jesus as a "great teacher" on the same level with Socrates and Pythagoras. This is a positive statement about Jesus, but an unlikely thing for a Christian to say. A Christian would say that Jesus is God come to Earth in human form and thus far above mere men like Socrates and Pythagoras. A Christian would not say that Jesus lives on in his teaching, but that he lives on because he came back from the dead.

There is no evidence that Mara had any first-hand knowledge of Jesus. He is probably just commenting on news and rumors that he had heard. But he had heard of Jesus, knew that he was a philosopher or religious teacher, and that his own people, the Jews, had plotted his death. This implies that this information was common knowledge in Mara's time.

Josephus: Ambiguous View

A great deal of what we know about the history, politics, and daily life of Jesus' day comes to us from the Jewish historian Josephus. Josephus wrote about Jewish history and culture for a primarily Roman audience. In his book *Antiquities of the Jews,* written about AD 90-95, Josephus mentions Jesus.

This section from Josephus is highly debated. Many critics say that it is just *too* supportive of the Christian position to come from a non-Christian writer. Here's the paragraph as it appears in the copies of Josephus that we have today:

> Now there was about this time Jesus, a wise man, if it be lawful to call him a man; for he was a doer of wonderful works, a teacher of such men as receive the truth with pleasure. He drew over to him both many of the Jews and many of the Gentiles. He was Christ. And when Pilate, at the suggestion of the principal men amongst us, had condemned him to the cross, those that loved him at the first did not forsake him; for he appeared to them alive again the third day; as the divine prophets had foretold these and ten thousand other wonderful things concerning him. And the tribe of Christians, so named from him, are not extinct at this day.

> Josephus, Flavius. *Antiquities of the Jews.* 16:3:3.

The critics argue that Christians must have edited Josephus, either adding this paragraph to the text or changing what he had originally written. Bear in mind that we do not have original manuscripts of many – if any – ancient texts. We have copies of copies of copies. The oldest surviving copy of Josephus dates to AD 900-1000. Of course this is long before computers or even the printing press so copies were made by hand. Someone making a copy could make minor – or major – changes as he went along.

On the other hand, there are a number of reasons to believe that the text as it has come down to us is indeed the original text of Josephus, or close to it.

The text is the same in the oldest copies of Josephus that we have, and the oldest quotations of Josephus. If we had some old copies that included this paragraph and others that did not, there would be an obvious case to question which was authentic. But we have quotations going to back to at least Eusebius in circa AD 320, i.e. 130 years after the book was written, a blink of the eye in historical research, and they quote it exactly as we have the text today.

The paragraph fits in the context of the book. It is in the middle of a chapter on problems that afflicted the Jews during the time of Pilate. It comes between a story about a protest against a tax to build an aqueduct that ended with Pilate ordering soldiers to beat up and kill the protestors, and a story about four Jewish outcasts traveling to Rome and getting into trouble there for trying to con people out of money. That is, it is a chapter about trouble-makers who brought problems on the Jewish people. It is exactly the sort of context in which we would expect a Jew to describe Jesus. It is not at all the context in which we would expect a Christian to insert a phony, flattering reference to Jesus.

Josephus makes a very brief reference to Jesus later:

So [the high priest] assembled the Sanhedrin of judges, and brought before them the brother of Jesus, who was called Christ, whose name was James, and some others, and when he had formed an accusation against them as breakers of the law, he delivered them to be stoned.

Josephus, 20:9:1

Without the earlier explanation of who Jesus was, this passage would be cryptic: The brother of whom? This makes it unlikely that the section on Jesus is a complete invention. The original version of Josephus must have said something about Jesus. The paragraph we have may have been altered, but it cannot be a complete invention.

While the paragraph sounds very sympathetic to Christianity on first reading, it could be read differently. The statement, "He was Christ", does not necessarily mean that Josephus accepted him as the messiah, but might just mean that he called himself Christ or that others called him that. It is also a necessary set-up for the later reference. The statement that his followers did not forsake him and that the "tribe of Christians" is still around is a statement of fact that does not imply agreement with their beliefs. "If it be lawful to call him a man" may be deference to Christians, like someone unfamiliar with titles of nobility might ask, "Do I call him 'your majesty'?" It may even be intended sarcastically.

If Josephus did not like Jesus, he would not have considered the statement that Jewish leaders condemned him to death to be embarrassing. As is clear from his book on the revolution against Rome, *The Jewish War*, Josephus had no qualms about executing opponents.

Some have pointed out that the Greek word (Josephus was originally written in Greek) for "truth" is "alethe", while the word for "strange things" is "aethe", just one letter different, in Greek as well as in English. If there was a one-letter copying error, the original text may have said that Jesus was "a teacher of such men as receive *strange things* with pleasure"

Such interpretations change the paragraph from a pro-Jesus statement to a slighting reference, the sort of thing we would expect from someone talking about a cult leader.

In 1972, Professor Schlomo Pines of Hebrew University in Jerusalem published an article on an Arabic version of Josephus. Arabs translated Josephus into their own language and passed down copies independently of the European version. In the Arabic version, this paragraph reads:

At this time there was a wise man who was called Jesus. His conduct was good and [he] was known to be virtuous. And many people from among the Jews and the other nations became his disciples. Pilate condemned him to be crucified and to die. But those who had become his disciples did not abandon his discipleships. They reported that he had appeared to them three days after his crucifixion, and that he was alive; accordingly he was perhaps the Messiah, concerning whom the prophets have recounted wonders.

> Josphus. As quoted in Gary Habermas. *The Historical Jesus.* Joplin, Missouri: 1996. pp. 193-194.

Differences in wording should be no surprise: We are comparing an English translation of a Greek text to an English translation of an Arabic translation of a Greek text.

But let's look at the substantive differences. With some fairly minor changes, the Arab version significantly changes the tone. It does not include the most positive assertions, "if it be lawful to call him a man" and "he was the Christ". It mentions only Pilate as being responsible for his crucifixion, omitting any blame on the Jews. It adds "they reported" in front of the statement that Jesus rose from the dead, making this a claim made by his followers rather than a statement of fact. And by re-arranging the words some, the statement about prophecies and wonders is attached to the Messiah, who may or may not be Jesus, rather than specifically to Jesus. Perhaps this is the original text and Christian copyists made minor alterations, either to clarify the text or to make it more "pro-Jesus". Or perhaps the Arab copyists wanted to make it less pro-Jesus.

The critics do not offer any historical or literary reasons to doubt the authenticity of this quote. The only reason ever given to doubt it is that critics find it too supportive of Christianity. They just know in their gut that Jesus is a fictional character, so any historical evidence that corroborates the existence of Jesus must be a fraud.

Conclusions

Note these references are all from before AD 130. (Well, Mara is uncertain, but likely before 130.)

What do they prove?

Some critics say that they do not prove that Christ existed, but only that Christians existed. There is an element of truth to this.

References like Pliny are not directly about Christ, but rather about Christians. Pliny's letters prove that Christians existed, but it could be argued that of themselves, they do not prove that anything they said about Jesus was true. But others, like Tacitus, Mara, and Josephus, specifically talk about Jesus. They are direct evidence that Jesus lived, was crucified under Pilate, etc.

Even the most general prove that Christianity existed and had spread throughout the Roman Empire by AD 100 or so, and that these Christians believed that Jesus had lived and was the Son of God. What they tell us is consistent with Christian claims, and difficult to reconcile with the idea that Jesus never lived. In AD 100 there were people still alive who had been living in Judea at the time this fictional man was supposed to have lived. If someone had just made up Jesus out of thin air, there would have been plenty of people who would say, "What? Who? There was no such person; what are you talking about?"

If someone was going to invent a mythical Jesus on which to base a new religion, the Jesus of the Gospels is not the sort of person they would have invented. The Gospels describe him as a very public figure: thousands of people following him, getting into conflicts with the top religious and political leaders, and ending up being put on trial and publicly executed. If these claims were complete fabrications, there would have been plenty of people who would have known it. Anyone living in the city of Jerusalem at the time Jesus was claimed to have made his "triumphal entry" and been tried and executed would have known instantly whether the story was true or not. Imagine if you were trying to invent a mythical person as part of some fraud today. Would you describe him as being honored with a parade through a major capital city, and being the subject of a sensational Supreme Court case? It would be much smarter to describe him as living an obscure life, so your claims about him would be difficult to refute.

Some ancient sources mention that Christians believed that Jesus performed miracles and came back from the dead. Of course non-Christian sources do not accept these things as true. If someone said that he believed in the resurrection, I think he would automatically be called a "Christian", so to say non-Christians didn't believe these things is pretty much true by definition. But they agree that Christians made these claims; there is no mention of debate about this. That is, the earliest sources we have say that Christians were making these claims. These are not later additions to Christianity, but part of the original message.

Neither these nor any other ancient references to Jesus that I have read debate whether he existed, whether he was crucified under Pilate, or any other basic facts about his life. Ancient writers did not debate whether Jesus existed any more than they debated whether Julius Caesar or Alexander the Great existed. They all accepted that he lived: the question was whether he performed miracles and came back from the dead. It was not until fairly recent times that critics came up with the "no such person" argument.

It is fair to be cautious about taking any one source uncritically. But when many ancient sources say the same or similar things, and none contradicts it, that is very persuasive. On any less controversial subject, this would be taken as virtual certainly.

[Important sources for this section were: Habermas, Gary. *The Historical Jesus*. Joplin: College Press, 1996. pp. 187-208. And: Bruce, F. F. *Jesus and Christian Origins Outside the New Testament*. Grand Rapids: Eerdmans, 1974. pp. 19-53]

5.14. Quirinius, the Missing Governor

The Bible says that Jesus was born during a census taken "when Quirinius was governor of Syria". But Quirinius did not become governor of Syria until AD 6 – ten to twelve after Jesus was supposed to have been born.

First, some background.

Our present system of numbering years was invented in AD 525 by the scholar and monk Dionysius Exiguus. He set the starting date of his calendar, AD 1, at the year that he calculated Jesus was born.

The Jewish historian Josephus, writing circa AD 100, tells us that Herod died shortly after a lunar eclipse. This must have been the eclipse of March 13, 4 BC. He also talks about Quirinius becoming governor and taking a census, linking it to dates in Roman history that would place it at AD 6.

Here's where we run into a problem. The Bible says that Jesus was born before the death of Herod. That would mean he could not have been born later than 4 BC. But Luke tells us that Quirinius was in charge of the census that led Jesus' parents to go to Bethlehem: "In those days Caesar Augustus issued a decree that a census should be taken of the entire Roman world. (This was the first census that took place while Quirinius was governor of Syria.)" [Luke 2:1-2] So he would have had to be born after Quirinius became governor. Thus he had to be born before 4 BC and after AD 6, which of course is impossible.

This is an interesting criticism in that there are at least four possible replies. There is a case to be made for each of them.

Possibility 1: Questioning Josephus

Perhaps Josephus is wrong in his dates. Maybe Herod didn't really die until well after the eclipse, or Quirinius may have become governor sooner than Josephus indicates. If the Bible contradicts Josephus, who says that Josephus must be right and the Bible must be wrong?

I have never heard any serious scholar discuss this possibility, either to defend it or to refute it. We can keep it in mind, but let's move on to other possible replies.

Possibility 2: Translation Problem

The Greek word translated "first" in Luke 2:2 is "protos". This can also mean "before". The same Greek word is translated "before" elsewhere in the book of Luke. So this might be a translation problem. The correct reading might be, "This was before the census that took place when Quirinius was governor of Syria."

Luke was certainly aware of the census that Josephus talks about, as he mentions it in Acts 5:37. But nothing in the text makes clear whether this was the same census as the one he talks about in Luke 2 or a different one.

If Jesus was born during a census that was not the AD 6 census, it would be quite plausible for Luke to make some effort to point this out. There was a lot of political opposition to the AD 6 census. It resulted in riots and assassinations. Someone writing about another census in the same time period might want to make clear, "I'm not talking about *that* census, I'm talking about a different one." It is like a modern writer discussing an event that happened during a hurricane in Louisiana, carefully noting, "Not Hurricane Katrina, this was a different hurricane before that."

On the other hand, Greek scholars generally say that while the word "protos" can mean "before", that is an unlikely reading given the wording of this sentence.

This reply is tempting because it reconciles Luke with Josephus and Roman historians and is exactly the sort of thing that a careful historian would be likely to write. But is it a legitimate reading of the Greek or is it a stretch?

Possibility 3: Two Terms

In 1764 a stone tablet was found near the Italian town of Tivoli. Archaeologists call it the "Lapis Tiburtinus", Latin for "tablet of Tibur", Tibur being the name of a Roman town in the region. This tablet was like modern historical markers or plaques: It was erected to honor a local hero, briefly summarizing his achievements. In this case, it mentions that this person was "twice governor of Syria".

Unfortunately, the edges of the tablet eroded away over the centuries, including – maddeningly – the name of the person! Could it be Quirinius? If so, Quirinius first term as governor may have been earlier, at the time of Jesus' birth.

The parts of the Lapis Tiburtinus that we can read tell us other things about the career of this person, for example that he also served as a senator and as a general in Asia. These match what we know about Quirinius from Roman sources. And of course we know that Quirinius was governor of Syria at least once. We don't know of anyone else who was governor of Syria twice. There are not many people who would match all of the details on this tablet, and Quirinius is one of them, so it *could* be about Quirinius. But with no name on the tablet, we can't say for sure.

Note that Luke says that this was the "*first* census that took place while Quirinius was governor". This implies that there was a second. Luke may have been distinguishing a census taken during an earlier term of office from the more well-known census in AD 6.

So Quirinius might have been governor of Syria twice, and been involved with a census both times, and Luke is referring to the first time.

This is probably the most common reply that Christians give to this criticism today.

Possibility 4: Trouble-Shooter

When we read in an English translation of the Bible that Quirinius was "governor of Syria", it is easy to read "governor" as a specific job title, like "governor of New York". But the Greek word that Luke uses, "hegemon", is not a specific job title, but a general word for government official. He uses the same word in chapter 3 to refer to Pilate, who was a prefect, an office lower than provincial governor, and then again to refer to the emperor, (obviously) the highest office.

So when Luke calls Quirinius a "hegemon", he does not necessarily mean that he held the specific title "governor" at this time. Perhaps Quirinius held some other office that had him involved with the census.

The Christian writer Tertullian, writing circa AD 200, says that Jesus was born during a census by Sentius Saturninus. Saturnius was governor of Syria from about 9 BC to 6 BC, which would be about the right time. (Tertullian's point in bringing this up is to say that anyone who doubts that Jesus was a real person born to a real human mother can look up the record of his birth in the census rolls.) [Tertullian. *Against Marcion*. Book IV.]

So perhaps Quirinius was not actually the governor of Syria at the time of Jesus' birth, but held some other office.

One critic dismissed this possibility as ridiculous. He points out that from Roman historians we know that Quirinius had been a senator and a consul and a general before this time, and to suppose that he would then take a job as an assistant to a governor was like saying that "a former president of the United States got a job as a shift manager at McDonald's". [Carrier, Richard, PhD. "Luke vs. Matthew on the Year of Christ's Birth" http://www.errancywiki.com /index.php?title=Legends&rcid=41896. 2006. Retrieved November 2010.] Cleverly put, but no one is suggesting that he took an entry-level job. (And, I might point out, it's almost as ridiculous as suggesting that after being President of the United States, Jimmy Carter would be personally hammering nails on low-income housing.)

According to Roman historians, in 1 BC, Emperor Augustus asked Quirinius to act as a guide to his grandson Gaius Caesar on a trip to Syria and Armenia. Augustus planned for Gaius to succeed him as emperor and wanted the young man to get some experience in government. (The plan was ruined when Gaius was killed in battle.) He also acted as an unofficial advisor to Tiberius, Augustus's step-son and later emperor himself, when he was in Rhodes. [Tacitus. *Annals*. Book III] Augustus needed someone to keep these young men out of trouble while maintaining the fiction that they were in charge.

So on at least two occasions, the Emperor Augustus asked Quirinius to act as some sort of unofficial or semi-official advisor in politically delicate situations. He also spent a significant chunk of his career in and around Syria.

Judea at the time was a politically explosive region. Augustus had set up Herod as a puppet ruler, but now he had lost confidence in him: A few years later he took power away from Herod's son and exiled him to Gaul, the opposite end of the empire. Judea was on the brink of revolt, there was violence a few years later that ultimately led to a complete rebellion. Perhaps Augustus asked Quirinius to help out in a politically difficult situation.

The circumstances might have been like the president calling in a former senator or cabinet officer and saying, "Hey Bob, we're having some real problems in the State Department. The present Secretary of State is in way over his head, but I can't fire him and put you in charge because he has too many powerful friends, and besides, that would be admitting that this administration screwed up when we appointed him in the first place. Would you be willing to go over there as my personal representative and see if you can clean things up?" Most people would consider such a request an honor, not a degrading demotion.

Also, note that the Gaius mission came just a few years after the birth of Jesus. If Quirinius had just been in Syria as a trouble-shooter a few years before and done a good job, he would quickly come to mind as someone to escort the heir-apparent to the same region. He would have proven his ability and know the area.

So while there is no specific historical record to back up this theory, it is plausible that Augustus might have sent Quirinius to Syria as a trouble-shooter during a difficult time.

Conclusion

Any of these four replies could be the truth. Frankly, we just don't have enough information to say for sure. But while we can't give a definitive answer that exonerates Luke, there are a number of possibilities.

When there are reasonable scenarios under which statements in a book would be true, speculation that none of these scenarios is the actual truth and so the book *might* be false is not much of an argument. We could use such arguments to "prove" any book to be false. You could always invent might-have-beens that contradict any claimed facts.

5.15. Nonsense Census

The Bible says that Jesus' parents, Joseph and Mary, had to travel to Bethlehem to register for a census that was ordered by Caesar Augustus. But according to Roman historians, there never was any such census. Not only is there no record of such a census, but the idea that everyone would be required to travel to an ancestral homeland would be wildly impractical – the Romans would never have done such a thing. Nor would they have required a man to bring his wife.

Here's the Bible's account of the subject:

> And it came to pass in those days *that* a decree went out from Caesar Augustus that all the world should be registered. ⋯ So all went to be registered, everyone to his own city. Joseph also went up from Galilee, out of the city of Nazareth, into Judea, to the city of David, which is called Bethlehem, because he was of the house and lineage of David, to be registered with Mary, his betrothed wife.

> Luke 2:1-5

No Record?

When the critic says that there was no such census, he means that Roman historians do not record such a census. We are talking about events that happened – or are claimed to have happened – 2000 years ago. Many things happened back then of which no record exists today. Every now and then archaeologists dig up a city that was previously unknown or lost. In this book alone two such cities come up for other reasons: Ebla (see issue 5.1) and Hattusas (see issue 5.4). If all knowledge of an entire city can be lost, record of one census could easily be lost.

There are many events in ancient history that are known from only one source. For example, to the best of my knowledge, Plutarch is the only ancient historian who reports that Julius Caesar was kidnapped and held for ransom when he was young. (If you know some other source for this, fine, take a different example.) If a modern scholar categorically stated that Plutarch was lying or deluded when he said this because no other ancient writer confirms it, no one would take him seriously. Of course the fact that Plutarch tells this story doesn't prove it's true. Our confidence would be greater if other writers told the same story. But the fact that no other historian tells the story certainly does not prove it is false. Every historian has his own perspective. Every historian includes some events that others do not. This doesn't prove they're lying; it just proves that they are not all colluding.

While doing research for this book, I stumbled across an interesting historical fact that I had not previously known: Almost everything we know about Pontius Pilate, the governor of Judea who was involved in Christ's crucifixion, comes to us, not from Roman history books, but from Jewish and Christian sources. The only surviving mentions of Pilate in Roman sources are in connection with his role in Jesus' death. If there had never been a Jesus, today there would probably be no surviving Roman references to Pilate. [Bruce, F. F. *Jesus and Christian Origins Outside the New Testament.* London: 1974. p 23]

So even if there were no surviving references from Roman historians to this census, that would not prove it didn't happen. We have the record in Luke. Why do we need another?

Acts of Augustus

That said, Roman histories may in fact mention this census. When Caesar Augustus was an old man, he wrote a summary of what he considered the highlights of his reign, known as the "Res Gestae Divi Augusti", or "Acts of Augustus". Number 8 on the list is that he conducted three censuses: one in 28 BC, one in 8 BC, and one in AD 14.

Augustus's 8 BC census might well be the census mentioned in Luke. Most modern scholars believe that Jesus was born somewhere between 6 BC and 4 BC. In those days before telephones and the Internet, communications were slow. In those days, as in these days, bureaucracy was slow. A census ordered in 8 BC would not have really gotten underway in a remote corner of the empire like Judea for several years.

Even if this particular census was not the one in the Bible, still, we see that Augustus boasts that he commissioned three censuses. Other records of the period describe other censuses ordered by Rome. There are some references to a census that was conducted every 14 years. The Romans had a passion for this sort of record keeping and bureaucracy. It is not at all unlikely that there were other censuses whose details are not preserved.

Egyptian Papyrus

What about the criticism that the Romans would not have ordered people to return to an ancestral home?

A papyrus discovered in Egypt records an edict by G. Vibius Maximus, the Roman governor of Egypt, stating, "[I]t is necessary to command all who for any reason are out of their own district to return to their own home, in order to perform the usual business of the taxation ..."

This was not the census of Luke. The Egyptian census occurred in AD 174 to 175, clearly much later than Luke's. But the point is that we have here a Roman decree that people must return to their homes for a census, like Luke describes. Critics reply that this is not a requirement to return to the home of an ancestor, but rather that travellers and migrant workers must return home, or that people were required to register in the city of their birth. Maybe, but they have no way of knowing that.

Even if this is so, Joseph was born in Bethlehem and so was required to return there to register. The fact that Bethlehem is called Joseph's "own city" could mean that he lived there or was born there. Luke's comment about "house and lineage of David" may not mean that the Romans required everyone who was descended from David to go to Bethlehem to register, but rather may be an editorial comment explaining how Joseph came to be born in Bethlehem, i.e. because his family had lived there for centuries.

Sexist Census

Why did Mary have to go to Bethlehem also? When critics dismiss this as absurd, they are just assuming that Roman censuses never included women. Who says? Besides, the Bible doesn't say that the Romans required her to go, but simply that she went. The couple was basically newlyweds. The trip was at least three or four days each way, plus some time there. It's not hard to imagine a new bride wanting to go with her husband rather than stay behind while he goes off alone for a week or two. They likely did not know that they would not be able to find a hotel when they arrived and would end up sleeping in a stable. She might have understood that the trip would be hard, but not how hard.

Conclusion

In an autobiographical statement, Augustus proudly tells of commissioning three censuses of the Roman world. The second of these might well be the census that brought Mary and Joseph to Bethlehem. That is, we might have direct corroboration of the Bible story from Emperor Augustus himself.

We can't prove this is the same census. But even if it's not, it's apparent that Augustus ordered numerous censuses to be conducted throughout the empire. Other details that Luke mentions are consistent with Roman censuses. There is nothing unbelievable or surprising about the Biblical account.

5.16. Lost Child

The story of [the boy Jesus'] discussion with the doctors in the Temple is proved to be mythical by all the circumstances that surround it. The statement that his mother and father left Jerusalem, believing that he was with them; that they went a day's journey before discovering that he was not in their company; and that after searching for three days, they found him in the Temple asking and answering questions of the learned Doctors, involves a series of tremendous improbabilities. ... [A]dd again the unlikelihood that a child would appear before serious-minded men in the role of an intellectual champion and the fabulous character of the story becomes perfectly clear.

Gauvin, Marshall. Did Jesus Christ Really Live?
1922

The critic claims that the story of the boy Jesus at the temple is impossible for two reasons: One, his parents would never have lost him like this. Two, a group of scholars would not be impressed by a young boy.

Lost Child

On the first point, one must conclude that the critic never had children. Almost every parent I know has a story about the time one of their children disappeared and they searched frantically before finding him, often going into a panic worrying that the child had been kidnapped or was hurt in an accident and was now lying bleeding to death somewhere, or something equally terrible.

The Bible tells us that when his parents finally found him, "His mother said to Him, 'Son, why have you done this to us?'" [Luke 2:48]

Isn't this exactly what you would expect a mother to say to a child who has been missing for over a day?

Impressed Scholars

I don't find it at all difficult to imagine a group of old college professors being impressed and amused by a young boy who seems knowledgeable far beyond his years.

If Jesus really was God in human form as the Bible claims, he would presumably have known far more than any of these professors. They might well have been amazed at this little boy's incredible knowledge. Even if there was nothing miraculous going on here, if Jesus was simply a bright young boy, it's not hard to imagine the professors finding him interesting. I've often seen old men fawn over a child.

Unlikely versus Impossible

Many criticisms of the Bible rely on an argument that an event described is unlikely. So what? The Bible is not saying that these events happen all the time, just that they happened this once.

The same could be said of any history book. The fact that some event is unlikely hardly proves that it didn't happen. If someone claims that a certain interesting event happened, and you object that the odds against it are a 1000 to 1, he may quite rightly reply that this was the 1 time in a 1000. That's why it's interesting. History books don't normally record the commonplace; they record the extraordinary.

To prove that a claimed event never happened it is not sufficient to prove that it is unlikely. You must either prove that it didn't happen on this particular occasion, or you must prove that it is literally impossible.

Conclusion

I don't see anything improbable about these events at all. I've personally seen parents lose their children and old men fawn over children many times. The critic here doesn't even make a convincing case that the reported events are unlikely. We are expected to dismiss a claimed eye-witness account as a lie based on a statement of someone who wasn't there that, in his subjective opinion, in total absence of any specific evidence, it sounds unlikely to him.

5.17. Jesus' Trial

The trial of Jesus as described in the Gospels could not possibly have happened that way. The story there does not conform to the laws of Israel about how trials must be conducted. These regulations are clearly spelled out in the Mishnah, the book of Jewish law that was followed at the time. For example, the Gospels say that the trial was at night, while the Mishnah requires trials to be held during the day. The Gospels say that Jesus was tried and sentenced on the same day, while the Mishnah requires sentencing to be two days later ("on the third day", counting the day of the trial as the first day) to give the judges time to reconsider their decision. The Gospels describe the judges questioning Jesus and trying to trap him into making damaging confessions, while under Jewish law there had to be a clear charge before the trial began: judges could not fish for charges during the trial. And of course the description of Jesus being spit on and physically assaulted in the courtroom is absurd: no such thing was allowed. Some scholars have identified as many as 18 points on which the Gospel stories of the trial of Jesus conflict with actual Israeli legal procedures.

The funny thing about this criticism is that Christians not only admit that these discrepancies exist, but routinely preach sermons about them!

The assumption behind this criticism is that government officials always follow the letter and the spirit of the law meticulously, and that there could not ever, possibly, in the entire history of the world, be such a thing as an unfair trial or of a defendant railroaded by a biased court.

But of course we all know full well that unfair trials happen all the time in real life. There are the outrageous "show trials" of the former Soviet Union and modern North Korea and Iran, where everyone knows that the accused's fate was decided before the trial began, and the only purpose of the trial is to force him to publicly confess, usually after he has been tortured. The only thing in question in these trials is whether the governments that conduct them believe that anyone will be fooled into thinking that this trial has anything to do with justice. Even in places where fairness and justice are taken more seriously, like the United States and western Europe, people who are unpopular for their political or religious beliefs, or for their race, or who the judge or jury see as individually a dislikable person, do not always get a fair trial. Often-cited examples in America include Sacco and Vanzetti (1920), who many believe were convicted because of their anti-government political beliefs rather than any evidence of actual criminal acts; the Tulia 46 (1999), a group of mostly poor black people railroaded on drug charges by police and courts who seemed to assume that all black people must be drug dealers; and the Duke Lacrosse team (2006), who were pre-judged because they were rich white boys and thus "obviously" racist and corrupt.

The fact that there have been unjust trials throughout history does not prove that the Gospel stories of Jesus being given an unjust trial must be true. But it does prove that the Gospel stories cannot be refuted by simply pointing out that the trial as described would have been illegal. You can't prove that something didn't happen just by pointing out that, if it had happened that way, it would have been illegal. People do illegal things all the time. That's why we have police and courts. It is not unheard of for government to do illegal things. It happens so often that we have numerous words and phrases to describe it, like "corruption" and "abuse of power".

There is nothing impossible or unbelievable about the idea that a group of officials could use the power of the government as a legal lynch mob. It happens all the time.

5.18. Shroud of Turin

Christians claim that the Shroud of Turin is the cloth that Jesus was buried in. They claim the image on the shroud was a side-effect of the resurrection. But Carbon-14 dating has proven that the Shroud of Turin was made in the Middle Ages, and so must be a fake. Therefore, Jesus never came back from the dead – if he ever lived at all.

For those unfamiliar with the Shroud of Turin, a bit of background: In the city of Turin, Italy, there is a piece of cloth, 14 feet 3 inches long by 3 feet 7 inches wide, bearing the image of a man. The image shows his front and his back, joined at the head, as if he lay on the cloth and it was folded over him and then the image made. There is a detailed history of the cloth from about 1350 and fragmentary history before that. For centuries the owners have claimed that it was the cloth that Jesus was wrapped in when he was buried.

Christianity does not depend on the Shroud of Turin. If the shroud is a fake, that doesn't prove anything about Jesus or Christianity. Even if it could be proven that the shroud was the burial cloth of Jesus, that of itself wouldn't prove that Jesus was the Son of God or that he came back from the dead.

In April, 1983, *Stern*, a German magazine, published excerpts from "The Hitler Diaries". According to the article, the diaries had been lost in a plane crash and hidden for almost 30 years. Historians were excited about the new insights these diaries could give into the history of the Nazi regime. But it was eventually discovered that the diaries were a forgery. They were actually written by a dealer in historical memorabilia for the money and the fame he would get for "discovering" them.

Did the fact that the Hitler Diaries turned out to be a fraud prove that Adolf Hitler never lived, or that World War II never happened? Of course not. Likewise, if the Shroud of Turin proves to be a fraud, that doesn't prove that Jesus never lived or didn't come back from the dead.

That said, the case for the Shroud of Turin is much better than the media reports might lead you to believe.

Arguments against the authenticity of the shroud:

1. Carbon-14 dating puts the shroud at about AD 1300.
2. There are two medieval documents that question the authenticity of the shroud.

Arguments for the authenticity of the shroud include:

1. There are references to the preserved burial cloth of Christ dating back to the second century AD. Many of these references include descriptions and drawings that closely match the shroud.
2. Pictures of Christ in art dating back to the 5th Century resemble the image on the shroud.
3. A number of points about the image on the shroud do not conform to misconceptions commonly held in the Middle Ages. The nails are through his wrists and not his palms, which we now know is how the Romans did it. He has a pigtail, which we now know was a common style in first century Palestine. Etc.
4. The cloth is woven in a style typical of the ancient Middle East and not of Medieval Europe.
5. The cloth includes threads made from a type of cotton native to the Middle East and not Europe.

6. Pollen and mites found in the shroud are native to Palestine, Turkey, and Constantinople. These are places that old documents say the shroud was in, and that it would have passed through on the way to Europe.

7. Numerous details about the shroud match the Biblical account of Jesus burial, and none contradict it.

8. The image is a negative. People always thought the image looked decidedly strange. When the first photograph of it was taken in 1898, the photographer was surprised to see that the negative of the photo looked like a positive. Why would a medieval forger have made a negative image? Where would he have even gotten the idea?

9. Attempts to reproduce the image have consistently failed. The image is not a painting – there is no trace of paint pigments on the cloth. The image is a chemical change to the fibers of the cloth similar to the browning of food when you cook it, but somehow showing the image even in places where it could not have been in contact with the body. The image is only about 500 nanometers thick, that is, 1/2 of 1/1000 of a millimeter. A popular theory among the scientists who have studied the shroud is that the image was produced by a burst of radiation.

[Stevenson, Kenneth and Habermas, Gary. *The Shroud and the Controversy*. Nashville: 1990. pp. 209-213 et al]

Every method of determining the date and history of the shroud that has been thought of except one indicates that it comes from Palestine before the second century. The one contrary piece of evidence is the Carbon-14 test. Therefore, the critic concludes, the shroud is a medieval forgery and all the other evidence is a bunch of curious anomalies that cannot be explained.

This is a common ground rule adopted by Biblical critics: One piece of evidence against the Bible trumps one hundred pieces of evidence supporting it. Even if, as in this case, it isn't even really an argument against the Bible, but a highly tangential point.

5.19. The Resurrection Scam

The Bible says that Jesus Christ came back from the dead. But how do we know that the Bible writers were telling the truth? They had a very obvious reason to make up the whole story: To set themselves up as the leaders of a new religion. Then they could become rich and famous, and have hordes of followers who would obey their every command. What if it was all just one big scam? It may have been the biggest scam in history.

Let's suppose, for the sake of argument, that after Jesus' death the eleven disciples made up the whole story about his coming back from the dead and appointing them to carry on his work. (Twelve minus Judas equals eleven.) Or maybe there never was such a person as Jesus at all, and they just invented him. Or maybe there was a Jesus but he never knew these men. Whatever. Let's suppose this was all just one big scam so they could become rich and powerful.

If so, the scam quickly went bad.

In AD 44, about the same time that the first books of the New Testament were being written, James Ben-Zebedee, one of the original twelve disciples, was executed by order of the governor. His head was cut off. Within a year two other early leaders were also killed. If this was all a scam, this should have made the surviving conspirators hesitate. Were they going to get rich and famous after all? Or would they all end up being killed? Well, maybe they figured that James just had bad luck, and now there was one less person to divide the loot.

In AD 54, Philip, another of the disciples, was killed in Heliopolis. He was whipped and crucified. Surely a very unpleasant way to die. But the remaining disciples apparently stuck to their story.

In AD 60, Matthew, author of the first Gospel, was killed in Ethiopia.

A few years later the authorities in Jerusalem came to James – the other one of the twelve named James, and author of one of the books in the Bible – and asked him to stand up publicly and stop these wild rumors that were spreading about this Jesus person. James was a widely respected community leader, and they thought people would listen to him. But when he got up to speak, instead of refuting the stories, he said they were all true. So they had him dragged to the top of a building and thrown off the roof. When they discovered that he was still alive after hitting the ground, they incited a mob to stone him to death. When he survived that, finally someone bashed his brains out with a club.

When James got up to give his speech he knew that the authorities would not like what he planned to say. Maybe he didn't know that they would kill him, though the fact that five of his associates had already been killed would have been a clue. At the least he knew that they would make things unpleasant for him. He could have avoided all of this by simply backing down on his story about Jesus coming back from the dead. They might well have rewarded him for helping to stop this movement. If it was all a con game, why would he stick to the story when it could only result in him getting into serious trouble, and when the authorities gave him an easy out?

Andrew was crucified on an X-shaped cross in Edessa.

Mark, author of the first Gospel to be published, was killed by a mob in Alexandria, dragged to death.

Peter was crucified in Rome. He was crucified upside down at his own request, because, he explained, he didn't think he was worthy to die in the same way that Jesus did.

Jude was crucified in Edessa in AD 72. Bartholomew was beaten to death by a mob in India. Thomas was killed with a spear, also in India. Simon the Zealot was killed in Britain in AD 74.

[Fox, John. *Fox's Book of Martyrs*. 1563. Ch 1.]

If this was a con game, these men must have been either incredibly optimistic or incredibly stupid. As one by one they were tortured and killed, they all still stuck to their story. It is possible that at the beginning they thought that this was a route to fame and fortune. But within a few years it became clear that it was more likely a route to a violent death.

Of the original twelve disciples, the Bible says that Judas killed himself, and of the remaining eleven, both Christian and secular historians tell us that ten died violent deaths. Only one, John, managed to live long enough to die of natural causes, and he had some close calls along the way. Several were given the opportunity to recant their story before they were killed. As the deaths were spread across twenty years, they had plenty of time to think about whether this plan was going well.

I suppose the disciples did become famous, but none of them ever became rich. They had devoted followers, but these followers didn't treat them to lives of luxury and cater to their every whim. About the most they could do was to help them hide from the soldiers and the mobs trying to kill them. If this was all a con game, it was the most *unsuccessful* con game in history.

And if this was all a con game, we are asked to believe that, when faced with torture and death, *not one* of the eleven decided to call it quits. Even the Romans and the Jews, who were trying to stamp out this new religion, never claimed that any of the disciples ever changed his story. Every single one of them stuck to his story right up to the end.

I could believe that a con man would miscalculate and end up getting himself killed in a scheme that he thought would bring him fame and fortune. I suppose I could believe that one or two men might keep trying to make a scam work when it should have been obvious that this plan was a loser and that any rational person would switch to chain letters or insurance fraud or politics or some other scam that had a better chance of success. But to believe that these eleven men set out to foist a scam on the world, and *all eleven* stuck to their story as they were threatened and beaten, that they watched their co-conspirators be tortured and killed, and *not one* ever thought to say, "Hey fellas, only kidding, never mind, just a gag you know, I think I'll be heading out of town now" ... I find that incredibly difficult to believe.

Maybe Jesus didn't really come back from the dead. But these eleven men believed he did. They were so sure, they were willing to be tortured and killed before they would say differently.

Critics sometimes reply that many people throughout history have been willing to die for their religion. If this proves that their religion is true, then, say, the Koran is proven by the willingness of Moslem suicide bombers to die.

The difference is that whether the resurrection was real or a lie, the disciples knew it. They were there. They did not believe it because they read it in some holy book, or because their priest told them. If someone today gives his life for Christianity, you could plausibly argue that he was fooled by a smooth-talking evangelist. That could not possibly be true of the original disciples. They knew.

6. Mathematics

6.1. Matthew Genealogy Count

Matthew chapter 1 says that there were 14 generations from the Babylonian exile to Christ. But he only lists 13 generations.

This shows up on a lot of critics' lists of "contradictions". But as this occurs in a single section written by one author, the real criticism is not so much that it is a contradiction as that Matthew can't count. (As "mathematics" goes counting to 14 is pretty elementary, but I didn't know what other category to put it in.)

Matthew breaks his genealogy into three parts of 14 generations each. Here are the people Matthew lists in each part:

From Abraham to David:

1. Abraham
2. Isaac
3. Jacob
4. Judah
5. Perez
6. Hezron
7. Ram
8. Amminadab

9. Nahshon
10. Salmon
11. Boaz
12. Obed
13. Jesse
14. David

From David to the exile:

1. Solomon
2. Rehoboam
3. Abijah
4. Asa
5. Jehoshaphat
6. Joram
7. Uzziah
8. Jotham
9. Ahaz
10. Hezekiah
11. Manasseh
12. Amon
13. Josiah
14. Jeconiah

From the exile to Jesus:

1. Jeconiah
2. Shealtiel
3. Zerubbabel
4. Abiud
5. Eliakim
6. Azor
7. Zadok
8. Achim
9. Eliud
10. Eleazar
11. Matthan
12. Jacob
13. Joseph
14. Jesus

Well, there are 14 names from the exile to Jesus. What's the problem?

In order to say "14 from Abraham to David" and "14 from David to the exile", Matthew counts Abraham to David; and then Solomon, the guy after David, to Jeconiah. But then when he says "... and 14 from the exile to Jesus" he counts Solomon to Jeconiah to get 14, and then counts Jeconiah to Jesus to get 14. That is, he ends the first group with a different person than he uses to start the second group, but the second group ends with the same man who also starts the third group. Yes, this is inconsistent.

Before we come to conclusions, we must note something else: The genealogy has gaps. In 1 Chronicles 3:10-16, we also find a genealogy from David to Jeconiah. It includes three extra names between Uzziah and Jotham: Joash, Amaziah, and Azariah; and one extra name between Josiah and Jeconiah: Jehoiakim.

This is not a mistake or a deceit: It is common in Hebrew genealogies to skip over generations to make the list more concise. The phrase "son of" can mean a son in the literal English sense of the word, or it can mean "descendent", as an English-speaking person might say "We are all sons of Noah". Indeed in the very same chapter Matthew begins with a super-summary genealogy: "The book of the genealogy of Jesus Christ, the Son of David, the Son of Abraham" [Matthew 17:1]. Clearly Jesus was not the immediate son of David nor David the immediate son of Abraham. Matthew makes no secret of the fact that he is omitting some generations.

When Matthew breaks Jesus' genealogy into these three neat fourteens, he is not saying that there is some incredible coincidence or divine pattern. It is just a handy literary device. Perhaps Matthew intends some important symbolism here, some mystical significance to the number fourteen. Or it may simply be a way of organizing the list, or a mnemonic device.

In any case, in order to make the generations add up to fourteen, he has to leave out four names in the second set to trim it down, and he has to re-cycle one from the second set to the third to pad it out. (He couldn't just include Jehoiakim in the second set and use Jeconiah exclusively in the third set because this would not have brought the genealogy all the way to the exile.) It seems likely that the third set includes all the generations that existed, or Matthew would have simply included one more, i.e. omitted one less, to complete the fourteen, rather than recycle Jeconiah. But Matthew wasn't going to invent a name to make fourteen. It is legal to omit real names. It is not legal to invent fake names.

Conclusion

Matthew was perfectly capable of counting to fourteen. (He didn't even need to take off his shoes to do it.) For some reason he wanted to divide Jesus' genealogy into three sets of fourteen. We can debate why he wanted to do this, whether it has some deep spiritual significance or was simply a handy organizational device, but for whatever reason, he did it. To make it add up, he had to leave out some names here and change the way he counted from one set to another. This is not a mistake a contradiction. It is simply an organizational trick to fulfill a literary device.

6.2. Biblical Value of Pi

For any circle, dividing the circumference by the diameter gives a constant value, called π (pi). According to the Bible, π is equal to exactly 3. See 1 Kings 7:23: "And he made the Sea of cast bronze, ten cubits from one brim to the other; it was completely round. Its height was five cubits, and a line of thirty cubits measured its circumference." That is, it says that the diameter of this basin is 10 and its circumference is 30. 30 divided by 10 gives exactly 3.

But π is not 3, but 22/7. So if the diameter of the basin was 10 cubits, then the circumference would have been 220/7 cubits, or 31 3/7. Therefore, the Bible is in error.

The flaw to this argument is the unscientific idea of an "exact measurement".

A *count* can be exact. If you ask me how many people are in a room, I may be able to tell you "exactly 23" or whatever the number is. But a *measurement* cannot be exact. It can only be accurate to the limits of the equipment used to take the measurement.

Scientists refer to this as the number of "significant figures". As one chemistry tutorial I found on the web put it:

Care must be taken when determining the number of significant figures to use. Your driver's license may state that your height is 5 feet 3 inches, or 5.25 feet. Measuring a little more carefully, we may find that your height is found to be 5.257 feet. However if you said you were 5.257186 feet tall the scientific community would look upon that measurement with serious skepticism because you stated your height accurate to the nearest micron!

Clemson University Physics Department. "Physics Tutorial: Significant Figures". http://phoenix.phys.clemson.edu /tutorials/sf/index.html. Jan 27, 2006 (Retrieved Oct 27, 2009)

Beginning chemistry and physics students often make the mistake of reporting the results of a calculation to more significant digits than is warranted by the accuracy of their measurements, simply because their calculator shows that many digits. For example, suppose a student is asked to calculate velocity. He is told that this is distance traveled divided by time. He measures the distance as 4.1 feet and time as 1.7 seconds. So he plugs 4.1 divided by 1.7 into a calculator and reports that the velocity is 2.411764706 feet per second. Then he is surprised when the teacher tells him this is wrong. His measurements were only accurate to 2 significant digits, thus the calculation cannot be accurate to more than 2 significant digits. The correct answer is 2.4 feet per second.

Students often say, "But isn't it better to show more digits rather than fewer? Isn't more always better?" The answer is no. Giving more digits implies that you have more precise measurements than you really have.

When I took chemistry in high school, we had a question on a test that said (not an exact quote – I'm quoting as best I remember it from 30 years ago), "A beaker contains 200. grams of water. You add 0.43 grams of potassium nitrate. What is the total weight of the mixture?" A student who answered 200.43 grams was marked wrong. To be marked correct the student had to say 200. grams. That is, the student was required to recognize that 200. grams is only accurate to within 1 gram. 0.43 grams is less than this precision, and so adding this amount is just lost in the rounding error.

Another common student mistake is to say, "The correct measurement is 12.842, so Sally was wrong when she said it was 12.8". But as there is no such thing as an exact measurement, it is incorrect to say that a less precise measurement is "wrong". In this case, 12.842 is also just an approximation. With more precise equipment, we could add yet more digits to the measurement. The limit is not when we finally get to an "exact" answer, but rather when we either reach the limits of our instruments or when further precision is meaningless. Like, to take the earlier example of measuring a person's height, at some point things like how much you press the person's hair down when you put the ruler on top of his head, or whether flakes of dead skin on the bottom of his feet count as part of his height or not, lead to ambiguities in the measurement that are greater than the precision of our measuring tool.

So the question becomes, when 1 Kings says that the basin was 10 cubits in diameter and 30 cubits in circumference, how precise were those measurements? Modern scientists have conventions about how to express numbers in ways that make the number of significant digits clear. But we cannot apply these conventions to the book of Kings, because those conventions were not invented yet when it was written, and in any case the text makes no claim to being a scientific or engineering treatise, it is just giving a general description of the size and shape of various objects. I'm sure that even the most rigorous modern physicist will casually say "the grocery store is two and a half miles from my house" without using the technical conventions when he is not speaking or writing in a technical context.

As no fractions are included, it's unlikely the numbers are precise to more than the nearest one cubit, i.e. to more than two significant digits. As both numbers are multiples of ten, they might be precise only to the nearest ten cubits, i.e. to one significant digit. Let's suppose for the sake of argument that they are accurate to two digits.

Then by the modern conventions, the reported diameter of 10 means 10 plus or minus 0.5, or somewhere between 9.5 and 10.5. This gives a calculated circumference between 29.8 and 33.0. The reported circumference of 30 means somewhere between 29.5 and 30.5. There is plenty of overlap between these two ranges, so there is no reason to conclude that there is any error here.

Indeed, the objection as stated leads to an impossible requirement. Even if we were describing an abstract math problem rather than a physical measurement, so that we could state that the diameter is exactly 10, the circumference cannot be expressed in any finite way. π is what is called a "transcendental number" or "irrational number": It cannot be expressed as a fraction. ("Irrational" here does not mean "crazy" but "not a ratio". Despite what you may have thought in math class.) If you write π as a decimal number, it takes an infinite number of digits. No value of π given with a finite number of digits is "exact". One of my math teachers said that the only way to exactly state the value of π is to say "pi". This is not entirely true: you could also give a rule or formula, but the point is valid. If the Bible had said that the circumference was 31 cubits, the critic could say, No, no, π is really 3.14, so the right answer is 31.4 cubits. If the Bible had said 31.4, the critic could insist it should be 31.42. If the Bible had said it was 31.4159265, the critic could have insisted it say 31.41592654. Et cetera, forever.

Many critics express their objection with words like "but π is really 22/7". They seem to mean "exactly 22/7", which is flat wrong. π is *approximately* 22/7. This is a slightly more precise approximation that 3, which is, after all, 21/7. Both are approximations.

Conclusion

The critics who claim that the Bible is unscientific on this point are themselves the ones who are being unscientific. They are displaying a complete ignorance of the concept of "significant figures". Many display ignorance of the fact that π is an irrational number, or that there are such things as irrational numbers.

6.3. Present Population from Two People

If the world was really created just a few thousand years ago with just two people, how did we get the billions of people we have today? There's no way two people could multiply into billions in just a few thousand years.

The historian James Ussher (1581-1656) estimated that the world was created in 4004 BC. This is the most recent date I've heard seriously proposed. Could the entire present world population have come from one couple in just 6000 years?

Let's do the math. What would be the rate of population growth to get from 2 people to today's 6 billion in 6000 years? Is it a reasonable number?

The calculation is straightforward enough. Let r be the rate of population growth. Then:

$$2 \times (1+r)^{6000} = 6 \times 10^9$$
$$(1+r)^{6000} = 3 \times 10^9$$
$$6000 \times \log(1+r) = \log(3 \times 10^9)$$
$$6000 \times \log(1+r) \sim= 9.4771$$
$$\log(1+r) \sim= 0.001580$$
$$1+r \sim= 1.0036$$
$$r \sim= .0036$$

That is, the average population growth rate would have been about 1/3 of 1% per year.

How does that compare to historical growth rates? This is well below the current average world growth rate of 1.1%. Current population growth rates are probably above the historical average because of more reliable food supplies, better health care, etc. No one knows what the population of the world was before about 1750, when it is estimated at 800 million. By a similar calculation, to get from 800 million to 6 billion in 250 years would require a growth rate of about 0.8%, still over double the "Eve-to-today" number.

Some object that there have been great disasters that have reduced the world population, and we must factor these in. In fact most disasters only reduce the world population for a few minutes or at most a few hours. About 120 million babies are now born each year, or over 300,000 per day. The 2010 earthquake in Haiti killed 230,000 people. It took the world 17 hours to replace them. Hurricane Katrina killed 1,800 people. It took 8 minutes to replace them. World population at the end of World War 2 was higher than it was when the war started: 2.2 billion in 1939 versus 2.3 billion in 1945.

The only two events in history that have reduced world population for more than a day are the Black Death and Noah's Flood.

The Flood is generally dated around 2500 BC, or 4500 years ago. To get from 8 people (Noah and his wife and three sons and their wives) to 6 billion today, using the same algorithm as above, gives $r \sim= .0045$, or less than 1/2 of 1% per year. Again, well below the growth rates since anyone has been keeping records.

The fact that it's possible doesn't prove that it's true, of course. But there is nothing about the story in Genesis that is not biologically and mathematically possible.

6.4. Israeli Population Unbelievable

Genesis says that just 70 Jews moved to Egypt with Joseph and Jacob. But Exodus says that when they left just a couple of hundred years later, there were over 2 million. There's no way 70 people could multiply into 2 million in just a few hundred years.

The underlying issue in this argument is the same as in issue 6.3.

Yes, originally there were 70 descendants of Jacob in Egypt. This number did not include women who married into the family. Based on the statement in Acts that 75 people moved to Egypt with Jacob, and four – Joseph, his wife, and their two sons -- were already there, the Jewish population of Egypt at that time must have been 79. (See issue 7.3.) But let's give the critic the benefit of the doubt and say 70.

According to Exodus 12:40, the Jews were in Egypt for 430 years. Numbers 1 tells us that they took a census of the men eligible for military service, at least 20 years old and physically fit. The count came to 603,550. From this people estimate that the total population, adding in women, old men, children, and the handicapped, was about 2 million.

So the growth rate would have been:

$$70 \times (1+r)^{430} = 2 \times 10^6$$
$$(1+r)^{430} \sim = 29 \times 10^3$$
$$430 \times \log(1+r) \sim = \log(29 \times 10^3)$$
$$430 \times \log(1+r) \sim = 4.46$$
$$\log(1+r) \sim = .0104$$
$$1+r \sim = 1.024$$
$$r \sim = .024$$

That is, it would have taken an average population growth rate of 2.4%. This is an above-average rate but quite plausible. There are many countries today, mostly in Africa and the Moslem world, with higher growth rates. Liberia, Kuwait, Congo, and Ethiopia have growth rates over 3%. The Republic of Maldives reports a population growth rate of 5.6%.

These are not technologically advanced countries, so no one can claim that such growth rates are only possible with modern medicine and nutrition.

According to Josephus, the Israelis were only in Egypt for 215 years. He says that the 430 years of Exodus 12:40 is the time from when Abraham arrived in Canaan to the Exodus, which included the time in Egypt but also a period before that. [Josephus, Flavius. *Antiquities of the Jews*. AD 94. 2:15:3.] It's not my purpose here to defend Josephus, but to defend the Bible. But for what it's worth, if we perform a similar calculation using Josephus' 215 years, we get a population growth rate of 4.9%. This is high but not unprecedented.

Apparently the critic ridiculed the Bible's math without first doing the elementary algebra himself.

7. Internal Contradictions

7.1. Two Creation Stories

You say you believe the creation story in Genesis. Which one? There are two creation stories, one in Genesis chapter 1 through chapter 2 verse 4, and another beginning in 2:5 and going through the end of the chapter. These stories contradict each other.

1. The Genesis 1 story says that man and woman were created together, after the animals. The Genesis 2 story says that the man was created first, then the animals, then the woman.

2. Genesis 1 says the world began with watery chaos. Genesis 2 says it was a barren desert.

3. Genesis 1 says God created by speaking things into existence. Genesis 2 describes him making things with his hands.

It is true that Genesis gives two accounts of creation. The critics say that Genesis 2 was written centuries before Genesis 1, and the two stories later slapped together. See issue 4.3 for a discussion of this theory, the Documentary Hypothesis.

The more realistic explanation is that Moses did not personally write Genesis, but rather compiled and edited information written by earlier authors. These authors signed their sections with the "toledoth colophons" found throughout Genesis. See the end of issue 4.3 under "Toledoth Colophons" for more on this theory of the authorship of Genesis. But briefly, Genesis is divided into sections each ending with the signature of the author: Noah, Shem, Terah, and so forth. The second creation story is part of the section signed "This is the book of the account of Adam". The first creation story is the only section which is not signed with a name. Instead it says "This is the account of the heavens and the Earth when they were created." This section may have been written or dictated directly by God.

This theory is consistent with the content of the two creation stories. The first story, the one written by God himself, describes events that happened before the first human being was created. According to this account, humans were created at the very end of the creation week. So no human could have been an eye witness to most of the events of creation. The only way a human could know what happened is if someone who was there, such as God or an angel, told him.

The second story, the one written by Adam, is written from a human point of view. After a quick introduction, "Before any plant of the field was in the earth ...", this account relates things that happened to Adam or that he could readily have witnessed.

It is not surprising that an account written by Adam would not describe created things in the order that God created them, but rather in the order that Adam encountered them. If I wrote an autobiography and discussed the various U.S. states in which I have lived, I would likely list them in the order that I lived there. You wouldn't expect me to list them in the order that the states entered the union.

Even if Genesis was written personally by Moses, as opposed to edited, there is no great mystery in the two stories. Genesis 1 is an overview of the creation of the universe. Genesis 2 is specifically about the creation of man. Writers often find it helpful to begin with an overview to put the entire subject into perspective, and then to step back and go into detail about the part of particular interest. Like, if I was reading a book about the Battle of the Bulge in World War 2, I wouldn't be surprised if it began with an overview of the entire war to put this battle into perspective, and then went back to explain the details of the battle.

Let's look at the three claimed contradictions.

Man or Beast?

Genesis 1 clearly says that birds and animals were created before humans. Genesis 2 describes the creation of Adam, and then it says, "Out of the ground the LORD God formed every beast of the field and every bird of the air, and brought them to Adam ..." [Genesis 2:19] This certainly sounds like it is saying that the birds and the beasts were created *after* Adam.

But note that the problem here comes entirely from the tense of the verbs in Genesis 2: "formed" and "brought". When we read this in English, it sounds like its saying that this is the next event in a series of events.

But ancient Hebrew does not have all the complex tenses that English (and many other languages) have. Hebrew has just two tenses: "perfect" and "imperfect". The perfect tense indicates action that is completed; the imperfect tense is action that is not completed. So when translating Hebrew to English, the same imperfect-tense Hebrew verb could be translated, for example, "he is looking", "he will look", or "he has been looking". A perfect-tense verb could be translated "he looked", "he will have looked", or "he had looked".

Thus in Genesis 2, the sentence translated in the King James as "the LORD God formed every beast of the field ... and brought them unto Adam", could with equal fidelity to the Hebrew be translated "Now the LORD God *had formed* out of the ground all the beasts of the field and ... brought them to the man". This is how it is translated in the New International Version. (Italics mine.) That is, an equally valid translation of Genesis 2 is that God had created the animals earlier, and now he showed them to Adam. An understanding of Hebrew tenses quickly resolves the apparent contradiction.

Regarding the creation of man and woman, Genesis 2 says that God created the man first, then took his rib – or more literally, a piece of his side – and made the woman from this. So yes, Genesis 2 describes the creation of man and woman as being separate acts.

Genesis 1 simply says "So God created man in His own image; in the image of God He created him; male and female He created them." [Genesis 1:7]

So where's the contradiction? Genesis 1 says that God created both male and female humans. It doesn't say they were created simultaneously. The critic seems to be claiming that just because both events are mentioned in the same sentence, they must have happened at exactly the same time. But nothing in the wording of Genesis 1 or of elementary logic requires this. If I say, "Bob had two children", would you conclude that because I mentioned both children in the same sentence that the children must have been twins? If I say, "Bob got married and had two children", would you take this to mean that not only must the children be twins, but that the wedding must have occurred in the maternity ward at the same instant that the children were being born?

Yes, if we didn't have Genesis 2, you could read Genesis 1 and assume that both man and woman were created at the same moment. But the words could equally well mean that they were created separately, just by the same God. In order to find a contradiction here, you have to pick the reading that leads to a contradiction, and then insist that must have been the writer's intent. The only reason to do that is if you are going out of your way to find a contradiction.

Wet or Dry?

Critics say that Genesis 1 begins with a world covered with water, while Genesis 2 begins with a desert world. They claim that Genesis 1 was written in Babylon, known as "the land between the rivers"; while Genesis 2 was written in Judah, a land on the edge of the desert, and so each writer brought the perspective of his homeland to the story.

It is true that Genesis 1 begins with a world covered in water. Genesis 2 begins with a world that is barren in the sense of no plants, but it's not a dry desert. It clearly says "a mist went up from the earth and watered the whole face of the ground".

The stories readily fit together. Genesis 2 does not begin at the beginning. It doesn't mention the creation of the Earth itself or of the land and seas, but starts with these things already existing. The only question is where Genesis 2 fits in the chronology of Genesis 1 Genesis 1 says that God created the waters, then he separated the water and caused dry land to emerge, then he created plants. Genesis 2 begins with dry land with no plants, then talks about the creation of plants and humans. It begins after God created the dry land but before he created the plants. So it must begin at the time of Genesis 1 verse 10, after verse 9 and before verse 11. There's no problem fitting the two stories together at all.

Mouth or Hands?

Critics say that Genesis 1 describes God creating by speaking things into existence, while Genesis 2 has him making things with his bare hands. Many critics say that Genesis 2 is an older and more primitive story, while Genesis 1 represents a more sophisticated intellect.

In order to see a contradiction here, you have to not only interpret the descriptions of God's actions in a highly simplistic, anthropocentric way, but then you have to also mix up two verses.

Both the Genesis 1 and Genesis 2 accounts of creation are high-level summaries. It says that God created the dry land, but it doesn't spell out the individual continents and islands. It says that God created humans, but it doesn't spell out all the organs or explain the details of biochemistry. This isn't surprising: A full technical discussion of everything God had to do to create the universe would have been long and tedious. People have written many large books on tiny details of creation, like how subatomic particles interact or the function of a single component within a living cell. Much of this would be incomprehensible to people who lived before modern science. Actually most of the science behind what God did to create the universe would be incomprehensible to the most brilliant scientist today. God's purpose was not to confuse but to enlighten, so the story is related in simple terms.

We could try to read Genesis 1 and 2 as if God had a human body. That is, we could interpret statements in Genesis 1 like "God said, Let such-and-such happen" to mean that God spoke verbally using human or human-like vocal cords. We could interpret statements in Genesis 2 like "God planted a garden" and "he took one of his ribs" to mean he did these things with human or human-like hands. But Genesis never says that God created by making things with his bare hands. It just says that he "formed man" [Genesis 1:7], "made every tree" [v 8], etc. It says he "made", but it doesn't say whether this was with his hands, with his voice, or with power tools.

Even if we read these verses in this simplistic, anthropomorphic sense, the supposed contradiction still doesn't hold water. Genesis 1 describes God's creation of most things with words like, "God said, 'Let there be light.'" He speaks things into existence. But when it gets to the creation of people, the language changes: "Then God said, 'Let Us make man in Our image ... ' So God created man in His own image; in the image of God He created him; male and female He created them." [Genesis 1:26-27]. That is, when it gets to the creation of man, the language changes from "saying" to "making" and "creating". Genesis 2 says God "made man".

That is, Genesis 1 does not say that God "spoke" people into existence while Genesis 2 says that he "made" people. Genesis 1 says that God "spoke" light into existence and that he "made" people, while Genesis 2 doesn't mention light and says that he "made" people. The "contradiction" between Genesis 1 and Genesis 2 is that the words used to describe how God created light in Genesis 1 do not match the words used to describe how God created people in Genesis 2. Umm, so what? The words used to describe how God made humans in both cases are pretty similar.

More realistically, Genesis 1 does not mean that God created by simply speaking, nor does Genesis 2 mean that God created by making things with his bare hands. These words are a simplification of what God actually did to make it understandable by humans.

I work as a software engineer in real life. (Sadly, I make very little money from writing.) When I try to describe software development to non-technical people, I speak in simplified language and analogies. I've often said things like, "The computer thought that …" But of course a computer doesn't literally think. I've said, "The computer is trying to …" or "The computer wants to …" even though it has no volition. Etc. Statements like this certainly do not convey the complete truth of what is happening, but neither could you fairly say that they are false. They are simplifications, intended to help a non-technical person understand what they need to understand without bogging down the conversation with a long and unnecessary technical discussion. It is likely that the same is true of Genesis 1 and 2.

When Genesis says that God spoke some things into existence but "made" others, is that just a difference in wording, or does this mean something significant? I suspect that if we understood the full reality of what God did, we would find that the words used are technically accurate while being easy to comprehend. But that's just speculation.

Side Note: Secondary to Man

Many critics say that the Biblical account of the creation of Adam and Eve demonstrates that Christians look down on women. Genesis says that the woman was created second, after the man, so clearly the writer thought women were less important than men.

Furthermore, Eve is created from Adam's rib, which makes her a by-product, an afterthought.

This is not a question of fact but a philosophical interpretation, so it is really outside the scope of this book. But I've heard it so often that I thought I'd throw in a quick reply.

Yes, the Bible says that the woman was created from Adam's rib, or more literally, from his side. It is not clear how this makes her inferior to Adam. The woman was made from the genetic material of an intelligent creature. The man was made from dirt. That sounds more favorable to the woman to me.

Thomas Aquinas, a Catholic theologian of the 13th century and often considered the leading Catholic theologian of all time, wrote that the woman was not created from man's head, to be his master; nor from his feet, to be his slave; but rather from his side, to be his companion. [Aquinas, Thomas. *Summa Theologica*. 1:92:3]

If the fact that man was created first makes woman less important, then we must also conclude that both men and women are less important than bugs. After all, the Bible says that bugs were created before people. The order of creation is water – land – plants – fish – land animals – man – woman. This is clearly from simpler to more complex. The man was created first because you make a rough draft before you make a masterpiece. The sequence is from less important (to God) to more important. The woman was created last because she was God's greatest accomplishment, the crowning achievement of creation.

7.2. Has Anyone Seen God?

Gen 32:30 states, "...for I have seen God face to face, and my life is preserved." However, John 1:18 states, "No man hath seen God at any time..." Both statements cannot be true. Either there is an error of fact, or an error of translation. In either case, there is an error. And if there is an error, then infallibility of the Bible (in this case the King James Version) is falsified.

A typical defense used here is to look up the meaning of the original Hebrew / Greek, read that one of the words can have multiple meanings, and then pick the meaning that seems to break the contradiction. For example, the Christian might argue that "seen" or "face" means one thing in the first scripture, and something completely different in the second.

P. Wesley Edwards. "Bible Errors and Contradictions". http://www.freethoughtdebater.com /tenbiblecontradictions.htm Sept 1, 2004 (retrieved Oct 23, 2009)

There are two issues raised here: one general and one specific.

Multiple Definitions

Let's discuss the general issue first. The idea that a word might have two different definitions, and that we have to read it in context to know which is meant, is not some far-out idea invented by Christians desperate to explain away contradictions in the Bible. Open any English dictionary and you will find many words with multiple definitions, normally numbered 1,2, 3, etc. We all interpret language from context clues every day. If a man says "I love hamburgers" and later says "I love my wife", we do not normally assume that he means the word "love" in the same way in both sentences. We do not think he means that he enjoys killing and eating his wife or that he enjoys romantic getaways with hamburgers.

One of my favorite examples of multiple definitions is the word "fast". It usually means "moving swiftly", but when talking about a knot it means "securely tied". So if I say "The boat is fast" do I mean that it is moving rapidly across the water, or that it is securely tied to the dock? Or consider the definitions of the words "flies" and "like" in "Time flies like an arrow" and "Fruit flies like a banana".

This is rarely a problem in real life. Every now and then an author writes something where the applicable definition is not obvious. This kind of confusion is the basis of many jokes. Hollywood gets endless amusement from words or phrases that can have both an innocuous meaning and a sexual meaning.

As the Bible is translated from several foreign languages, there is the extra problem that we should consider the possible meanings of the word in the original, rather than the word used to translate it. The only surprising thing is that this creates as few problems as it does.

It is not at all unreasonable to say that "to see" could have both a literal meaning and a figurative meaning.

Substance and Manifestation

In this particular case, though, the most obvious resolution of the claimed contradiction comes not in examining the exact definitions of words but rather in thinking a little about the nature of God.

The critic cites John 1:18. Let's go back just a few paragraphs and read the fuller context:

> In the beginning was the Word, and the Word was with God, and the Word was God. ... And the Word became flesh and dwelt among us.
>
> John 1:1, 14

So God is a spirit, that is, an invisible being, but he took on human form, and thus became visible.

Now the contradiction evaporates. No one has seen God in his spirit form. But people did see him when he took on human form. God has put on a visible form for the benefit of human beings on a number of occasions.

Infrared radiation is invisible to the human eye. But with the aid of night-vision goggles you can see it, or rather, you can see an electronic representation of infrared radiation. So it is quite reasonable to say both "You cannot see infrared radiation", i.e. with the naked eye, and "You can see infrared radiation", i.e. with night-vision goggles. Each statement must be understood in the proper context.

7.3. How Many Went to Egypt?

According to Genesis, after Joseph became prime minister of Egypt, he sent for his father and brothers to join him. But how many came? Genesis 46:26, says 70. But when the story is retold in Acts 7:14, it says 75 people.

There is a slight difference in who is counted. Genesis gives a precise list of who made up the 70 people, by name. Acts just gives a number without listing names. We can't tell exactly who make up the difference. Still, there isn't much mystery.

The 70 in Genesis includes Joseph and his two sons, who were already in Egypt. Genesis specifically says that not including Joseph and his two sons, there were 66 descendants of Jacob who travelled with him (Jacob) to Egypt. It says this made 70 in Egypt: Jacob himself, 66 of his children, grandchildren, and great-grandchildren, and the 3 already in Egypt. 1+66+3=70. It explicitly says that this count does not include the wives of Jacob's sons. The writer later says that the 70 are those who "came from his [Jacob's] body", so apparently the wives are not counted because they are not *descendants* of Jacob. Jacob's two wives, Leah and Rachel, as well as the other two women by whom he fathered children, Bilhah and Zilpah, are not included in the count nor is any reason given why they are excluded. Genesis 33 tells us about the death of Rachel. Perhaps the other three had died by this time also.

Acts 7:14 says, "Then Joseph sent and called his father Jacob and all his relatives to him, seventy-five people." Joseph presumably did not send for himself, nor for his own sons who were already in Egypt with him. So they are not included in the 75. It is not clear if the 75 includes Jacob himself. Let's assume for the moment that it does not. "All his relatives" would presumably include his daughters-in-law, unlike the count in Genesis. We are told in Genesis 38:12 that Judah's wife was dead. That leaves at most ten other brothers' wives. If all of them were still alive, we would then have 66 descendants plus 10 wives makes 76. If one of the other brothers' wives was also no longer alive, that would get us 75. If Jacob is included in the 75, then to make the total add up we would have to assume that a third daughter-in-law was also no longer alive. (Or, perhaps, did not accompany her husband to Egypt for some other reason.)

I've seen several sources on the Internet that say that Simeon's wife was dead by this time, but none gives a citation and I cannot find any Bible reference or other source for this. The *Book of Jasher* says that Simeon married his sister Dinah. This subtracts one from the count because otherwise Dinah would be counted twice. But it doesn't help, because Jasher goes on to say that Simeon had a second wife, Bunah. [*Book of Jasher.* 45:2-3] (Some claim that this is the same Jasher mentioned in Joshua 10:13 and 2 Samuel 1:18, but this is debated. Our oldest copies go back to only the 17th century.)

Conclusion

The counts are not the same because there are some differences in who is included. Acts does not include Joseph and his sons, but it does include his sisters-in-law. We do not know how many of his brothers had a living wife to bring with him, but eight of the eleven would give the right total, or nine if Jacob is not included in the count. Either is a plausible number.

7.4. Who Killed Saul?

The Bible gives two contradictory accounts of the death of King Saul. 1 Samuel says that Saul killed himself to avoid being captured by his enemies. But 2 Samuel says that he was killed by an Amalekite soldier.

It's true that both 1 Samuel and 2 Samuel talk about the death of Saul. Let's see what they actually say. 1 Samuel says:

> Now the Philistines fought against Israel; and the men of Israel fled from before the Philistines, and fell slain on Mount Gilboa. Then the Philistines followed hard after Saul and his sons. And the Philistines killed Jonathan, Abinadab, and Malchishua, Saul's sons. The battle became fierce against Saul. The archers hit him, and he was severely wounded by the archers. ... Therefore Saul took a sword and fell on it.
>
> 1 Samuel 31:1-4

The account in 2 Samuel says that a man came to David and told him that Saul and Jonathan were dead.

> So David said to the young man who told him, "How do you know that Saul and Jonathan his son are dead?" Then the young man who told him said, "As I happened by chance to be on Mount Gilboa, there was Saul, leaning on his spear; and indeed the chariots and horsemen followed hard after him. Now when he looked behind him, he saw me and called to me. And I answered, 'Here I am.' And he said to me, 'Who are you?' So I answered him, 'I am an Amalekite.' He said to me again, 'Please stand over me and kill me, for anguish has come upon me, but my life still remains in me.' So I stood over him and killed him, because I was sure that he could not live after he had fallen."
>
> 2 Samuel 1: 5-10

Read these two selections carefully. 1 Samuel does indeed say that Saul killed himself rather than be captured or killed by the enemy army. Does 2 Samuel say that an Amalekite soldier killed him? Not

- 228 -

quite. It says that an Amalekite soldier *claimed* to have killed Saul. This is not the same thing at all.

The Amalekite had a very obvious reason to lie. He made this claim to David. Saul was king. David wanted to replace him as king. Saul had tried to kill David many times to put an end to his ambitions. The Amalekite might well have expected David to reward him for killing his enemy. (He was wrong, by the way: If you read on in 2 Samuel, you will see that David had him executed for murder. But this action was a surprise to almost everyone.)

When Christians say that we believe the Bible is completely true, we don't mean that we believe the contents of all quotes are true. When the Bible says that a person said X, if the Bible is true, that means that the person really did say X. Whether X itself is true is a different question.

There are many places in the Bible where someone is quoted as making a statement that is later identified as a lie. Ananias and Sapphira are quoted as lying about their gift to the church. [Acts 5] Potiphar's wife lied about Joseph assaulting her. [Genesis 39] Samson lies to Delilah about the secret of his strength and Delilah lies to Samson about why she wants to know. [Judges 16]

To take a silly example: The Bible says, "There is no God". It's true. See Psalm 14:1: "The fool has said in his heart, 'There is no God'." Would anyone seriously suggest that the Bible contradicts itself because it says that God exists and then quotes someone as saying that he does not?

You can accurately quote someone who is mistaken or lying without being mistaken or a liar yourself, as long as you make clear that you are quoting someone else. You may point out that the person is not telling the truth. You may say that you do not know if he is telling the truth or not. You may simply state that this is what he said without comment. As long as you do not say that his statement is true, you are not lying by accurately quoting a liar.

Suppose a reporter says, "Senator Jones denies that he accepted a bribe." Later Senator Jones is convicted. Does that mean the reporter was lying? Surely not. He didn't say that Senator Jones was innocent, just that Senator Jones claimed that he was innocent. Indeed, suppose the reporter changed a quote to what he believed to be true. Suppose he quoted Senator Jones as confessing that he had accepted a bribe, when in fact Senator Jones claimed to be innocent. Whether it turned out that the senator was guilty or not, such a fabricated confession would be a lie. An accurate quote would be the truth.

When the Bible quotes someone, the Bible is true if and only if that is what the person actually said. Whether the original statement was the truth or a lie has nothing to do with whether it was accurately quoted.

7.5. Age of Jehoiachin

The book of Kings says that Jehoiachin became king of Israel when he was eighteen years old and that he reigned for three months. Chronicles says that that he became king when he was eight years old and that he reigned for three months and ten days. This is two contradictions in one sentence.

> Jehoiachin was eighteen years old when he became king, and he reigned in Jerusalem three months.
>
> 2 Kings 24:8

> Jehoiachin was eight years old when he became king, and he reigned in Jerusalem three months and ten days.
>
> 2 Chronicles 36:9

Age

The difference between the ages is likely a copying error. In Hebrew, as in English, the difference between "eighteen" and eight" is just a few letters different.

If the original manuscript used digits instead of spelling out the numbers, then the difference is just one small mark. In ancient Hebrew, letters were also used for digits, somewhat like Roman numerals use the same symbols for both letters and digits. In Hebrew, the first nine letters were used for 1, 2, 3, ... 9, the next nine letters were 10, 20, 30, ... 90, and the remaining four letters were used for 100, 200, 300, and 400. Hebrew only has 22 letters so that's as far as they could go. (Later they used alternate forms of some of the letters for 500 through 900, but that's a later development and isn't relevant here.) This would be like an English-speaking person using A for 1, B for 2, C for 3, etc; then J for 10, K for 20, L for 30, etc.

Under this system, the smallest Hebrew letter, Yod, drawn as a little hook-shape (י), ends up being 10. Therefor, 8 is ח and 18 is חי. It is not difficult to imagine a copyist skipping over a single small mark like that.

Technicality for the detail-oriented: In Hebrew the symbols for the largest numbers normally come first. As Hebrew is written right to left, this means the largest numbers are on the right. But because the same symbols are used for both letters and digits, some numbers look like words when written in this order. To avoid confusion or distraction, numbers are therefore sometimes written out of sequence. Note that unlike Arabic numbers, where 18 and 81 are totally different numbers, in Hebrew the order doesn't really matter. 10+8 is the same as 8+10. 18, when written 10+8, looks like the word for "life". so instead it was routinely written 8+10.

If it is a copyist error, is the correct number 8 or 18? There are several reasons to believe that the correct number is 18.

First, it is more likely that someone would drop a word or a letter than that he would add one.

Second, our present copies of 2 Kings consistently say "eighteen". Most of our copies of 1 Chronicles say "eight", but some Hebrew manuscripts, as well as the Septuagint (an ancient translation into Greek) and Syriac (another old translation), say "eighteen".

Critics respond that this is a cheap way out: They find a contradiction in the Bible, and Christians weasel their way out by saying that we just know that the originals have no contradictions so this must be a copying mistake.

There is validity to this objection, but the reality is that we cannot rule out the possibility of copying errors. In this case, a copying error seems very likely. See issue 4.6 for more discussion of copying errors.

Length of Reign

This criticism is more easily disposed of. "Three months" versus "three months and ten days" is not a contradiction. If I ask a friend how long ago some event happened, and he says "three months ago", and later I ask someone else and they say "three months and ten days", I do not conclude that one of them was mistaken or lying, but simply that "three months" is a round number. If my friend said "three months and ten days", I might just as well cry, "That's a lie! It was really three months, ten days, and four hours!" If he says "three months, ten days, and four hours", I could insist it was four hours and ten minutes. Etc. Even if he gave the time to the second, I could quibble over tenths or hundredths of a second. A round number is not a lie.

7.6.   All the King's Horses

1 Kings says that Solomon had 40,000 stalls for his horses. 2 Chronicles says that he had 4,000.

> Solomon had forty thousand stalls of horses for his chariots, and twelve thousand horsemen.
>
> 1 Kings 4:26

> Solomon had four thousand stalls for horses and chariots, and twelve thousand horsemen whom he stationed in the chariot cities and with the king at Jerusalem.
>
> 2 Chronicles 9:25

Several possible resolutions of this apparent contradiction have been suggested.

Copying Error

The simplest theory is that this is a copying error. Some of the copies we have of 1 Kings give the number there as 4,000, matching Chronicles.

This isn't as obvious a copying error as the 8 versus 18 of issue 7.5. If the number was spelled out, in Hebrew forty thousand is "arboim alph" and four thousand is "arboth alphim". In digits it's a harder mistake to make in Hebrew than with modern Arabic numbers. See issue 7.5 above for a discussion of Hebrew numbers. The symbol for "four" is a totally different symbol from that for "forty". Forty thousand is 'ל while four thousand is 'ד . Still, someone going back and forth from the original text to the copy that he is making could read 4,000 and in his head think 40,000 and write that down, or vice versa.

Different Date

The two numbers do not necessarily refer to the same time in Solomon's reign. Solomon ruled for 40 years. Perhaps over that time he built more stalls, or demobilized some of his chariots and so didn't need as many stalls.

The main catch to this theory is that the number of horseman in both verses is the same. Would he have kept the same number of horsemen while changing the number of horses by a factor of ten? Well, maybe. Especially if the big number is the earlier number and he was demobilizing unneeded troops: Horses might have been more expensive to maintain than riders.

Horses versus Chariots

The wording of the two verses is different. Kings says "forty thousand stalls of horses for his chariots", while Chronicles says "four thousand stalls for horses and chariots". This could mean that Kings is counting stalls per individual horse, while Chronicles is counting stalls per chariot. There would have been multiple horses per chariot. Chariots are usually pulled by a team of several horses, and there were likely spare horses.

Conclusion

Personally I think the most likely explanation is a simple copying error. But the other two theories are also possible.

7.7. Counting Kingly Years

1 Kings 16:23 says that Omri became king of Israel in the 31st year of the reign of Asa king of Judah, and that Omri reigned 12 years. But then just a few verses later, verse 29, we are told that his son Ahab became king in the 38th year of Asa. So if Ahab became king in the 38th year of Asa, Omri must have only reigned 7 years, not 12.

There are many places in the Old Testament where the reigns of kings don't add up, like here. There's a simple reason for it.

In Western republics, we are used to leaders who have fixed terms of office. President George Washington began his reign on April 30, 1789, and served until March 4, 1797, when John Adams became the new president. Etc.

That's not how it was with ancient kings. They were not elected and did not have a fixed term of office. Basically, there were two ways that you could become king: One, by inheriting the kingdom from your father (or some other relative); and two, by overthrowing the previous king with a violent revolution.

Either way, the date of the start of your reign could be pretty fuzzy.

When you overthrew the previous king, does your reign start the day that you declared your intention to "run for office"? The date when you killed the previous incumbent? But maybe he escaped. The date when you declared victory in the war? The date when others acknowledged your victory? Etc.

When you inherit the title, things were not always as simple as the classic, "The king is dead. Long live the king!" As a king got old or sick, he often became too weak to run the country on a day by day basis. Or even if he was still healthy, after decades of running the country he might get tired of it and want to retire. But few were willing to just hand power over to their son. Either through an egotistical desire to hold on to power, or a reasoned belief that being king is a big job and his son needs some guidance while he gains experience, kings often shared power with their sons for many years. This is called a "co-regency".

So let's look now at just what the Bible says about Omri:

> Then the people of Israel were divided into two parts: half of the people followed Tibni the son of Ginath, to make him king, and half followed Omri. But the people who followed Omri prevailed over the people who followed Tibni the son of Ginath. So Tibni died and Omri reigned. In the thirty-first year of Asa king of Judah, Omri became king over Israel, and reigned twelve years. ... So Omri rested with his fathers and was buried in Samaria. Then Ahab his son reigned in his place.
>
> In the thirty-eighth year of Asa king of Judah, Ahab the son of Omri became king over Israel ...
>
> 1 Kings 16:21-23, 28-29

The most obvious reading of this text is that Omri reigned for 12 years. The first 7 years he reigned alone. Then he appointed his son Ahab as his co-regent, and they reigned together for 5 years before Omri died leaving Ahab to reign on his own.

Someone might object that we are told that Omri died before being told that Ahab became king. But if you read through all of the books of Kings and Chronicles, you will see that reigns of kings are routinely presented as a unit. That is, we are told the story of the life of king #1, then the life of king #2, then the life of king #3, etc. When two kings' lives overlap – as routinely happens when one is from the northern kingdom of Israel and the other from the southern kingdom of Judah – we are still given one complete life first, then the other. So the statement that Omri died might simply be summing up his life before we turn to the life of Ahab.

James Ussher, a prominent historian of the 1600's who was absolutely fanatical about determining exact dates of historical events, preferred a different theory. He said that the "31st year of Asa" is the year that Omri finally won the civil war with Tibni. Thus the 12 years includes the time when he was only king of part of the country, while the 7 years is the time that he ruled all of it. [Ussher, James. *Annals of the World.* 1658. para 501-507. (Pierce translation, 2003, p. 70)] I think this theory requires a more awkward reading, but I am reluctant to argue with so eminent an authority as Ussher.

7.8. Rainy Days

The Bible describes a drought during the time of Elijah. According to Kings, the drought lasted less than 3 years. "And it came to pass after many days that the word of the LORD came to Elijah, in the third year, saying, 'Go, present yourself to Ahab, and I will send rain on the earth.'" [1 Kings 18:1] It then goes on to describe Elijah meeting Ahab, announcing the end of the drought, and the rain quickly following, all within at most a few more days.

But James says, "Elijah was a man with a nature like ours, and he prayed earnestly that it would not rain; and it did not rain on the land for three years and six months." [James 5:17]

So Kings says the drought lasted less than 3 years, while James says it lasted more than 3 years.

The idea here is that if this happened "in the third year", that must mean less than three years. "In the first year" would mean within one year, etc.

It is true that James says the drought lasted 3½ years. No disagreement there.

Let's look at the statements about time as the story is told in 1 Kings:

> And Elijah the Tishbite, of the inhabitants of Gilead, said to Ahab, "As the LORD God of Israel lives, before whom I stand, there shall not be dew nor rain these years, except at my word. [1 Kings 17:1]

Then we're told that Elijah went to the Kerith Ravine and lived by a brook there. Then:

And it happened after a while that the brook dried up ... [1 Kings 17:2]

So he moves to Zarephath where he lives with a widow and her son.

... and she and he and her household ate for many days ... [1 Kings 17:15]

Now it happened after these things that the son of the woman who owned the house became sick. [1 Kings 17:17]

We go through the story about the widow's son, then:

And it came to pass after many days that the word of the LORD came to Elijah, in the third year, saying, "Go, present yourself to Ahab, and I will send rain on the earth." [1 Kings 18:1]

So we have the sequence of events: Announces the drought, "after a while" goes to Zeraphath, manages to get along there "for many days", "after these things" the widow's son gets sick, "after many days ... in the third year" goes back to see Ahab.

To find a contradiction here, you have to assume that when 18:1 says "in the third year" that this means in the third year after the drought began, that is, the third year after 17:1.

But when someone gives a chain of events like this and states a relative amount of time, if they do not explicitly link that time to an event, we normally understand them to mean "after the event I last mentioned". Like, suppose I said, "Bob graduated college, then five years later he met Sally and they got married. Six years later they moved to Pennsylvania." The normal understanding of that paragraph would be that Bob and Sally moved to Pennsylvania six years after they got married, not six years after he graduated college.

The most natural reading here is that Elijah went to see Ahab in the third year after the event described in the immediately preceding sentence, namely, the incident with the widow's son. The critic not only rejects the common-sense reading that the time should be relative to the immediately preceding event, but then leaps to the assumption that it is relative to the start of the drought. How does he know it's not the third year after Elijah moved to Zeraphath, or the third year after

Ahab became King, or the third year after any of the events in the preceding 16 chapters?

All the times other than that "third year" are casual "many days", "after a while", etc. so there's no way to add up the times. If the amount of time Elijah spent at Kerith and Zeraphath was six months or so, then the total length of the drought would be consistent with 3½ years.

When we are reading any book – not just the Bible, but any book – if there are two possible ways to interpret the words on the paper, and one leads to a contradiction while the other leads to consistency, we normally assume that the writer intended the way that does not lead to a contradiction. Even if this reading is not the most obvious or natural reading, we generally assume the reading that makes sense over the one that doesn't.

In order to find a contradiction here, the critic has to take an unnatural reading, and then insist that this is what the writer meant rather than the more natural reading. He has to go out of his way to interpret the words to make a contradiction.

7.9. Two Genealogies of Jesus

The Bible gives two contradictory genealogies of Jesus. Both say that Jesus' father was named Joseph, but Matthew 1 says that Joseph's father was Jacob, while Luke 3 says that Joseph's father was Heli.

This is admittedly a puzzling problem. Christians have offered two explanations.

The most common theory is that Matthew's genealogy is that of Joseph, while Luke's is that of Mary. The explanation is that as Joseph was not the natural father of Jesus, that Jesus' true descent came through Mary and not Joseph.

Personally I find this explanation unsatisfying, because nothing in the text justifies it. It does not say "Jesus was the son of *Mary*, the *daughter* of Heli", but "Jesus was the son (it was supposed) of *Joseph*, the *son* of Heli".

Eusebius gives another explanation in his book *History of the Church*, written circa AD 320. He says that he got his information from Julius Africanus, who in turn got it from members of Jesus' family.

Namely: Jesus' father Joseph was adopted, sort of. Matthew gives the genealogy through his natural father, while Luke gives the legal genealogy.

Under Hebrew law, under certain circumstances if a man died without having any children and his widow remarried, the first child by the second husband was considered for legal purposes to be the child of the first husband. He would inherit the first husband's land and property and would carry on his family name.

Eusebius points out that this is consistent with the text. Matthew says that "Jacob begot Joseph", while Luke says "Joseph the son of Heli". "Begot" indicates physical descent, while "son of" could be physical but could also be legal. Note that Matthew carefully does not say that Joseph begot Jesus, but rather that Joseph was the husband of Mary, who gave birth to Jesus.

7.10. O Little Town of Galilee

Everyone is familiar with the story of Jesus being born in Bethlehem. This story is in Luke. But John says that Jesus was born in Galilee.

I think most are familiar with the story in Luke about Jesus being born in Bethlehem: no room in the inn and being born in a stable and so forth. Matthew briefly states that Jesus was born in Bethlehem without discussing the circumstances. (See Luke 2 and Matthew 2.)

The critic contrasts these with this paragraph from John:

> Therefore many from the crowd, when they heard this saying, said, "Truly this is the Prophet." Others said, "This is the Christ." But some said, "Will the Christ come out of Galilee? Has not the Scripture said that the Christ comes from the seed of David and from the town of Bethlehem, where David was?"
>
> John 7:40-42

But wait! Did John say that Jesus was born in Galilee? No, he says that "some said" that Jesus was born in Galilee.

Why did they say this? Matthew clearly tells us that several years after Jesus' birth his family moved to Nazareth, a town in Galilee. "And he came and dwelt in a city called Nazareth, that it might be fulfilled which was spoken by the prophets, 'He shall be called a Nazarene.'" [Matthew 2:23]

So Matthew tells us that some people said that Jesus was from Nazareth in Galilee. John tells us that some people said that Jesus was from Nazareth in Galilee. It is difficult to see what the contradiction is here.

This brings us back to the same issue raised in 7.4. In order to find a contradiction, you have to assume that the writer agrees with everything that he quotes someone else as saying. That is very obviously not true here: The whole point of this paragraph in John is that he is saying that some people said that Jesus was the Messiah and others said that he was not. Obviously John cannot believe that both groups are correct. Obviously from the larger context John agrees with those who said that Jesus is the Messiah.

It is true that John does not specifically say anywhere in his biography that Jesus was born in Bethlehem. Either John didn't think it mattered whether Jesus fulfilled this prophecy, or he knew or believed that Jesus was from Bethlehem and so he did fulfill the prophecy.

John quotes many other prophecies and shows how Jesus fulfilled them. Several times he says that something had to happen so that the prophecy would be fulfilled. It is hard to believe that John would suddenly dismiss this one prophecy as irrelevant or unimportant when he placed so much importance on all the others.

John was the last of the four Gospels to be written. He might have taken it for granted that his readers would know that Jesus was born in Bethlehem and not find it necessary to point this out, just as someone writing a biography of George Washington today might not feel any need to explain that he was president.

But whatever John knew or assumes the reader knew, he does not say that Jesus was born in Galilee, but only that "some said" he was born in Galilee. There is no contradiction with Matthew and Luke.

7.11. O Little Town of Nazareth

Where was Christ born? According to the Gospels, he was habitually called "Jesus of Nazareth." The New Testament writers have endeavored to leave the impression that Nazareth of Galilee was his home town. The Synoptic Gospels represent that thirty years of his life were spent there. Notwithstanding this, Matthew declares that he was born in Bethlehem in fulfillment of a prophecy in the Book of Micah. ... Luke has it that his birth occurred at Bethlehem ...

Gauvin, Marshall. *Did Jesus Christ Really Live?*
1922

This criticism is related to the previous in that both are about Jesus' birth place, but the details of the criticism are different.

The criticism here is that the Gospels contradict, one place saying that Jesus was from Nazareth, another saying that he was from Bethlehem.

The claim isn't even that one Gospel writer contradicts another. All four Gospels refer to Jesus as being from Nazareth. Matthew and Luke clearly state that Jesus was born in Bethlehem.

Matthew's account clears up any thought that this is a contradiction:

> Now after Jesus was born in Bethlehem of Judea ... behold, an angel of the Lord appeared to Joseph in a dream, saying, "Arise, take the young Child and His mother, flee to Egypt, and stay there until I bring you word; for Herod will seek the young Child to destroy Him." ... Now when Herod was dead, behold, an angel of the Lord appeared in a dream to Joseph in Egypt, saying, "Arise, take the young Child and His mother, and go to the land of Israel, for those who sought the young Child's life are dead." ... And he came and dwelt in a city called Nazareth, that it might be fulfilled which was spoken by the prophets, "He shall be called a Nazarene."
>
> Matthew 2:1, 13, 19-20, 23

That is, the explanation for this claimed contradiction is that Jesus performed the amazing miracle of "moving".

According to Matthew, Jesus was born in Bethlehem, then his family moved to Egypt when he was about two years old, then a few years later they moved to Nazareth in Galilee.

I was born in New York, lived in Ohio for most of my life, and recently moved to Michigan. So when people ask me where I'm from, sometimes I say "New York", sometimes I say "Ohio", and sometimes I say "Michigan".

It's not at all surprising, then, that sometimes Jesus is said to be "from Bethlehem" and sometimes "from Nazareth". Jesus is far from the only person in the history of the world who could be said to be "from" more than one place.

7.12. Jesus Hometown

Matthew says that Jesus grew up in Egypt, while Luke says that he grew up in Nazareth. Matthew does not say anything about Mary and

Joseph living in Nazareth before the birth of Jesus. He says they lived in Bethlehem. Luke does not mention any trip to Egypt. The Gospels contradict each other on many points about where Jesus was born and grew up.

Matthew says that Jesus was born in Bethlehem without giving any explanation of how his parents came to be there. Some time after he was born the family moved to Egypt to escape from Herod. After Herod died they moved to Nazareth.

There are some indications in Matthew's account that the family stayed in Bethlehem for a year or more. He says that the Magi (Wise Men) came to visit Jesus in a "house" in Bethlehem, not in the stable, and that Herod sought to kill all the babies in Bethlehem "two years old and under". We don't know if Herod knew the exact date of Jesus birth. Maybe the two years was a broad range just to be safe. But either way, this indicates the family was in Bethlehem for more than the few days that might have been required to register for the census.

Luke says Mary and Joseph lived in Nazareth before they were married. They went to Bethlehem for the census (see issue 5.15), where Jesus was born. He mentions a trip to Jerusalem but there is no indication that they stayed there for longer than a brief visit. Then they "returned to Galilee".

All this only leads to a contradiction if you assume that Matthew and Luke intended to give a full account of everywhere that the family lived and traveled. But neither claims to be doing that. Both are giving very quick summaries of Jesus' birth and early years. Each takes only a page or two to tell its version of the first 30 years of Jesus' life, clearly not enough to give more than a few highlights.

So yes, Matthew doesn't say that Mary and Joseph lived in Nazareth before Jesus was born. But he doesn't say they lived in Bethlehem. He doesn't say anything about where they lived. He just says that Jesus was born in Bethlehem. My children were all born in Dayton, Ohio, but I never lived in that city. Our doctor recommended a hospital there, so that's where we went.

A simple reading of Luke might lead you to jump to the conclusion that the family moved to Nazareth promptly after Jesus was born. But just because he doesn't mention the time in Egypt doesn't mean he is denying that it happened. He just didn't have anything in particular to say about it.

Critics often say that the Bible contradicts itself because one account of a person's life or a certain time period doesn't mention an incident that another does. But this is not a contradiction; this is just two different perspectives. Suppose you read two biographies of some non-Biblical person, say George Washington. Would you expect that both would include exactly the same set of incidents from Washington's life? That there would not be one, single thing that he did that was mentioned in one and not the other? Each biographer has his own perspective. In the case of Washington, one writer might emphasize his political contributions and another his military career. One might strive to show how his career was shaped by his childhood education, while another emphasizes the influence of his peers and associates. Etc. Each will bring in events that contribute to understanding the point he is trying to make.

It's the same with the Gospels. Each writer has his own perspective on the life of Jesus, different things that he wants to emphasize, and so they mention different incidents, or describe the same incidents in different ways.

This is not a contradiction. This is just a different perspective.

7.13. Tax Collector's Name

What was the name of the tax collector who followed Jesus? Mark and Luke say that his name was Levi, but Matthew says that his name was Matthew. [Matthew 9:9, Mark 2:14, Luke 5:27]

It's unlikely that we are talking about two different people. In both cases the tax collector invites Jesus to his house for a dinner party with other tax collectors. The Pharisees ask why he associates with sinners, and Jesus replies that "it is not the healthy who need a doctor, but the sick". It is fairly unlikely that two tax collectors would both invite Jesus to a dinner party, and more unlikely still that the Pharisees would make the same challenge to Jesus about both parties, especially given that Jesus had a clever and pointed comeback.

The explanation is simple: Matthew and Levi are two names for the same person.

The idea of one person being called by two or more names is hardly radical. Most Americans have three names – first, middle, and last. There are lots of people in the Gospel who we are told had more than one name. Just among the twelve disciples, there are Simon Peter, Lebbaeus Thaddaeus, and Judas Iscariot. If you count the "son of"'s – which in English would be a last name, like "John*son*" – and nicknames that have a "the" in them, there are also James son of

Zebedee, John son of Zebedee, James son of Alphaeus, Thomas the Twin, and Simon the Zealot.

The name Matthew is from the Hebrew name "Matisya", meaning "gift of Jehovah". The Gospels tell us that Jesus gave Simon the nickname of Peter, meaning "Rock", like the American nickname Rocky; and that he gave James and John the collective nickname "Boanerges", meaning "Sons of Thunder". "Gift of Jehovah" might be the sort of nickname Jesus would give. In that case, Levi could be his given name and Matthew a nickname.

Note that it is Matthew who calls this person Matthew, and the other two writers who call him Levi. (John never mentions Matthew – or Levi – by name.) This contributes to the theory that Matthew is a nickname given by Jesus: someone writing about himself might embrace a nickname given him by Jesus, while others writing about him would use his legal name.

But this is speculation. His parents might have named him "Matthew Levi" at birth, or one or the other could be a nickname he picked up somewhere along the line.

Conclusion

Given the commonness of people with more than one name, the idea that Matthew and Levi could be two names for the same person is hardly a startling idea. This supposed contradiction is easy to resolve.

Side Note: Strange Bedfellows

Among Jesus' disciples are both "Matthew the tax collector", i.e. tax collector for the Roman government; and "Simon the Zealot", the Zealots being a revolutionary group trying to overthrow the Roman government. That would be a little like a modern group of twelve men including both an FBI agent and a member of Al Qaeda.

7.14. Sermon Venue

Both Matthew and Luke describe a sermon in which Jesus said, "Woe to you, scribes and Pharisees, hypocrites!", and condemned the Pharisees for being scrupulous about rituals while ignoring the important principles of justice and mercy. [Matthew 23:1-36, Luke 11:37-52] But Matthew says that Jesus gave this sermon while preaching to a crowd [Matthew 23:1], apparently at the temple (Matthew 24:1 tells us that Jesus "departed from the temple" after saying this), while Luke

says that he gave this sermon while at a private dinner with a group of Pharisees and lawyers. [Luke 11:37]

We find Jesus quoted using a catch phrase – "Woe to you, scribes and Pharisees, hypocrites" – and preaching some similar themes – rituals versus practical morality – in two different Gospels. But the events are clearly described as happening at two different places.

The critic concludes that the similarities in the two speeches mean this must be two accounts of the same speech, and the differences must therefore be contradictions. This criticism is based on the assumption that someone engaged in public speaking could not possibly use the same slogan in two different speeches, nor talk about similar ideas on two different occasions.

Anyone who has ever watched a political campaign can quickly see that this is not true. When a politician finds that a slogan goes over well with the crowds, he routinely uses it over and over.

Similarly, it would be quite surprising if a public figure gave a speech in which he said that some issue was extremely important and people really needed to do something about this ... and then he never mentioned it again. Politicians, reformers, preachers, and other public figures routinely hit on the same issues over and over again.

I used to give talks at churches and civic groups. I rarely spoke at the same place twice – once they heard me once, they no doubt concluded that they never wanted a boring speaker like me back again – so I basically had one speech that I just gave over and over again. Every time I gave it I'd make some changes to improve it and update it with new information. But I recycled many of the same words repeatedly.

In this case, while the speech in Matthew and the speech in Luke have many similarities, they also have many differences. Most obviously, I have been referring to both as "sermons" and "speeches", but this is not quite accurate. Matthew is describing a public speech. Luke is describing a conversation at a dinner. In Matthew Jesus stands in front of a crowd and gives a speech. In Luke people around the dinner table ask Jesus questions and he answers. They ask hostile questions and he gives strongly-worded answers – this was not a pleasant conversation. But it was a conversation and not a speech. Perhaps it would be more accurate to call it an argument.

What starts the conversation in Luke is that the Pharisees challenge Jesus for failing to wash his hands before eating – a religious ritual to them, not just a sanitary practice – and he replies by blasting them for placing great importance on these little rituals while ignoring fundamental moral principles like justice and caring for the poor. In Matthew he makes this same point as a straight statement rather than in a question-and-answer format.

Conclusion

There are a number of places in the Gospels where Jesus is quoted in two different places saying the same or similar words, but where other details in the accounts, like where he was or who he was speaking to or when he said it, are clearly different. Critics point to these as contradictions, like the Gospel writers couldn't get their stories straight on just where or when he made a certain speech. The easy resolution to such claimed contradictions is that Jesus talked about the same subject more than once, and used the same slogan or catch phrase in multiple speeches. Public speakers do this all the time.

7.15. Jesus' First Sermon

Where did Jesus preach his first sermon? According to Matthew, it was on a mountain. Indeed, Christians call it the "Sermon on the Mount". [Matthew 5:1-2] But according to Luke, it was on a plain. [Luke 6:17-20]

Like issue 7.14, to make a contradiction here you have to assume that the event described in Matthew is the same event described in Luke.

The two sermons have similarities. Both include Beatitudes ("Blessed are the meek ..." etc.), loving your enemies, and a warning against judging others. But that's about it. The sermon in Matthew talks about being salt and light, about marriage and divorce, and about taking oaths and giving to charity, all things not mentioned in Luke. The sermon in Luke has a series of "woes" after the "blessings" and a warning about the blind leading the blind, things not mentioned in Matthew. In other circumstances we might theorize that it was a long sermon and Matthew and Luke are each giving excerpts, i.e. different excerpts. But combining the differences in content with the differences in location makes it clear that this is not two accounts of the same sermon, but two different sermons in which Jesus happened to re-use a few themes.

The critic implies that Matthew and Luke each refer to the speech they relate as "Jesus' first sermon". Thus if they are describing the same sermon, we have a contradiction about the place, while if it is two different sermons, then we have a contradiction about which was first. But neither Matthew nor Luke says it is "Jesus' first sermon". In fact both indicate that this is *not* Jesus' first sermon. Matthew 4:17 says "From that time Jesus began to preach", and then relates several other incidents before getting to the Sermon on the Mount in chapter 5. That is, during chapter 4 he preached other sermons that Matthew did not quote. Luke 4:15 says "And [Jesus] taught in their synagogues" and relates various incidents before getting to the sermon in chapter 6. Again, during chapter 5 Jesus preached other sermons that Luke does not quote. Neither the Sermon on the Mount nor the "sermon on the plain" was Jesus' first sermon.

Jesus just used some of the same themes in more than one sermon.

7.16. Jairus' Daughter

Both Matthew and Luke relate the story of Jesus healing Jairus' daughter. According to Matthew, when Jairus approached Jesus his daughter was already dead. But according to Luke, she was sick but still alive.

Here are the two accounts. Both are interrupted by another story about another healing. For brevity and clarity I put "[other healing]" at the point of interruption in each.

> While He spoke these things to them, behold, a ruler came and worshiped Him, saying, "My daughter has just died, but come and lay Your hand on her and she will live." So Jesus arose and followed him, and so did His disciples. [other healing] When Jesus came into the ruler's house, and saw the flute players and the noisy crowd wailing, He said to them, "Make room, for the girl is not dead, but sleeping." And they ridiculed Him. But when the crowd was put outside, He went in and took her by the hand, and the girl arose.
>
> Matthew 9:18-25

And behold, there came a man named Jairus, and he was a ruler of the synagogue. And he fell down at Jesus' feet and begged Him to come to his house, for he had an only daughter about twelve years of age, and she was dying. [other healing] While He was still speaking, someone came from the ruler of the synagogue's house, saying to him, "Your daughter is dead. Do not trouble the Teacher." But when Jesus heard it, He answered him, saying, "Do not be afraid; only believe, and she will be made well." When He came into the house, He permitted no one to go in except Peter, James, and John, and the father and mother of the girl. Now all wept and mourned for her; but He said, "Do not weep; she is not dead, but sleeping." And they ridiculed Him, knowing that she was dead. But He put them all outside, took her by the hand and called, saying, "Little girl, arise." Then her spirit returned, and she arose immediately.

Luke 8:41-55

In some cases of stories that are similar but not identical, we may resolve contradictions by theorizing that they are two different incidents that happen to be similar. But that is extremely unlikely here. There are too many similarities between the stories: a ruler, a daughter, the interruption for another healing – and that story is very similar in both accounts – Jesus telling the relatives that the girl is not dead but sleeping, and Jesus taking her by the hand. It's hard to imagine that all these details happened on two separate occasions. It's the same incident.

Luke tells us that the daughter is "dying", but then a couple of sentences later he tells us that messengers arrive saying that the daughter is "dead". Matthew just tells us that the daughter is "dead". It may simply be that Matthew is leaving out details to make the story more concise. Instead of telling us that first the man said this and then later he said that, he simply tells us the last thing he said.

The catch to this is the interruption in the story for the other healing. In Matthew, we are told that the daughter is dead *before* the other healing. In Luke, we are not told until *after*. Perhaps Matthew does not consider the timing of the "interlude" important. Is such a discrepancy a "contradiction" or just a "simplification"?

Matthew tells us that the man said his daughter was dead. Luke does not quote the man, but states as a fact that she was dying. What the father said and the reality are not necessarily the same thing.

But if the messengers didn't arrive to tell the man that his daughter was dead until after the other healing, why did the man say she was dead before? Was he mistaken? Was he exaggerating or supposing the worst?

In the end, I admit I find this one slightly troubling. Yes, both accounts do say that the daughter was dead, but one tells us this before the interruption and the other after. Maybe this is just skimming over details, maybe it is a tiny technicality, but it is difficult to reconcile with absolute literal inerrancy.

7.17. How Many Angels?

How many angels were at Jesus tomb? Matthew and Mark say only one, but Luke says there were two.

> [T]here was a great earthquake; for an angel of the Lord descended from heaven, and came and rolled back the stone from the door, and sat on it. ... But the angel answered and said to the women ...
>
> Matthew 28:2, 5

> But when they looked up, they saw that the stone had been rolled away, for it was very large. And entering the tomb, they saw a young man clothed in a long white robe sitting on the right side; and they were alarmed. But he said to them ...
>
> Mark 16:4-6

> Then they went in and did not find the body of the Lord Jesus. And it happened, as they were greatly perplexed about this, that behold, two men stood by them in shining garments. Then, as they were afraid and bowed *their* faces to the earth, they said to them ...
>
> Luke 24:3-5

There is not necessarily any contradiction here. Matthew and Mark do not say that *only* one angel was present, it is just that they only mention one.

Suppose I told you, "I went to the hardware store yesterday and saw a clerk in the plumbing section, who told me where to find the water heaters." Would you conclude that I mean that this man was the only clerk in the store? A more likely interpretation is that he was the only clerk in the store relevant to my story.

Indeed, suppose I told you, "I went to Chicago where I saw my friend Bob." Would you conclude that I must mean that Bob was the only person in the entire city of Chicago? Far more likely is that Bob was the only person relevant to whatever I am trying to say. I don't mention the millions of others, not because I am unaware they exist, but simply because I am not concerned about them right now.

As Luke gives a specific number – two – it is fair to conclude that two angels were present. Matthew and Mark only mention one because he is the only one relevant to their account.

Mark's point is to tell us what the angel said to the women. So he says the angel was there and then relates what he said. Unless he had some reason to think that the number of angels was important, there was simply no reason to bring the other one up.

Matthew also wants to relate that it was the angel who moved the stone from the entrance of the tomb. Apparently it was this same angel who spoke to the women. Mentioning the second angel could have been an awkward digression. Like, "An angel of the Lord descended from heaven, and came and rolled back the stone from the door, and sat on it. And by the way there was another angel standing to the left of him. And then the angel – the first one I mean, the one on the right – said to the women ..." He apparently had no specific reason to mention the second angel, so he didn't interrupt the narrative with unnecessary information.

No writer can possibly include every detail. He has to choose those he considers important and relevant. The fact that one reporter of an event includes a detail that another omits isn't a contradiction.

7.18. Peter's Source

How did Simon Peter find out that Jesus was the Christ (Messiah)? According to the Gospel of Matthew, it was miraculously revealed to him by God. But according to the Gospel of John, his brother Andrew told him. Contradiction.

> He said to them, "But who do you say that I am?" Simon Peter answered and said, "You are the Christ, the Son of the living God."
> Jesus answered and said to him, "Blessed are you, Simon Bar-Jonah, for flesh and blood has not revealed *this* to you, but My Father who is in heaven.

Matthew 16:15-17

He [Andrew] first found his own brother Simon, and said to him, "We have found the Messiah" (which is translated, the Christ).

John 1:41

To make a contradiction of this one must assume that a person must come to a conclusion based on only one piece of evidence. But for such a serious question as, "Is this person the Son of God?" you would not simply accept the word of one person, not even your brother. He could be deceived himself.

Suppose you ask a friend, "Why did you invest in XYZ Corporation?" and he replies, "My stock broker told me it was a good investment." Later you hear someone else ask him the same question and he answers, "I studied their past performance on the Internet."

Would you say that he is contradicting himself and one of these statements must be a lie? Both answers might well be true. Perhaps his stock broker told him it was a good investment, and then he checked out the history to verify it. Or perhaps he was reviewing the history of various stocks, this one looked good, and then he asked his broker about it.

Either way, on important decisions a rational person doesn't leap to a conclusion based on the first thing he hears. He collects an array of information and looks for corroboration.

When Peter's brother told him he had found the Messiah, Peter did not just accept that as the final word on the matter. Nor would we expect him to. Peter went to see Jesus himself. He likely studied the scriptures and prayed for guidance. Andrew was the human agent who introduced him to Jesus, but God had to work on Peter's mind and heart to convince him that this was true.

It is not a contradiction to say that someone had more than one reason for his beliefs.

7.19. Bearing a Cross

Who carried Jesus' cross? John says that Jesus carried it himself; but Matthew, Mark, and Luke say that a man named Simon carried it for him.

Then [Pilate] delivered Him to them to be crucified. Then they took Jesus and led Him away. And He, bearing His cross, went out to a place called the Place of a Skull, which is called in Hebrew, Golgotha.

John 19:16-17

And when they had mocked Him, they took the robe off Him, put His *own* clothes on Him, and led Him away to be crucified. Now as they came out, they found a man of Cyrene, Simon by name. Him they compelled to bear His cross.

Matthew 27:31-32

The most likely explanation is that Jesus carried his own cross part of the way, and then Simon carried it the rest of the way.

Jesus had been severely beaten. While the Romans normally made the victim carry his own cross, Jesus may have been physically unable to do so. The likely scenario is that the soldiers initially required Jesus to carry his own cross, but then he collapsed, and so they grabbed a random passer-by and forced him to carry the cross the rest of the way.

Note that Matthew says the soldiers found Simon "as they came out". If we read back a few verses, they had taken Jesus to the Praetorium, which was basically the barracks or headquarters for the soldiers, so this is presumably what they were "coming out" of. They didn't bring Simon into the Praetorium for him to carry the cross. They found him along the way. So Simon couldn't have carried the cross from the beginning of this trip: someone else must have carried it part of the way. While Matthew (and Mark and Luke) don't specifically tell us that Jesus carried his own cross part of the way, examination of the text shows that Simon did not carry it the whole way, so someone else must have carried it at least out of the building. They don't tell us who, but nothing in the text is inconsistent with it being Jesus himself.

Meanwhile, John tells us that Jesus was carrying the cross as he "went out". It doesn't say that he carried it the whole way, just as he "went out", i.e. out of the Praetorium.

We could question why Matthew doesn't mention Jesus carrying the cross part of the way and John not mentioning Simon. But the fact that a writer doesn't mention every detail of an event doesn't mean that he is denying that these things happened. This is why reporters and historians like to get multiple accounts of the same event: One witness may mention facts that others do not.

In each case, the writer recorded what he thought was important or relevant to the points he was trying to make. Different writers had different perspectives and so thought different things relevant.

Critics often leap on these sort of omissions and call them contradictions. But a little thought will tell us that no writer can possibly tell us every single thing that happened. The fact that two people reporting on the same event do not relate stories that are word-for-word identical is hardly proof that one or both are lying.

Think of any time you've told someone else about an event you participated in or witnessed. (It may be something of earth-shaking importance like a crucifixion, or something trivial like an amusing mishap you suffered on vacation.) Did you relate every single thing that happened? Did you identify every person present, every word that was said, every move that was made, the weather conditions and room lighting, etc.? Surely not. You mention the things that were interesting or important.

Suppose I told you that on my family's last vacation, we went to a Civil War museum, where we saw such-and-such interesting exhibits. Later my daughter tells you that on our last vacation, we visited grandma. Would you conclude that one of us must be lying or seriously confused? But the explanation for this "contradiction" is simple: On our last vacation, we went to visit grandma, and while there we took a day to visit a Civil War museum.

When Christians offer this sort of common-sense explanation for claimed contradictions, the critic often replies, "Well, I suppose it *could* have happened that way. But you're just saying that to try to reconcile these two stories. You have no proof that that's what happened." Well, of course I have proof. We have two accounts of the same event. One mentions that A happened; another mentions that B happened. The logical conclusion is that both A and B happened. I freely admit that I am saying this to reconcile the two stories. When we have two accounts of the same event, the logical thing to do is to see if there is some way to reconcile them.

Conclusion

In this case, the alleged contradiction is easily resolved. Matthew says that Simon carried the cross. John says that Jesus carried the cross. A little study of Matthew shows that Simon did not carry it the whole way. So the logical conclusion is that Jesus carried it part of the way and Simon carried it the rest of the way.

7.20. Words on the Cross

According to the Gospels, when Jesus was crucified Pilate had a plaque attached to the cross identifying the person on it. While the four Gospels all agree that there was such a plaque, they give contradictory statements about the text on it:
Matthew 27:37 - "THIS IS JESUS THE KING OF THE JEWS"
Mark 15:26 - "THE KING OF THE JEWS"
Luke 23:38 - "THIS IS THE KING OF THE JEWS"
John 19:19 - "JESUS OF NAZARETH, THE KING OF THE JEWS"

In modern English, we make a careful distinction between an exact quote and a general statement of what the original said. If I were to write, "Abraham Lincoln said, '87 years ago our ancestors started a new country based on principles of freedom and equality'", you might well reply that I am misquoting Lincoln, that those were not his exact words at all. But if simply removed the quote marks and wrote, "Abraham Lincoln said that 87 years ago our ancestors ... " etc., no one would challenge my statement. If you use quote marks, we expect what is inside them to be an exact quote. If you say "he said that ...", then your statement will be accepted as accurate as long as it at least generally reflects what the speaker said.

Ancient Greek did not have quotation marks. They did not make this distinction. Quotation marks that you see in a modern English translation of the Bible were inserted by the translator. So no quote that we see in the Bible should be understood to be necessarily the exact words of the original. We should not read this as, "And the inscription said, quote, The King of the Jews, end quote", but rather more like, "And the inscription said that this is the king of the Jews."

Luke tells us that the inscription was written in three languages: Greek, Latin, and Hebrew. [Luke 23:38] The writers may be quoting from different language versions. For example, Matthew was a tax collector for the Romans, so he must have known Latin. Luke was a doctor in an age when Greece was the center of medical learning, so he must have been proficient in Greek. All four Gospel writers knew Hebrew so Mark or John could be quoting that language.

The Gospels are all written in Greek. If one or more of the writers is quoting the Latin or Hebrew version of the inscription, he would have had to translate it into Greek. It is not a surprise if two translations of the same text differ slightly. A difference like "The King of the Jews" versus "This is the King of the Jews" is the sort of difference we would expect to see between different translations.

Finally, we might note that even in English, just because something is in quotes does not necessarily mean that it is a word-for-word quote, especially if the writer is quoting spoken words. Reporters routinely clean up quotes by dropping out "umms" and "ahs", fixing grammar errors, and so on.

Conclusion

Ancient Greek did not distinguish exact quotes from paraphrases. No quote in the Bible can be assumed to be the exact words of the original. The minor differences between the quotes of the plaque in the Gospels are not a contradiction, but simply different writers paraphrase or translation of the original text. As the original was in three different languages, they may be quoting different languages.

7.21. Centurion's Words

According to the Gospels, the centurion stationed by the cross was incredibly impressed by Jesus. But they contradict each other over what he said. According to Mark he said, "Truly this man was the Son of God." [Mark 15:39] But Luke reports that he said, "Certainly this was a righteous man." [Luke 23:47]

Jesus was on the cross for over six hours. There was plenty of time for the centurion to have said more than one sentence.

It takes an awfully pedantic critic to say, "Aha! You say that last night you said to your wife, 'Let's watch TV', but she claims you said, 'What's for dinner?' Clearly one of you is lying!"

7.22. Naming the Field of Blood

How did the place where Judas died come to be known as the "Field of Blood"? Matthew says it is because it was bought with blood money, i.e. the money that the priests gave to Judas in exchange for betraying Jesus. [Matthew 27:8] Acts says that it was because of the bloody death that Judas died there. [Acts 1:19]

This criticism assumes that there can be only one reason why a place got its name, and everyone must agree on the reason.

But it is easy to imagine people agreeing that something is a good name for a place, while disagreeing about the reason. Some could have said, "We should call this place the Field of Blood because it was bought with blood money" while others said, "Well, Field of Blood is a good name, but I was thinking of the bloody death that Judas fellow died here." If person A made up a name, and then person B misunderstood the reason for that name and went around telling people a different reason, so that some people thought the name came from person A's reason while others thought it came from person B's reason, who is to say what the "real" reason for that name was?

There are plenty of modern examples. For example, I can find at least three different stories for how the town of Protection, Kansas got its name: 1. It was a place relatively safe from Indian attack because of a nearby fort. 2. Three rivers that bounded the town gave protection from prairie fires. 3. For a protective tariff supported by the town during the 1884 election campaign.

Like many criticisms, this one assumes that there can be only one reason why people did something. In real life, people often have many reasons for any given action. Different people who do the same thing could certainly have different reasons for it.

7.23. Paul's Invented Quote

In Acts 20:35, Paul told people to "remember the words of the Lord Jesus, that He said, 'It is more blessed to give than to receive.'". But there is no record in the Gospels of Jesus ever saying any such thing. Either Paul just invented this quote, that is, he is lying, or the Gospels are in error for not giving this quote.

Nowhere do the Gospels claim that they are relating every single word Jesus ever spoke. Elementary logic would tell us that no biography can be that comprehensive. If the Bible told us everything Jesus did and said over the course of 30 years, it would take 30 years to read it. There is nothing surprising in someone quoting a statement from Jesus not mentioned in the Gospels.

This statement is consistent with quotes from Jesus found in the Gospels. There are many places in the Gospels where Jesus talks about showing compassion for the poor.

Paul may have attended a sermon by Jesus where he heard this, or he may have heard it from one of Jesus' followers after his conversion, or he may have read it in Q or some other early written source (see 4.1).

In any case, the idea that Jesus may have said things that are not recorded in the Gospels is not a mystery. It is inevitable from the plain fact that the Gospels are not thousands of pages long.

8. Miscellaneous

8.1.　You Think You're Right

You Christians think you are right and everybody else is wrong. There are many religions in the world. No one has a monopoly on truth.

Christians believe that we are right. Well, duh. Whenever people disagree, each side thinks that they are right and the others are wrong. What else could you possibly think? Who would say, "I believe X is true, but I know it's really false"?

I don't claim that Christianity has a "monopoly on truth" if by that you mean an assertion that the Bible is the only source of truth. I don't know of any Christian who says that. There are many ways that one can gain knowledge, from scientific experiments and historical research to intuition to listening to gossip. Some are more reliable than others. Many produce truth at least some of the time. What I do claim is that Christianity is true, and when others make claims that contradict Christianity, that they are wrong.

If I made such a statement about almost any other set of ideas, no one would consider it remarkable. If I say that I believe that the theory of gravity is true and that any contradictory theory is false, no one would accuse me of being arrogant and intolerant. Okay, there's not a lot of disagreement about that one today. Suppose a medical researcher says that he believes that a certain disease is caused by a virus, and that competing theories held by other medical researchers, say a theory that it is caused by a genetic defect, are false. You may agree with him, you may disagree, you may admit that you do not understand the evidence well enough to have an opinion. But you would not denounce him as arrogant and intolerant just because he has come to a conclusion.

People who like to think of themselves as "tolerant" often say that all religions are just different roads to God and that all are equally true. Even the briefest examination of different religions will show that this cannot be so. Jews, Christians, and Moslems say that there is one God. Hindus say that there are many Gods. Atheists say that there is none. We can't all be right. Zero, one, many: that would seem to cover all the possibilities. One of us must be right and the others wrong.

Suppose we held a convention to discuss all these different religions that are just different roads to God. Would you ask for directions to that convention? Why? It shouldn't matter whether you head north, south, east, or west. They are all just different roads to the same place, right? In real life, of course, they aren't. If you want to get to a building whose address is 42 Foobar Road, you pretty much have to take Foobar Road to get there.

It is, of course, conceivable that some statements from Christianity are true and others are false; that some statements from Islam are true and other false; etc. Perhaps Christians are right when they say that Jesus is the Son of God, while Moslems are right when they say that Mohammed is God's greatest prophet. But Christians cannot be right when they say that Jesus is the Son of God, if Moslems are right when they say that he is not. One could fairly say that each claim must be debated individually. But each claim is still true or false, and I am not ashamed to say that I have come to a conclusion about some debated questions.

If a person declares that something he believes is true because he said so and he doesn't need any logic or evidence, and if you disagree you are a moron, and there should be laws to silence anyone who tries to spread different ideas, *that* would be arrogance and intolerance. I will gladly join you in criticizing people who take such a position. I suppose you could find some Christians who take this position. But you can also easily find atheists who take this position about their beliefs.

Let me make clear that "he won't listen to any counter-arguments" is not at all the same thing as "he is not convinced by my counter-argument". Just because someone does not agree with you does not make him intolerant or an idiot. He may simply find your arguments unconvincing. Even if your argument is, in fact, completely valid and he is wrong to dismiss it, that does not mean he has not considered it.

A funny thing about this criticism of Christianity is that the people who make it routinely do exactly the same thing themselves. Atheists love to say how arrogant Christians are for insisting that they are right and all other beliefs are wrong. But I've never heard an atheist say, "I don't believe there's a God, but I could be wrong." Or, "I'm an atheist, but you know, those Christians have a lot of good points." No, atheists say that they are right and Christians are wrong. Then when we say the same about our position, they are (or pretend to be) shocked and offended.

People who boast about their tolerance are some of the most intolerant people around. They show no tolerance for people who disagree with them. They are quick to denounce anyone who says that tolerance is not the greatest good or the only good. If someone says, for example, that he believes homosexuality to be morally wrong, the champions of tolerance instantly denounce him as a "homophobe". What happened to their respect for all beliefs? Why doesn't the belief that homosexuality is morally wrong deserve equal respect with the belief that all sexual preferences are morally neutral?

You say that it is wrong to impose your beliefs on others. Okay, great. Then don't impose that belief on me.

You say that there is no such thing as "truth"? Oh. Is that statement true?

If you believe that Christians are wrong about some claim that we make, fine, let's examine the evidence. But don't condemn us for saying that we believe what we believe, for saying that the things that we claim are true are in fact true. That's just silly.

8.2. Who Created God?

Christians claim to solve the problem of how the universe came to exist by saying that it was created by an all-powerful God. But this just moves the problem back a step. Where did this God come from?

If God created everything, who created God?

First Cause

People who offer this rebuttal to the Christian argument from First Cause apparently haven't understood the argument.

I really shouldn't say "the Christian argument", as it goes back to at least Aristotle in the 4th century BC. This is, of course, well before Christianity existed, and I don't think there is any evidence that Aristotle ever read the Hebrew Scriptures. Nevertheless, Aristotle argued that there must be a "first cause", "first principle", or "prime mover" behind all things:

> But evidently there is a first principle, and the causes of things are neither an infinite series nor infinitely various in kind. For neither can one thing proceed from another, as from matter, ad infinitum (e.g. flesh from earth, earth from air, air from fire, and so on without stopping), nor can the sources of movement form an endless series (man for instance being acted on by air, air by the sun, the sun by Strife, and so on without limit). Similarly the final causes cannot go on ad infinitum,-walking being for the sake of health, this for the sake of happiness, happiness for the sake of something else, and so one thing always for the sake of another.
>
> Aristotle. *Metaphysics*. Book 2, Part 2.

To put it in modern language, everything we see in the universe has some cause. Aristotle talked about "cause" in multiple senses of the word. To move, something must be pushed or pulled – whether by physical contact or by magnetism or whatever. For an object to come into existence, it must be made of materials that existed before. For an intelligent being to act, he must have some motivation. Etc. Aristotle called forces, pre-existing materials, or intelligent beings acting, all examples of "causes".

Suppose we look at some event, say, the book fell off the shelf. What caused this? Someone must have put it on the shelf in the first place. How did this person get the strength to put it on the shelf? He got energy from food. How did he get the food into his body? He ate it. Where did the food come from? It grew somewhere. How did it grow? Energy from the sun acted on chlorophyll. Where did the sun get its energy? Etc. For every action we can trace a cause, and a cause for that cause, and a cause for the cause for the cause, etc. (Of course there are often multiple causes for any given event, and any cause could trigger multiple results.)

But all of this had to start somewhere. There had to be some cause that was different from all other causes in that it itself was not caused by anything else, a "First Cause". If not, how did the whole process get started? There must have been something "moving yet unmoved", as Aristotle put it.

To put it in terms of creation, thing A may have been created by thing B, and thing B was created by thing C, and so on. But at some point we must come to an object or being which was not created, but which exists independently of all other things, and which was the prime source for the creation of everything else. We call this thing "God".

To respond to this argument by demanding, "But then who created God?" misses the whole point. The conclusion of the argument is that there must have been something which was not created, which somehow exists with no prior cause.

Aristotle, along with most Christian thinkers, goes on to conclude that this being must be "eternal". This is an often misunderstood word. As used by the ancient Greeks and by ancient and medieval Christian thinkers, it does not mean "lasting forever", but rather "existing outside of time". If God exists outside of time, then he is not subject to the problem of needing a cause that came "before" him, because there is no such thing as "before" to a being outside of time.

Improbability

One critic gives this rebuttal to the argument from First Cause:

> A God capable of continuously monitoring and controlling the individual status of every particle in the universe cannot be simple. His existence is going to need a mammoth explanation in its own right.

> Dawkins, Richard. *The God Delusion.* New York: 2006. p. 149

Indeed, this critic devotes an entire chapter of this book to rebutting the argument from First Cause, which he calls the "argument from improbability". By "improbability" here he refers to the creationist argument that it is wildly improbable that anything organized and complex beyond a trivial level could arise by chance.

But, the critic replies, any "God" capable of creating stars and planets and living things must itself be highly organized and complex. Thus God is even more improbable then the things his existence is supposed to explain. If it is improbable for an amoeba to spring into existence by chance, surely it is even more improbable for God to spring into existence by chance. God is far more complex than an amoeba.

Well, of course! I don't know any Christian scholar who would say differently. No one is saying that our reply to evolution is that the planets and living things did not evolve by chance ... but God did! Again, the critic has either missed the point of the argument from First Cause or he is conveniently ignoring it. The whole point of the argument is that there must be some being whose existence is very different from that of the beings we routinely encounter, in that it is *not* the result of a predictable, materialistic chain of causation. It must be fundamentally different: causing yet uncaused, moving yet unmoved. It must either exist outside of time as we know it, so that it cannot be said to have a "beginning"; or in some other way be uncaused.

The Christian says that the universe and life did not evolve, but were created by God. The evolutionist then replies that this answer is unsatisfactory because it does not explain how God evolved. Even if you don't understand the argument from First Cause, surely you do not honestly suppose that the creationist thinks that God evolved.

Objection 1: No beginning

There are coherent objections that can be made to the argument from First Cause.

One is to propose that the chain of causation extends infinitely into the past. Every cause has some prior cause, with no beginning. The universe has no beginning.

Modern physics shoots this theory down. One of the fundamental principles of physics is that the universe is, slowly but surely, running down. This is called "entropy". It is so fundamental that it is one of the three "Laws of Thermodynamics". The first law of thermodynamics is conservation of mass/energy: Matter and energy can neither be created nor destroyed, though they can be converted into each other. The second law is entropy: While energy cannot be destroyed, it tends to become evenly distributed. As useful work requires different energy levels – water will flow downhill but not uphill, heat will flow from hot areas to cold areas, etc. – this means that energy becomes less and less usable. The third law basically says that entropy cannot be reversed. As a wit once put it, the Laws of Thermodynamics amount to: 1. You can't win. 2. You can't even break even. 3. You have to play the game.

What does this have to do with the argument from First Cause? If entropy is slowly but surely increasing, then after some finite amount of time, all the energy in the universe would become unusable. Physicists refer to this as the "heat death" of the universe, because all energy would be converted to unusable, evenly-distributed heat. We don't know exactly how long this would take, but we know it would happen eventually. In fact we are able to do useful work, so this clearly has not yet happened. Thus, the universe cannot be infinitely old.

The critics come up with many fanciful solutions to this problem, like theorizing that there has been an infinite series of universes, and that as each universe dies it somehow magically gives birth to a new universe. I can't prove this wrong, but there is zero evidence that it is true. Amusing speculation, perhaps. Or a desperate attempt to salvage their dogma in the face of contradictory scientific evidence.

Objection 2: Godless Cause

Another objection is to concede that there was a First Cause but to deny that this First Cause is the same thing as God. Aristotle was not quite prepared to say that the First Cause was God:

> (1) God is thought to be among the causes of all things and to be a first principle, and (2) such a science [of creating things] either God alone can have, or God above all others.

Aristotle. Metaphysics. Book 1, Part 2.

That is, Aristotle thought God is or could be *a* first cause, but he was not necessarily *the* first cause.

The argument in its most basic form does not begin to prove that the First Cause is the God of the Bible. Many atheists postulate a "Big Bang" that created the universe, and while I've never heard one of them describe it in the language of the First Cause, that is basically what they are claiming.

Aristotle went on to say that the being or force that created good, beauty, and reason must have possessed a knowledge of good and beauty and reason, else where did these things come from? It is difficult to see how a random, chaotic explosion could produce order, never mind good and beauty and reason.

Objection 3: Rebuttal from Ignorance

Others object that the idea of a being that exists outside of time is incomprehensible and impossible. Christians reply that the existence of such a being is the inevitable result of logic, and therefore the fact that you find this concept difficult to understand is irrelevant. Much of modern physics, from black holes to quarks to relativity, challenges our intuition and comprehension, but this is not grounds for saying that it must be false.

Conclusion

There are rational objections that can be made to the Argument from First Cause. But ignoring the logic and the explanation and re-asking the original question isn't one of them.

It is no answer to say that a being as complex as God could not have evolved by chance. No one is saying that God evolved. The whole point of the argument is exactly the opposite.

No one claims that this argument proves the existence of the God of the Bible. It doesn't tell us everything that God is. It does tell us something he isn't. He doesn't have a cause, like most beings that we are familiar with. The argument proves that there must be a being which causes but is uncaused. This sounds an awful lot like what we mean when we say "Creator God".

Some try to extend the argument to deduce attributes of God. For example, the creator of things that are good and beautiful must have knowledge of goodness and beauty. By studying the universe he created, we can come to conclusions about the nature of God.

8.3.   Born Gay

The Bible says that homosexuality is morally wrong. But today we know that there is a genetic basis to homosexuality. Some people are simply "born gay". It is completely natural, people born this way have no control over it, and there is nothing wrong with it. Condemning homosexuality is out-dated and intolerant.

We could find fault with the science behind this claim.

The critics claim this argument got major scientific corroboration from a study done by researcher Simon LeVay and published in the journal *Science* in 1991. He claimed that he had found a biological basis for homosexuality.

The gist of the researcher's paper was this: He obtained tissue samples from the brains of 41 dead bodies in Los Angeles and New York. He classified 19 of the corpses as homosexual men, 16 as heterosexual men, and 6 as heterosexual women. He found that a certain section of the brain known as "the third interstitial nucleus of the anterior hypothalamus", or INAH3 for short, was about twice as large in the heterosexual men as in the homosexual men, and about the same size in the homosexual men as in the heterosexual women. Therefore, he concluded, a smaller INAH3 causes a man to become a homosexual.

There are some highly questionable things about the way this study was done.

One, the sample size was far too small to be meaningful for a serious biological study. His findings could simply be the normal random variation that you always find among small groups of people. This point is especially telling given that he did *not* find that all the homosexuals had smaller INAH3's than all the heterosexuals. Rather, the numbers for both groups overlapped. It was simply the average that was higher for the heterosexuals.

The researcher studied other parts of the brain as well, and found no statistically significant differences. For example, he says that he expected INAH2 to also show differences, but it did not.

Pick 40 or so friends or co-workers. Divide them into groups based on something that is unlikely to have a physical basis. Say, Democrats, Republicans, and whatever other parties may be represented. Then observe hair and eye color, measure height and shoe size, find month of birth, and in general take all the statistics and measurements you can think of. It is quite likely that, with such a small group, sooner or later you will come up with some measurement, purely by chance, that turns out to be different for the Democrats than for the Republicans. If you take enough measurements on a small enough sample, sooner or later you'll find one that fits any desired theory

Two, the researcher never explained in his paper how he determined the sexual orientation of the dead people. Presumably the dead people were not able to tell him. In his paper he refers to the heterosexual males and females as "presumed heterosexual", which rather implies that he had no definitive source of information.

All of the homosexuals in this study died of AIDS. This naturally brings up the question: Is a smaller INAH3 associated with homosexuality, or is it a symptom of AIDS? Countering this argument, six of the heterosexual men also died of AIDS, and the researcher reports that the size of INAH3 in the heterosexual AIDS victims was not significantly different from that in the heterosexual non-AIDS victims. Of course now we're down to sample sizes of ten and six.

Three, let's suppose it really is true that INAH3 is smaller in homosexual men than in heterosexual men. That still leaves the question of cause and effect. The critics simply assume that a small INAH3 causes a man to be a homosexual. It is equally plausible that the reverse is true: that being a homosexual causes a man to have a small INAH3. Suppose we measured the size of the biceps of weight-lifters versus that of non-weight-lifters. I expect that we would find that weight lifters have bigger biceps. Would it be fair to therefore conclude that being born with big biceps causes a man to become a weight lifter? It would be much more sensible to conclude that regular weight-lifting increases the size of the biceps. If the INAH3 section of the brain is, indeed, associated with male heterosexual activity, then it is not at all hard to imagine that it might grow and develop as one "exercises" it by performing male heterosexual acts.

Thus, I have serious doubts about the scientific validity of this research. But it doesn't matter. Christians already agree with the premise – if not the details of the genetics behind it, at least with the basic idea.

The Bible says that homosexuality is sin. The Bible also says that we are all born sinners.

Behold, I was brought forth in iniquity,
And in sin my mother conceived me.

Psalm 51:5

> For all have sinned and fall short of the glory of God.
>
> Romans 3:23

I don't know if anyone is specifically "born gay". But we are all born sinners. The only question for the Christian is whether we are born predisposed to specific sins, or only to sin in general.

The Christian and the critic agree that human beings are born with a natural tendency to do things that the Bible calls "sin". Where we disagree is the conclusion to be drawn from this fact. The critic says that because some people are born gay, therefore there is nothing wrong with being gay. The Christian says that this does not follow at all.

Suppose that it was proved that some people are "born racists", that there is a "Klan gene", and that if someone is born with this gene, he will inevitably grow up to be a racist. Would we conclude that it is unjust to criticize racists because they can't help how they were born, and that we should accept racism as just another "alternative lifestyle"? It would be disappointing if we learned that some people will be racists no matter what anyone tries to do about it, and that the problem of racism is virtually unsolvable. But this would not make racism good. Likewise, even if it were proven that some people are "born gay", this would not make it good.

Conclusion

The Bible says that all human beings are born sinners. Among the things it calls sin are stealing and adultery and greed and homosexuality. So according to the Bible, some people will be "born gay". The critic says that scientific research proves that some people are "born gay". So the critic examines the world around him and discovers that what the Bible says and what he observes in the world are the same. Therefore, he declares, the Bible has been proven wrong.

8.4. Heavy Rocks

If God can do anything, can he make a rock so heavy that he can't life it? If he can't make such a rock, then there is something he can't do. If he can make this rock and then can't life it, then there is something he can't do. Either way, there is something God can't do.

This criticism takes a general statement, "God can do anything", and attempts to apply it strictly literally.

Language is not that simple. It's like the paradox, "All generalizations are false." That statement is a generalization. Is it false? The Bible itself points out that not all generalizations it contains should be taken as having no exceptions. In 1 Corinthians 15:27-28 Paul quotes from Psalms to tell us, "For [God] 'has put everything under [Jesus] feet.'" But then he explains, "Now when it says that 'everything' has been put under him, it is clear that this does not include God himself, who put everything under Christ." [(NIV)]

The straight answer to the question is: No, he can't.

Technically, the question is meaningless in light of elementary astronomy. Is this rock bigger than the Earth? If so, what does it mean to "life it"? How do you speak of lifting something that is bigger than the Earth? Lift it above what? Physicists define "weight" as the gravitational force exerted on an object. An object not within the gravitational field of a planet (or some other massive body) does not have any weight, so it cannot be said to be "heavy".

Presumably God is able to lift any rock smaller than the Earth, because he was able to move the Earth and put it into its orbit. Any rock bigger than the Earth is pretty much by definition not a "rock" but a "planet". To make the question applicable to a planet, it could be reworded, "Can God make a *planet* so *massive* he can't *move* it?" Clearly, the answer is no. No matter how big it is, the application of force would move it by some amount. Any given force might move it by only a small amount, but it will move it.

So are there things God can't do? Yes. This bothers me not at all. See 8.5 for more things that God can't do.

8.5. Evil in the World

The Bible claims that God is good, and that he is all-powerful. So why does he allow evil in the world? Why doesn't he put a stop to it immediately?

The existence of evil in the world proves that there cannot be a good and all-powerful God.

What Religion?

Are we talking about Biblical Christianity here, or about some other religion?

Nowhere does the Bible say that God prevents all evil in the world. Quite the contrary, the Bible repeatedly says that the world is full of evil. "The imagination of man's heart is evil from his youth."

[Genesis 8:12] "There is none righteous, no, not one." [Romans 3:10] "[Men are] filled with all unrighteousness, sexual immorality, wickedness, covetousness, maliciousness; full of envy, murder, strife, deceit, evil-mindedness; they are whisperers, backbiters, haters of God, violent, proud, boasters, inventors of evil things, disobedient to parents, undiscerning, untrustworthy, unloving, unforgiving, unmerciful." [Romans 1:29-31]

If there is some religion that teaches that their God does not allow any evil in the world, and so the world is full of loving people with no hint of hatred or violence or deceit or greed ... that would be a nice religion to believe in, I guess. But you only have to look at the world around you to see that it isn't true. There is evil everywhere. Just like the Bible says.

People who make this argument are making up their own religion, a religion that flatly contradicts the Bible. Then they look at the world around them and see that it isn't true. And so they declare that the Bible has been proven wrong. Excuse me? The Bible says that the world is full of evil. We look around us and we see that the world is full of evil. So on what point was the Bible proven wrong?

Maybe you'd like to believe in a God who prevents all evil. But that's not how the God of the Bible says he operates. If there is some religion that teaches that, it's not Christianity.

Impossible Things

So why doesn't God work that way? Why doesn't God just end all the evil in the world? If God can do anything, then he could do this.

As noted in issue 8.4, a statement like "God can do anything" is very general, and we should be cautious about taking it literally. Christians believe that God is all-powerful, so he can do anything that requires power. But it's easy to think of problems that don't require power.

Suppose I asked you to make a triangle with four sides. Barring some trick answer – redefining the words or some such – it can't be done. But suppose you had four really strong men to help. Then could you do it? What if you had a nuclear power plant to supply the energy? This sounds like a joke or a riddle. Making a four-sided triangle is a logical impossibility. Having more power doesn't help.

God gave people free will. He considers free will a great good, perhaps the greatest good.

If people have free will, then some will choose to do evil. It is a logical impossibility to have free will and also to always do what God wants, just like it is a logical impossibility to make a four-sided triangle. More power doesn't help.

God could, I suppose, instantly strike someone dead the instant he does anything evil. But then the evil-doer would have no opportunity to repent. Plus, if people knew that any violation of God's rules would result in instant death, that wouldn't be real freedom.

Suppose the government said that you have absolute freedom of speech. You can say anything you want. Of course, if you say anything critical of the government, you will be immediately arrested and tortured. But you are completely free to say anything you like. Would that be real freedom?

Conclusion

There is evil in the world because God allows people free will. It's that simple. The Bible clearly and repeatedly states that the world is full of evil, so the fact that there is evil in the world cannot possibly be said to prove the Bible wrong. The Bible is very obviously correct on this point.

8.6. Cruel God

The God of the Bible, and especially the Old Testament, is too judgmental and harsh. I can't believe in a God like that.

As one atheist friend of mine put it, "The God of the Old Testament doesn't exist for me."

Critics point to places in the Bible where they believe that God was too tough on some sin, dishing out excessive punishments for minor offenses, or for acts that the critic doesn't think are morally wrong at all. Or they will say that God is cruel to the victims of sin by being too soft on the villain. For example, they say that God was cruel in ordering the Canaanites to be wiped out, and was cruel in the opposite way for failing to ban slavery.

We could reply by trying to defend God point by point. The Canaanites engaged in wide-spread sexual immorality, and then disposed of the resulting children by child sacrifice, burning innocent babies to death. I can't imagine a crime more deserving of capital punishment than torturing a child to death.

God put limits on slavery. Perhaps he knew that this was the best that could be achieved given that he allows people free will. (See issue 8.5.) Jesus said that God hates divorce but nevertheless allowed it because he knew that a complete ban would not be obeyed, so regulating it was more productive. Maybe he followed the same principle with slavery.

But all this is beside the point. Whether or not you or I approve of something that the Bible says God did has nothing to do with whether it really happened.

The critic says that he does not approve of things God did in the Bible. Therefore, he does not believe in this God. That is, he declares that this God does not exist.

We could discuss exactly what the Bible says about slavery and what it means. But such a discussion would be irrelevant to the question of whether what it says is true. No one questions that slavery has existed in the world. There was slavery in the United States until 1865. Does the critic insist that, because he does not approve of slavery, that therefore the history books that say slavery existed must be wrong? If the history books say that the Confederacy condoned slavery, and slavery is evil, then therefore the Confederacy must never have existed.

Of course that reasoning doesn't follow at all. Reality does not change just because you don't like it.

The critic here is saying that not only does he demand that God live up to the critic's standard, but if God refuses, the critic condemns him to non-existence. Retroactively.

Unfortunately for the critic, he just doesn't have that power. He cannot wish God or anyone or anything else out of existence. Reality does not bend to the critic's whim.

Conclusion

Let's grant the critic's premise for the sake of argument. Suppose he is correct that the God of the Bible is cruel and capricious. A rational response might be to seek ways to escape or hide from his anger. It might even be rational to sink into despair at the thought that an all-powerful being seeks to do us harm. An irrational response is to declare that it cannot be true because you don't like it.

Note that this criticism contradicts 8.5. First the critic complains that God is too lenient because he fails to punish evil quickly and harshly enough. Then he complains that God is too cruel because he punishes evil too quickly and too harshly.

8.7. No Judgment

People who have had near death experiences consistently report that the after-life is a place of love and acceptance. They report no "judgment day". This disproves the Bible's claim that some go to Heaven and some to Hell.

Of course this criticism is the opposite of the criticism of issue 2.27. Atheists argue that near-death experiences (NDEs) should be dismissed as frauds or hallucinations. People of a New Age or liberal theological bent accept NDEs as real, but then see them as proving Christianity wrong on the nature of the after-life.

Some aspects of NDEs match the Bible very well. People describe meeting the souls of friends and relatives who had died before them. They describe having a "spiritual body" that can pass through walls, etc., like Jesus post-resurrection body, and like the body described by Paul in 1 Corinthians 15.

Other aspects of NDEs do not match anything in the Bible. One of the most prominent and widely-known elements is the part about going through a dark tunnel. I don't know of any place in the Bible that says that at the time of death we pass through a tunnel. Of course there's nothing in the Bible that says we don't. But it's not something one would have predicted from the Bible.

One key element has been pointed to as contradicting the Bible. In his classic book, *Life after Life*, Dr. Moody reported that all the NDE patients he interviewed had positive experiences. They meet a "being of light" who radiates total love and acceptance. This being guides them through a review of their life. But this review is not a judgment of whether the person's life was good or bad. Rather, when the person did fail, the being of light indicates how he should learn from this experience and do better next time. [Moody, Dr. Raymond, MD. *Life after Life*. Covington, Georgia: 1975. pp. 45, 73, et al]

Curiously, though, later in the same book he says that people who had attempted suicide consistently had unpleasant experiences, in which it was made clear to them that suicide was not an acceptable action. [Moody, p. 103] What are we to make of this apparent contradiction? Did Dr. Moody's wishes for what he hoped the after-life was like cloud his reporting? Or is there some way to reconcile these statements?

In *Life after Life*, Moody says that no one reported seeing a Heaven or Hell. In his follow-up book, *Reflections on Life after Life*, written two years later, Moody says that he has collected additional accounts, and that some of these people report seeing a "city of light" as well as a "realm of bewildered spirits". He describes the latter as being a gray area where people wander aimlessly and morosely. The implication is that they are people who are unable to separate themselves from the present life. None of his subjects report actually being in the realm of bewildered spirits themselves, but only of having observed others there. [Moody, Dr. Raymond. *Reflections on Life after Life*. Covington, Georgia: 1977. pp. 152-158.] The city of light is consistent with Biblical descriptions of Heaven, or the New Jerusalem of Revelation. His realm of bewildered spirits is only vaguely comparable to Biblical statements about Hell: there is no fire and no torment. It sounds more "unpleasant" than "terrifying".

Dr. Maurice Rawlings, another NDE researcher, found many cases of unpleasant experiences. He concluded there were almost as many frightening experiences as pleasant ones. But he observed that while people who had frightening experiences would talk about them immediately after being revived, they were unable or unwilling to talk about them later. Rawlings was a practicing physician who regularly treated dying people, and thus regularly talked to people right after they were resuscitated. Moody, Kubler-Ross, and other researchers normally spoke to patients days, weeks, or even years later. Rawlings speculated that the unpleasant experiences were so frightening that people's minds blocked them out. [Rawlings, Dr. Maurice. *Beyond Death's Door*. New York: 1978, p. 45 et al] Another theory consistent with Rawlings findings is that people may be unwilling to talk about them once the initial panic reaction is past: the experience is too unpleasant and too revealing of their own corrupt nature.

Rawlings descriptions of frightening experiences are consistent with Biblical descriptions of Hell. People report darkness, fire, fear, and despair.

Finally, as we are talking about the supernatural, we must consider what God would allow and what Satan would attempt.

God gives us only limited information in the Bible about life after death. He makes clear that Heaven is a wonderful place and Hell is a terrible place, but beyond that, he says little. Perhaps he has a reason for this. Perhaps it is all beyond our comprehension. Perhaps he doesn't want us to be too preoccupied with details about Heaven and Hell. Whatever the reason, if he didn't want to tell it all 2000 years ago, the same reasons may hold true today, and so God is only allowing limited information to be revealed.

Moody mentions that some people have suggested to him that NDEs are deceptions by Satan. He quickly dismisses this idea by saying that NDEs are filled with light and love and people routinely come away from them with a renewed commitment to show love to others. Satan would not want to encourage love and caring. [Moody, p. 112] But this is naïve. Presumably Satan's primary goal is to keep people out of Heaven. If he can do this by giving them a small measure of love and happiness here on Earth, in exchange for an eternity of separation from God and suffering, this would be a good plan from his point of view. If he can convince people that there is no judgment, that as long as you are a "good person" and try hard that everything will be fine, this would be a very viable strategy.

So why do accounts of near death experiences not report a judgment, Heaven and Hell? Perhaps Dr. Rawlings is right that people who saw Hell couldn't deal with the experience and blocked it out. Perhaps people who returned from death did not get to the point of judgment. Perhaps unsaved people who have pleasant NDEs are being deceived by Satan. Or some combination of these.

9. Conclusions

9.1. Multiplication of Charges

At this point some may say, "Oh, so you have an answer for everything. But there are so many problems with the Bible that all your excuses start to wear thin. If there were just one or two criticisms and you managed to offer alternative explanations, I might accept that. But there are dozens, hundreds! If even a few of these charges are true, your precious Bible collapses."

To this I reply, Multiplication of charges is not evidence. When critics bring up charge after charge, and every charge proves to be unsubstantiated, unprovable, or demonstrably false, is the logical conclusion that the Bible is full or errors but we just can't quite pin them down, or that the critics are desperately searching for some charge that will stick?

Suppose that Senator Hamner and Senator Nale are engaged in a heated political campaign. At one point Hamner charges that Nale has sexually harassed female campaign workers. Nale denies the charge, and many women who have worked for him come forward to say that he has always behaved properly to them and that they cannot imagine there being any truth to these charges. A reporter asks Hamner about this rebuttal, and he says, "Well, maybe I can't prove that, but you know, Nale took a bribe from XYZ Corporation in 1986!" Nale denies this charge as well. He points out that he was not even involved in politics in 1986 so no one would have any reason to bribe him. He produces bank records to show he had no unusual income in that period. Hamner replies, "Okay, maybe he didn't do that one. But he did lots of other terrible things. I have proof that Nale is a thief! I can't show it to you now, but trust me, I have absolute proof. And he may have killed someone once! And he tore the tag off a mattress! And ... and ... and ..."

At this point, would you conclude that with all these charges that Hamner is hurling at Nale, some of them must be true? Or would you conclude that Hamner is a liar hurling out one false charge after another?

Let me clarify that I do not mean to imply that that all criticisms of the Bible are deliberate lies. I am sure that many people who question the Bible are honestly seeking the truth.

What I do mean to say is that when it comes to logical arguments, you cannot make up for quality with quantity. Two weak arguments do not make one strong argument. An argument that is not backed up by solid evidence has a net weight of zero. Ten times zero is still zero. A million times zero is still zero.

9.2. Extraordinary Evidence

There is a common pattern to discussions between Christians and their critics that goes something like this: The Christian presents some evidence that supports the Bible. He points out that this evidence is at least as strong as that used to support many propositions that are widely accepted. For example, the Christian will point out that there are more surviving historical references to the resurrection of Jesus Christ than to Julius Caesar's conquest of Gaul, so as historians routinely accept that Caesar really did conquer Gaul, by the same standard they should accept that Jesus really rose from the dead. The critic replies that he cannot rebut this evidence per se, but he demands a higher standard of proof for Christian claims, on the grounds that, "Extraordinary claims require extraordinary evidence".

There is some plausibility to this slogan. If someone tells you that there is a red Toyota in the parking lot, you probably just take his word for it. If he tells you there is a 40-foot stretch limo in the parking lot, you may go to the window to see for yourself. If he tells you there is a flying saucer from the planet Altair 4 in the parking lot, even seeing it for yourself would likely not be enough. Just because there's a saucer-shaped object in the parking lot doesn't prove it's from another planet.

But is this a valid standard, or just laziness? If "extraordinary claims require extraordinary evidence", who decides what is "extraordinary", and how much evidence will be sufficient? At best, "extraordinary claims" means "claims that are inconsistent with prevailing theories". That is, any challenge to the status quo. At worst, "extraordinary claims" means "claims that contradict my prejudices".

If you tell an ardent Democrat that a Republican is guilty of corruption, he may readily believe it on little evidence, because that's what he expects of Republicans. Tell him that a fellow Democrat is guilty of corruption, and he wants to see solid proof. Ditto if it's the other way around.

If someone has spent years studying and thinking about a subject, I certainly don't expect him to change his mind based on one newspaper story claiming contradictory evidence. It is fair to say, "I know a hundred facts backing up my position. I can't refute this claim off the top of my head, but I'm not going to throw out conclusions I've come to over many years based on one claim that I haven't even had an opportunity to examine."

But the critic often goes far beyond this. He makes clear that *no* amount of evidence will convince him. He knows that there is no God, that miracles are impossible, etc. So it doesn't matter what evidence the Christian produces to prove these claims. He knows they are impossible, so any evidence *must* be a mistake or a hoax or flawed in some way. It just has to be.

If a critic insists that he knows the truth on philosophical grounds before he examine the evidence, then what is the point of even looking at the evidence? He is not going to be convinced no matter what. This attitude makes rational discussion impossible. It is fundamentally anti-scientific: Evidence and experiments are unnecessary because the critic already knows the truth.

It's rather ironic that the critic often describes this anti-scientific attitude as "scientific". He likes to think that the ideas he believes in are scientific, so refusing to listen to contrary evidence must be scientific.

Do extraordinary claims require extraordinary evidence? Or are claims that contradict what I want to believe to be dismissed regardless of the evidence?

9.3. Impossible Standards

Often when a critic brings up some claimed error or contradiction in the Bible and the Christian offers a resolution, the critic relies, "Well, yes, *maybe* it really happened that way. You can always come up with some hypothetical scenario to explain away the problem. But you can't prove it."

That is, the critic insists that if one interpretation of the available facts is bad for the Bible, and another interpretation upholds the Bible, we must assume that the anti-Bible interpretation is the truth. If the critic can think of any scenario, no matter how far-fetched or crazy, under which the Bible would turn out to be wrong, then that must be the preferred interpretation. If the Christian says otherwise, he's desperately clinging to unproveable dogma.

Forget the Bible for a moment. Suppose you were reading any book, the instruction book for your newest electronic toy or a history book or whatever. You find a statement that doesn't seem to be true. Perhaps you try to follow the instruction book and the gadget doesn't seem to work. Is the likely explanation that the book is full of errors? Or is it more likely that you have misunderstood it?

When reading any book, people normally work on the assumption that the book is accurate until there is strong evidence otherwise. If the book makes a statement that could be interpreted in two ways, and the first way leads to a contradiction while the second does not, we assume the writer intended the second way. If a statement sounds like an error but we can imagine a reasonably plausible set of facts that would make it true, we give the author the benefit of the doubt and assume that something like that is probably what happened. If the book mentions an event that we cannot corroborate from other source but which doesn't contradict other sources, we work on the assumption that it happened like the author says.

But the critic insists that we take the opposite approach with the Bible. If there are two ways to reasonably interpret a sentence in the Bible and the first leads to a contradiction or an error while the second does not, the critic insists that we must read it the first way. Like, when we read in the Bible that there was a census at the time of the birth of Jesus, and then we read in Roman histories of a census at about this same time, we can't prove that this is the same census, but it certainly sounds plausible. But the critic insists that we assume that it is *not* the same census, and then insists that there is no other record of this census. If the Bible mentions an event that we do not find in secular history, the critic insists that we must assume it never happened. Instead of giving the Bible the reasonable benefit of the doubt, the critic insists that the Bible must be assumed to be in error or lying unless we can prove 100% that it is true.

I don't make this demand of atheists' books. I refuse to accept it as the standard of evaluation for the Bible.

9.4. A Review of Weak Arguments

I can't hope in any book of modest length to cover every attack made on the Bible. However, we see some of the same flawed arguments show up repeatedly in many of these attacks. If you see an attack that has not been covered here, you might consider some of these common flawed arguments. Could it fall into any of these categories?

(I don't claim that such a list of logical fallacies is original. People have been making lists like this since at least Aristotle. This list is just tailored specifically to criticisms I often hear of the Bible.)

9.4.1. Because I Said So

Critics often present their intuition as proven fact.

For example, they will declare that miracles are impossible. How do they know? Witnesses say that they have seen a miracle. Obviously the witness must be mistaken or lying, because miracles are impossible. It doesn't matter what evidence is offered, it is irrelevant, because the critic knows that miracles are impossible.

The critic's intuition trumps all facts or evidence.

In its extreme form, the critic resorts to simple ridicule. "Do you know that there are people so stupid that they actually believe in Noah's Ark? Ha ha ha!" Substitute any number of things from the Bible for "Noah's Ark". The critic presents no evidence why this idea is so absurd. The fact that he finds it unbelievable is supposed to be all the evidence we need.

Ask yourself: What evidence or logic does the critic offer to back up his claim? Are we supposed to believe it because he has proven that it is true, or just because he says so? Beware of any argument that hinges on "I just can't believe that …"

9.4.2. Appeal to Authority

The critic says that you must believe something because a respected authority says it is so. This is just a step up from "because I said so". Here it is, "because a high muck-a-muck said so".

For example, critics will often say "historians say that ..." or "all scientists agree that ..." Such broad generalizations are rarely true. On these controversial subjects, there are serious scientists or historians or whatever experts on both sides.

Even if it is true that most scientists agree, do they agree because they have all carefully studied the evidence and found it persuasive? Or do they agree because it fits their preconceived ideas? Science has certainly proven to be a very effective means of gaining knowledge. But just because someone is a scientist doesn't mean that everything he says is based on scientific evidence.

What makes the scientist being quoted an authority? Scientists have accomplished some amazing things, from discovering how gravity works to inventing the computer. But the people who make these anti-Bible arguments are rarely people who have made important discoveries themselves. The argument here comes down to: Great scientists like Newton and Pasteur and von Braun accomplished amazing things, I call myself a scientist, therefore you should believe me like you would believe Newton and Pasteur and von Braun. The funny thing about this is that Newton and Pasteur and von Braun were all Bible-believing Christians. The critic is trying to claim the authority of these great men in order to contradict everything that these same men said.

Ask yourself: Why does this authority believe this? If he was convinced by solid evidence, show me the evidence and I'll have to believe too. If he doesn't have evidence, then his belief is just an unsubstantiated opinion. Either way, the fact that the authority believes it is irrelevant. What matters is the evidence.

9.4.3. Non-Sequiturs

The critic presents some facts that the Christian concedes are true, but then draws a conclusion from them that does not follow.

Just because someone's facts are accurate doesn't mean that his conclusions are. Just because you can't refute his claimed facts doesn't mean that you have to concede the argument. Critics often present facts that Christians agree with completely, but we draw totally different conclusions from them.

Ask yourself: So what? Suppose we grant everything the critic has said up to this point. Does that prove what he claims it proves?

9.4.4. Contradiction by Coincidence

If two stories from the Bible are similar but also have important differences, the critic insists that the similarities prove that they must be two accounts of the same event, and the differences are therefore contradictions, proving that one or both accounts are wrong. The possibility that the two stories are about two different events that happen to have similarities is ignored or discounted.

Ask yourself: Is this one story or two? How do we know that both stories describe the same event?

9.4.5. Contradiction by Omission

Critics claim there is a contradiction when the Bible gives two accounts of the same event, and one mentions details that the other does not.

Suppose you saw two stories in the news about a political rally, and one said that Senator Jones gave a speech and another said that Governor Smith gave a speech. Before you concluded that the stories contradicted each other, you would consider the possibility that there might have been more than one speech.

If one account said that Senator Jones gave a speech and another account said that he was invited but refused to come, that would be a contradiction. Just not mentioning him, even if he was there, is not a contradiction.

When it comes to the Bible, if one account mentions a person being present and a different account doesn't mention that person, this is held up as a contradiction.

Ask yourself: Is this really a contradiction, or just two accounts that include different details?

9.4.6. Words in Your Mouth

The critic invents some idea and claims that Christians believe this. Then he demonstrates that it isn't true, and thus he has proven Christianity false. The Christian points out that he doesn't believe this, or that the Bible says no such thing, and the critic replies that now he is trying to weasel out.

The critic invents his own religion which he calls "Christianity". Then he proves this religion false, and claims to have disproven Christianity.

Ask yourself: Does the Bible really say that? Or is this just something that the critic assumes Christians say or thinks Christians are likely to say?

9.4.7. Guilty Until Proven Innocent

If something in the Bible could be taken in two ways, and one of those ways leads to a contradiction or implausibility while the other way leads to no problem, the critic assumes that the problem reading is what is intended.

When we are reading a book looking for information rather than looking for things to attack, we try to interpret the text in the way that makes the most sense, rather than going out of our way to come up with readings that lead to problems. Suppose I am reading, say, the instruction manual for my latest computer toy, and I find a statement that seems to contradict a previous statement or that just can't be true. My first reaction is not to declare that this book is full of errors. Rather, I study the book and try to figure it out. I consider whether I misunderstood the writer's intent the first time I read the statement, or if there is some other resolution.

But when it comes to the Bible, the critic always insists on the interpretation that leads to trouble.

Ask yourself: If a statement in the Bible leads to a contradiction or doesn't seem to be true, is this interpretation the most natural reading? Is it the only plausible reading?

9.4.8. Secular Trumps Christian

If some evidence comes to light that contradicts the Bible or appears to contradict the Bible, the critic immediately accepts this evidence as definitive and the Bible as wrong. The possibility that the Bible might be correct and that the contradictory evidence is a mistake is not considered.

If a non-Christian source conflicts with a Christian source, the non-Christian source is always assumed to be right. Any suggestion that the Bible might be right and the other source wrong is not allowed.

If there are ten pieces of evidence that support the Bible and one that contradicts it, the one that contradicts it is taken as conclusive and the supporting evidence is dismissed as a set of curious anomalies.

Ask yourself: Is evidence against the Bible being given more weight than evidence for the Bible? If there is evidence on both sides, why is the evidence against the Bible considered more persuasive?

9.4.9. Non-Verbatim Quotes

The critic finds a quote that is not word-for-word and calls this an error or a contradiction.

In real life, people routinely make non-verbatim quotes. A report might say, "Senator Jones said that the country should support the president's economic policy." Suppose a recording reveals that Senator Jones exact words were, "The nation should support President Miller's plan to fight unemployment." We would not normally say that the reporter was lying or misquoting Jones. We understand that every quote is not necessarily word for word.

This is sometimes confused in the Bible because modern translations use quote marks, which to some people implies a word-for-word quote. Ancient Greek and Hebrew, however, did not have quote marks. This is a modern invention.

Ask yourself: When someone says two Bible quotes of the same original statement contradict, is it just a difference in the exact words, or is the meaning really changed? If the translator had not added quotation marks, would the claim of a misquote hold water?

9.4.10. Quoting False Statements

The critic claims the Bible is in error for quoting someone who makes a statement that is not true.

When we are reading a news story and the reporter says that someone made such-and-such a statement, we do not say that the reporter is lying if the statement quoted turns out to be false. As long as the reporter accurately quoted the source, the reporter is telling the truth. Whether the person quoted is telling the truth or not has nothing to do with the accuracy of a quote. Indeed, if the reporter changed a quote to make it conform to what he believes to be the truth, he would be misquoting the source, and could fairly be accused of lying. Accurately quoting a liar does not make you a liar.

Ask yourself: When the Bible quotes a statement that is inaccurate or that you believe to be inaccurate, is the Bible saying that this statement is true, or simply that the person said it?

9.4.11. Bogus Artifacts

People who are interested in the Bible, Christians or otherwise, sometimes declare that some historical artifact or archaeological find confirms the Bible. Further research later indicates that this discovery was a mistake or a hoax. There have been a number of reported discoveries of Noah's Ark, none of which has yet stood up to scrutiny. The Shroud of Turin and the James Ossuary are current subjects of debate. The critic then declares that this disappointment proves the Bible false.

It proves nothing of the kind. The existence of counterfeit money does not prove that there is no such thing as real money. The existence of Elvis impersonators does not prove that there never was a real Elvis.

Ask yourself: If this artifact or document really is a mistake or a fraud, how does that prove that the real thing never existed?

9.4.12. Imputed Ignorance

Critics often spin their theories on the assumption that the people in Bible times were not just ignorant of modern science, but were mind-bogglingly stupid.

They will explain away claims of miracles by supposing that ancient people mistook some common event for an amazing supernatural act. The critic will say that they mistook a sunset for a miraculous appearance of God, or that they were unaware that it is impossible by any known law of nature for people to walk on water. They'll say that some statement in the Bible demonstrates scientific ignorance by insisting that we interpret the Bible to mean something that people at the time would know was not so just as well as any modern scientist.

Ask yourself: When the critic says that the Bible is scientifically ignorant, is this claim based on more recent discoveries? Or are they supposing that the people of the time couldn't look around them and see the obvious? Is there a way we could read the part of the Bible in question that does *not* require us to assume that everyone present was stupid?

9.4.13. Scientific Ignorance

The critic claims that the Bible is wrong about some scientific question, when there is no scientific evidence to back up his statements.

The critics often imagine themselves to be "scientific". But often they demonstrate profound misunderstandings of what the scientific method is all about. They often confuse science with materialism. They think that "science" means "denying the supernatural" rather than "supported by experiment and observation". On other occasions they demonstrate simplistic views of science or outdated theories. They question how there could be light before the sun was created, apparently unaware that photons can exist independent of the sun.

Ask yourself: When the critic talks about science, does he have experiments and observation to back up his statements, or is he just using "science" as a synonym for "things I like to believe"?

9.4.14. Made-Up Facts

Sometimes the critic just makes up facts.

In general I work on the assumption that people I disagree with are being intellectually honest. I expect to disagree about how to interpret the facts. I expect to disagree about starting premises. I expect that there will often be honest dispute about what the facts are. But I also expect that my opponent will not cite "facts" that he knows to be false or that he just made up. Sadly, this is not always the case.

Ask yourself: What is the source of the claimed facts? Is this source unbiased? Is it reliable?

9.5. A Realistic Standard

In theory, if you could find just one error or contradiction in the Bible, that would prove that it is not the inspired word of God. Even one error, no matter how small, means that it is not infallible, by definition.

But to apply this test in practice would require that the critic is himself infallible. For you to say that some statement in the Bible is false assumes that you know the truth. How can we be certain that you are right and the Bible is wrong, and not the other way around?

In practice, to make a solid case that the Bible is wrong you would have to show multiple errors with a high degree of certainty for each. To really prove it you would have to show a pattern of errors.

Don't misunderstand me here. I'm not suggesting that we should ignore claims of error in the Bible. Quite the contrary, we should take them very seriously. If I didn't think that, I wouldn't have written this book.

The Bible-believing Christian is in a much stronger position than, say, the evolution-believing atheist. One outspoken atheist wrote:

> What would be evidence against evolution, and very strong evidence at that, would be the discovery of even a single fossil in the wrong geological stratum ... But not a single

solitary fossil has ever been found before it could have
evolved.

Dawkins, Richard. *The Greatest Shown on Earth.*
New York: 2009, pp. 146-147

In fact such out-of-place fossils are discovered all the time. In
1986 a fossil bird was discovered in Texas, called Protoavis Texensis,
in strata supposedly 75 million years before when the first birds are
claimed to have evolved. The coelacanth, a fossil fish, was supposed to
have been extinct for 80 million years, and then it turned out that
fisherman in South America were regularly catching them and eating
them.

I have never heard an evolutionist say that evidence like this
that contradicts their theory had led him to conclude that the whole
thing was a mistake. Rather, they used to say, "This forces us to revise
our theories on the evolution of [whatever creature]". They would talk
about how excited they were about these new discoveries and new
challenges. But that's getting old, so in recent years they've come up
with a new response:

Often, however, the fossil record doesn't fit the cladogram
[predicted evolutionary tree], a difficulty well known to
paleontologists and systematists. In fact, the cladistic
revolution in the 1970s and 80s was motivated in large
measure by evolutionary theorists setting aside
stratigraphy -- the fossil record -- as determining phylogeny
[ancestry] ... Ghost lineages are the unobservable
predictions of the phylogenetic branching ... based on our
assumption of common descent, which tells us the ghosts
were there.

Paul Nelson. "Seeing Ghosts in the Bushes"
Evolution News and Views. 2010.
http://www.evolutionnews.org
/2010/02/seeing_ghosts_in_the_bushes_pa031061.ht
ml. Retrieved Sept 2010.

That is, if the evidence contradicts the theory, they conclude
that there must be invisible "ghost evidence" that would confirm the
theory if only we could find it.

I wouldn't dream of going that far defending the Bible.

If you, Mr. Critic, can show a pattern of errors in the Bible,
then yes, you have won the argument. But don't expect the Christian to
concede the debate because you bring up a handful of points that we

can't answer. You don't give up your beliefs because Christians bring up points for which you can't come up with a good answer. You simply reply that, yes, you don't have all the answers, but you believe the weight of evidence is on your side. Sometimes there are points you can't answer because of your own limitations: You can't be expected to know it all. Allow us the same reserve.

9.6.   So What?

What difference does all this make?

On almost every point where critics claim that the Bible is in error, careful study shows that in fact the Bible is true. Given that, I am confident that if we had all the evidence, the few remaining criticisms would also evaporate.

Whenever it can be tested, when it talks about science and history, the Bible has proven to be true. It is reasonable to wonder, then, if it might also be true when it talks about things that we cannot test, like Heaven and Hell and salvation.

What if, just suppose, it is right about these things? That is worth considering. And what does it say on these matters? The most important things it tells us are:

(1) All human beings are sinners. We do not live up to God's standard. While people will deny this, we all know this is true. I doubt there is anyone who has never lied, never been selfish, never been hateful, or who has never stolen anything in his life. As G. K. Chesterton once wrote, "Certain new theologians dispute original sin, which is the only part of Christian theology which can really be proved." [Chesterton, G. K. *Orthodoxy.* Ch 2] Sometimes we justify ourselves by pointing to others whose sins are worse. But God's standard is perfection. He does not grade on a curve. We may make excuses for our sin, we may say that we're not really all that bad, but we all know that we are sinners.

(2) God says that the penalty for sin is Hell. We can debate exactly what Hell is. Some say that when the Bible talks about Hell as a place of fire and brimstone that this is just a metaphor. Maybe so. But it must be a terrible place for the Bible to describe it with such a metaphor. We may say that it is not fair for God to send us to such a place when our sins aren't really all that big. But fair or not, that's what God says he does.

(3) But there is an easy way out! God came to Earth as a man, Jesus of Nazareth, to pay the penalty of our sins for us. How can one

man take the penalty for another's crime? We tend to think of the punishment for a crime being a prison sentence. If you were convicted of a crime, could someone else volunteer to serve your prison sentence for you? Probably not. But suppose the penalty was a fine, maybe a very big fine, more than you could possibly pay. And then suppose some very rich person came along and offered to pay your fine for you. In this case, it is the judge himself who offers to pay your fine for you.

A friend of mine once said that she thought that Christianity, if true, was very unfair. After all, she said, Christians believed that someone like her, who did not believe in Jesus but who was basically a good person -- who had never killed anyone or stolen anything big and so on – someone like her would spend eternity in Hell. But someone who had spent his entire life stealing, killing, raping, kidnapping, whatever, could accept Jesus on his deathbed and spend eternity in Heaven, escaping any penalty for his crimes.

At the time I tried to come up with some explanation why Christianity was fair. But much later I realized that she was right. Christianity isn't fair. God never said that he would give us what we deserve. He offers something so much better. We all deserve to spend eternity in Hell. But instead we are offered a free gift: A complete pardon for all that we have done wrong, and a reward that far exceeds anything we have done right. God is not fair! He is generous! All you have to do is accept his free gift.

And immediately Jesus stretched out His hand and caught him, and said to him, "O you of little faith, why did you doubt?"

Matthew 14:31

Of making many books there is no end, and much study wearies the body.

Ecclesiastes 12:12 (NIV)

INDEX